Anatomy of a Controversy

Anatomy of a Controversy:
the Debate over *Essays and Reviews*
1860–1864

JOSEF L. ALTHOLZ

SCOLAR PRESS

Published by
SCOLAR PRESS
Gower House
Croft Road
Aldershot
Hants GU11 3HR
England

Ashgate Publishing Company
Old Post Road
Brookfield
Vermont 05036
USA

British Library Cataloguing in Publication Data

Altholz, Josef L.
    Anatomy of a Controversy: the Debate Over
    "Essays and Reviews", 1860–64.
    (Nineteenth Century Series)
    I. Title   II. Series
    941.081

ISBN 1 85928 040 4

Typeset in 10 point Garamond by Manton Typesetters, Louth, Lincolnshire and printed in Great Britain at the University Press, Cambridge.

Contents

Preface		ix
1	On Controversy	1
2	Broad Church?	3
3	The Essayists	9
4	The Essays	15
5	Early Responses	34
6	The Great Reviews	39
7	Censures	50
8	The War of the Pamphlets	64
9	Tracts into Tomes	73
10	The Case in Court	85
11	Verdict	95
12	Appeals	101
13	Acquittal	108
14	Condemnation	117
15	Aftermath	129
16	Epilogue	136
17	The Night Battle	141
Notes		145
Selected Bibliography		189
Index		191

The Nineteenth Century

General Editors' Preface

The aim of this series is to reflect, develop and extend the great burgeoning of interest in the nineteenth century that has been an inevitable feature of recent decades, as that former epoch has come more sharply into focus as a locus for our understanding, not only of the past but of the contours of our modernity. Though it is dedicated principally to the publication of original monographs and symposia in literature, history, cultural analysis, and associated fields, there will be a salient role for reprints of significant texts from, or about, the period. Our overarching policy is to address the spectrum of nineteenth-century studies without exception, achieving the widest scope in chronology, approach and range of concern. This, we believe, distinguishes our project from comparable ones, and means, for example, that in the relevant areas of scholarship we both recognize and cut innovatively across such parameters as those suggested by the designations 'Romantic' and 'Victorian'. We welcome new ideas, while valuing tradition. It is hoped that the world which predates yet so forcibly predicts and engages our own will emerge in parts, as a whole, and in the lively currents of debate and change that are so manifest an aspect of its intellectual, artistic and social landscape.

Vincent Newey
Joanne Shattock

University of Leicester

Preface

This study has had two incarnations. Its first, during the 1970s, was projected on a large scale as a complete history of the greatest crisis of Victorian faith, examined in all its ramifications. The appearance of Ieuan Ellis' *Seven Against Christ* in 1980 halted that project: though it was quite different from my work, it covered the same ground, and there was not room for two simultaneous monographs on *Essays and Reviews*. I spent the 1980s writing a book on the religious press. Then I found that I could return to *Essays and Reviews*, not as a revision of Ellis, but as a more precisely focused study of the controversy as a controversy, indeed the prototype of Victorian religious controversies. It was also more fun to do it that way: Victorians enjoyed a good controversy, and I could enjoy it with them.

The first project was assisted by a grant-in-aid from the American Council of Learned Societies; the reincarnation by a travel grant from the Western European Area Studies Center of the University of Minnesota. My thanks are due to the authorities of the British Library (and its Newspaper Library at Colindale); the Bodleian Library, Pusey House, Balliol and Keble Colleges, all of Oxford; the Archbishop of Canterbury for Lambeth Palace Library; the Institute of Historical Research and Senate House Library, London; and the University of Minnesota Library, for the use of their collections. My personal thanks are due to John Prest and the late John Sparrow at Oxford, William Brock and Joanne Shattock at Leicester, William Kellaway at the Institute of Historical Research, Merrill Distad, then at Toronto, and the late Walter and Esther Rhoads Houghton. I wish to thank Suzanne Haskins for the preparation of the manuscript. Especially I wish to thank the editors of *The Nineteenth Century: Leicester Studies and Texts* and Alec McAulay of Scolar Press for their willingness, in a publishing climate of reluctance to publish mere monographs, to publish a monograph which has no merit but mere merit.

Josef L. Altholz
Minneapolis
June 1993

On Controversy

Controversy, especially religious controversy, was the great spectator sport of Victorian England. The diverse movements and issues of this era of religious expansion periodically came to a head in major debates or controversies. Victorians took the issues of these debates seriously, and indeed many of them were momentous. But even more fascinating, and not yet systematically studied, is the process of controversy itself, carried to its perfection in the Victorian age. Controversy may be considered as a genre of human activity, which may be studied as one would study a genre of literature or art. This work is a study of a prototype of Victorian controversies; its subject was the greatest of that genre.

Essays and Reviews, published in 1860, was a composite volume by seven authors (six of them clergymen of the Church of England) which brought to England its first serious exposure to German biblical criticism. It evoked a controversy which included articles in newspapers, magazines and reviews, clerical and episcopal censures, a torrent of tracts, pamphlets and sermons, followed by weightier tomes (and reviews of all these), prosecution in the ecclesiastical courts, appeal to the highest court, condemnation by the Convocation of the clergy, a debate in Parliament (and letters and articles upon all these). The controversy lasted four years, drawing upon the resources of church and state, representing a crisis of faith contemporary with that provoked by Darwin's *Origin of Species* but more central to the religious mind, indeed 'the greatest religious crisis of the Victorian age'.[1]

Essays and Reviews was the culmination and final act of the Broad Church movement. The volume itself was modest in its pretensions and varied in the character and quality of its essays. Little of it was original, though it was new to most Englishmen. Yet this work touched Anglican orthodoxy on its most sensitive points and thus caused a controversy. Outwardly the conflict ended inconclusively, with the acquittal of two Essayists in the courts and the condemnation of the volume by the clergy. At a deeper level, it marked the exhaustion both of the Broad Church and of Anglican orthodoxy and the commencement of an era of religious doubt.

The issues raised in this controversy were substantial. All previous studies have been concerned with these substantive issues, usually with an interest in the current state of thought upon them. Men of letters have treated the subject superficially, describing the persecution of good liberals by bad literalists.[2] The only comprehensive study is by Ieuan Ellis, learned on the theological and critical background but confusing when dealing with the debate itself, so con-

cerned with the gravity of the issues that he misses the sheer zest of the controversy.[3] Most other studies are specific to individual figures in the debate.[4]

I am not without interest in the substantive issues,[5] nor can they be ignored
even in a study devoted to another purpose. However, this work will concern
itself primarily with the debate rather than the issues. This controversy illustrated 'the pathology of Victorian religion'[6] not only in its exposure of the less
attractive features of Victorian Christianity but also in its illustration of the
propensity to controvert and the methods of controversy of the time. The
debate proceeded through a number of stages usually defined by the chosen
medium of expression, and it both fed on itself and spun off several side-
controversies. In this study, it may be possible to establish some common
features characteristic of Victorian controversy in general.

It should be noted that this is an historical study. A student of religion[7] may
evaluate the theological merits or speculate on the religious significance; the
historian would not if he could. He prefers to cultivate his ignorance of the
present state of the argument. If he knows that the heresies of the Essayists later
became acceptable, then commonplace, then *passé*, he tries to forget this. Both
the orthodoxy and the liberalism of the 1860s were specific to their time. The
historian must relocate them in their time.

CHAPTER TWO

Broad Church?

There were two great parties in the Victorian Church of England, and there was one common orthodoxy.

The two parties are known for convenience as Low Church and High Church. The Low Church, or evangelicals, spiritual heirs of the Puritan tradition, stressed individual religious experience; their quasi-Calvinistic theology, based on the Bible alone, regarded the Atonement as the central doctrine of Christianity. Their initial momentum had produced the religious revival of the nineteenth century; but by the 1830s they had narrowed into a party, with exclusive tenets and a special cant. The High Church, which traced its roots to the early Anglican divines, had been revived by the Oxford Movement (or Tractarians) of the 1830s. Their emphasis was on the corporate Church rather than the individual and his Bible, a Church which had an authority of its own beyond state establishment, transmitted by the apostolic succession of the bishops. Their sacramental principles had, since the Oxford days, taken the distinctive form of ritualism. Their leading figure was E. B. Pusey, regius professor of Hebrew at Oxford.

The controversies between Low and High Church, which seemed to occupy most of church history from the 1830s to the 1850s, have obscured the fact that there was a real doctrinal consensus or common orthodoxy among them. It was rarely articulated. Indeed, it may well have been the chief function of the *Essays and Reviews* and related controversies to bring about the articulation of Anglican orthodoxy at almost the last period of its existence.

The assumptions of this common orthodoxy have been stated as: '(a) the transcendence of God; (b) the origin of the material world in an act of creation in time; (c) the claim of Scripture to be an authoritative revelation of truth otherwise unobtainable by man; (d) the happiness and salvation of souls as the supreme concern of religion'.[1] Two features of this definition are of concern here. The first is the insistence on an external revelation, given by God, and consisting of data to be received in faith. The second is the emphasis on salvation to the exclusion of any fundamental concern for morality. Both features posit a remote God supplying materials for faith in the revelation of Scripture, on the right reception of which salvation depends.

A theology resting upon an external written revelation faced challenges, beginning with the eighteenth-century deists, to the credibility, authenticity and accuracy of its Scriptures. The great Anglican divines of the eighteenth century, especially Joseph Butler (*Analogy of Religion,* 1736) and William Paley (*Evidences of Christianity,* 1794),[2] had produced a system of external evidences of revela-

tion, resting the case for Christianity on arguments from miracles which validated those who delivered the revelation, from the fulfilment of prophecies and
from the correspondence of types and antitypes in the Old and New Testaments. This evidential theology seemed to have routed the deists and provided
the staple of theological teaching, forming the minds of most of those who were
to take part in the *Essays and Reviews* debate. It may be described as an Anglican
scholasticism.[3] The evidences were spoken of as the 'foundations' of the faith,
and apologists sought 'to prove that the "Scriptures are authentic", and with that
established it must follow that "Christianity is true"'.[4]

That this orthodox apologetic, this rationalistic anti-rationalism, was alive
and well on the eve of the *Essays and Reviews* controversy was shown by the
reception accorded to the Bampton Lectures of 1858 by H. L. Mansel on *The
Limits of Religious Thought*. Seeking to place the Christian faith beyond the
reach of rational challenge, Mansel argued that the Absolute or Unconditioned
(God) was utterly beyond the power of human reason to understand. He thus
summarily dismissed both demonstration of the existence of God and attempts
to disprove it. This scepticism left it to God to supply truth to man through
revelation. Human reason was capable of examining only the evidences, not the
contents, of revelation. The evidences adduced by Mansel were the external
evidences of miracles and prophecy. These supplied the credentials of the Bible,
which must therefore be accepted in its entirety. 'If there is sufficient evidence
… to show that the Scripture, in which this doctrine is contained, is a Revelation from God, the doctrine itself must be unconditionally received, not as
reasonable, nor as unreasonable, but as scriptural.' Neither critical nor ethical
difficulties could be considered. 'If the teaching of Christ is not in any one thing
the teaching of God, it is in all things the teaching of men.'[5]

Paradoxically employing scepticism in defense of orthodoxy, staking the
truth of Christianity on its weakest point, Mansel won a momentary victory for
the orthodox apologetic. Although challenged by F. D. Maurice,[6] himself suspected of heresy, Mansel was hailed enthusiastically by the religious public as a
'champion of orthodoxy'[7] who had definitively put down rationalism. On the
eve of the *Essays and Reviews* controversy, the religious world was at once fearful
of rationalism and over-confident in the intellectual foundations of its faith.

But there were dissenters from this orthodoxy, intellectual nonconformists
within Anglicanism. Few in number, working as individuals or as small groups,
diverse as befitted upholders of diversity, they could hardly be called a party, still
less a movement. This tendency might best be called liberal Anglicanism,[8] but it
came to be known as Broad Church after that term was used in a celebrated
article in 1853.[9] The word Broad, by way of distinction from either High or
Low, had apparently been used at Oxford for some time and had surfaced in an
article by the liberal A. P. Stanley in 1850: the Church of England was 'by the
very condition of its being neither High nor Low, but Broad'.[10] The term Broad
Church is used here, with the understanding that, unlike the High or Low

Church, the Broad Church was not a movement or a party but a tendency of mind common to assorted individuals or small groups.

The Broad Churchmen had in common a rejection of a theology of passive acceptance of doctrines derived from a Bible validated by external evidences. More important than Christian doctrine was the Christian life, for morality was better suited than miracles to validate Christianity in modern times. The Bible was to be read with freedom, even by clergymen, to find its original, essentially spiritual message. The critical study of the Bible, using methods which German scholars had pioneered, was a duty owed to truth.

The founders of the Broad Church were Samuel Taylor Coleridge and Thomas Arnold, representing different approaches to these common themes. Coleridge, who had studied in Germany in 1798–99, provided a philosophical basis for the Broad Church in *Aids to Reflection* (1825). Revelation and grace were not interposed upon nature but were developed from it; faith was not opposed to reason but was the perfection of reason; Christianity was not a set of doctrines but a life, with the development of morality as its object. Coleridge rejected the evidential rationalism of Paley: 'Evidences of Christianity! I am weary of the word. Make a man feel the want of it; rouse him ... to the self-knowledge of his need of it; and you may safely trust it to its own Evidence'.[11] In his *Constitution of the Church and State* (1830), Coleridge stressed the 'nationality' of the Church, established by the State to guide the spiritual progress of the nation, with a special role of education. In his posthumous *Confessions of an Inquiring Spirit* (1840), Coleridge urged the duty of biblical criticism, reading the Bible afresh with no presumption of inerrancy, studying it as literature which, though inspired, had been developed by human hands: 'I take up this work with the purpose to read it for the first time as I should read any other work'. This only enhanced his sense of the Bible being inspired by God unlike any other book, for more than any other it reaches man's spirit: 'Whatever *finds* me, bears witness for itself that it has proceeded from a Holy Spirit'.[12] The Bible and Christianity are their own best evidences.

Thomas Arnold is remembered as the great headmaster of Rugby, but he was also the founder of the historical–critical approach to the Bible. Himself a classicist and Roman historian, he was attracted by B. G. Niebuhr's *History of Rome*, with its critical treatment of the classical sources of Roman history; and he kept in contact with German biblical scholarship through Christian von Bunsen, whom he had met in 1827. Arnold's great insight was the progressive nature of revelation, adapted to the knowledge and wants of those to whom it was first made, hence not always accurate in its details. The Bible must be examined historically and philologically, with no presumption of inerrancy. Its inspiration was general, not plenary, sufficient for its practical use as a guide to morality. Significantly, Arnold's *Essay on the Right Interpretation and Understanding of the Scriptures* (1832) is embedded in a volume of his *Sermons*, for he valued biblical exegesis chiefly as an aid to the promotion of morality. He was indifferent to dogmatic theology, prizing the connection of the Church with the State because the State helped to keep the Church from being overly dogmatic or exclusive. Arnold was linked to the later scholarly generation of Broad Church-men through his disciple and biographer A. P. Stanley.

Of the first generation of Broad Churchmen, the Cambridge friends Connop Thirlwall and Julius Charles Hare were the most active in bringing German critical scholarship to an England indisposed to receive it. Thirlwall remarked that 'it would almost seem as if at Oxford the knowledge of German subjected a divine to the same suspicion of heterodoxy which we know was attached some centuries back to a knowledge of Greek'.[13] In 1825 Thirlwall published a translation of Schleiermacher's essay on St Luke with an introduction in which he defended the German critical approach and dismissed the verbal inerrancy of Scripture. In 1828–32 Thirlwall and Hare published a translation of Niebuhr's *History of Rome*, provoking orthodox opposition which feared rightly that the techniques of historical criticism applied to Roman literature might be applied to biblical literature. Hare diffused his many talents, and his main significance for the Broad Church was as a connecting link among its various groups until his death in 1855. But Thirlwall, after completing his own Roman history, became bishop of St David's in 1840, and exercised a national influence through the publication of triennial Charges in which he magisterially surveyed the situation of the Church.

An element not within but to the side of the Broad Church formed around Hare's brother-in-law, Frederick Denison Maurice. Maurice is best remembered as the founder of the Christian Socialist movement in 1848, but his lasting claim to fame lies in his theological insight. Powerful in preaching, inept in writing, Maurice was the only truly prophetic figure associated with the Broad Church, focusing his theology on the person of Christ. This enabled him to reject all party dogmatisms and the Bible-worship which exalted the written over the living Word of God. In 1853 he was dismissed from his professorship at King's College, London, for denying the eternity of punishment. In 1859 he engaged in controversy with Mansel. But Maurice denied that he was a Broad Churchman, and in the controversy over *Essays and Reviews* he and his small band of followers took an independent line.

The next generation of the Broad Church, more academic in tone, centred on the Oxford friends Arthur Penrhyn Stanley, Benjamin Jowett and Frederick Temple. Their mentor had been Archibald Campbell Tait, who encouraged his students to engage in biblical study and learn German scholarship; but Tait left Oxford in 1842 to succeed Arnold as headmaster of Rugby and later became bishop of London. These men were involved in the campaign to reform and open Oxford in the 1850s, and some of the opposition their biblical works received may be traced to the reaction against university reforms. Stanley was at the heart of the group, which has therefore been called 'Stanleyite';[14] but Stanley was no leader, and his centrality was largely due to his personal and social qualities. Jowett had the last word on Stanley: 'He was a great spectator of life rather than a great actor in it'.[15]

Stanley, following up an unfinished project of Arnold, proposed to Jowett a commentary on the Pauline epistles based on the recent edition by Lachmann rather than the *textus receptus*. The resulting volumes appeared in 1855. Stanley's commentary on Corinthians was readable but superficial, 'Paul without ideas'.[16] But Jowett's commentary on Thessalonians, Galatians and Romans was a landmark in English criticism, a major effort to penetrate the mind of St Paul. Jowett's principle was to discard previous interpretations and to grapple directly with the text. In addition to his commentary proper, Jowett added a supplement of essays and dissertations dealing with larger aspects of his subject, voicing his opinions without reserve. An essay 'On the Imputation of the Sin of Adam' pointed out how slender was the biblical basis for this favourite theme of evangelicalism. In another essay he argued that 'Christianity is not a philosophy but a life ... The true use of philosophy in relation to religion is to restore its simplicity ... we return to Scripture, not to explain it away, but to translate it into the language of our own hearts, and to separate its accidents from its essence'. An essay on 'Natural Religion' drew no sharp distinction between natural and revealed religion, held that revelation was not confined to Jews and Christians, who had borrowed from others, so that their religion must be studied comparatively. But most startling was Jowett's essay 'On Atonement and Satisfaction', in which he vehemently expressed his moral indignation at the standard presentation of the Atonement in terms of penal substitution and satisfaction of God's justice: 'one cannot but fear whether it be still possible so to teach Christ as not to cast a shadow on the holiness and truth of God.'[17]

The dissertations were a direct assault upon orthodox opinions, especially those of the evangelicals. Jowett, who had just been made regius professor of Greek, was delated to the Vice-Chancellor and required to subscribe anew the Thirty-Nine Articles. This personal humiliation did not deter him. In 1859 he published a second edition, in which the essay 'On Atonement and Satisfaction' was actually sharpened:

> The doctrine of the Atonement has often been explained in a way at which our moral feelings revolt. God is represented as angry with us for what we never did; he is ready to inflict a disproportionate punishment on us for what we are; He is satisfied by the suffering of His Son in our stead ... The imperfection of human law is transferred to the Divine ... I shall endeavour to show, 1. that these conceptions of the work of Christ have no foundation in Scripture; 2. that their growth may be traced in ecclesiastical history; 3. that the only sacrifice, atonement, or satisfaction, with which the Christian has to do, is a moral and spiritual one ... the living sacrifice 'to do thy will, O God'.[18]

Stanley wrote a review in *The Times* hailing this work as 'the best kind of support which the cause of religion can receive in an age like ours'.[19]

Jowett's essay which appeared in *Essays and Reviews* had been intended for this second edition of the commentaries but was not ready in time for it. In Victorian religion, we cannot enter upon a controversy simply at its beginning. We find that we have stumbled upon a controversy (or controversies) already going on. The warfare between orthodoxy and 'Germanism' (or 'neology', as it was also called) was already under way.

CHAPTER THREE

The Essayists

Essays and Reviews was originated by a Broad Churchman of the second rank, Henry Bristow Wilson. A fellow of St John's College, Oxford, from 1825 to 1850, Wilson had been one of the 'four tutors' who protested against Newman's Tract 90 in 1841. In 1850 he received the college living of Great Staughton (Hunts). He gave the Bampton Lectures for 1851 under the title *The Communion of Saints*, emphasizing man's moral sense as the source of church unity, urging a broader comprehensiveness in the terms of communion in the national Church, and seeking recognition of the provisional nature of dogmatic statements in theology: 'all dogmatic statements must be held to be modalized by greater or less probability'.[1] This anticipation of *Essays and Reviews* was widely criticized.[2]

In 1855 Wilson was drawn into a publishing venture of the house of John W. Parker and Son. The elder Parker had managed Cambridge University Press from 1829 to 1854 and also served as publisher for the Society for Promoting Christian Knowledge, meanwhile building up his own publishing firm in London. He was joined by his son of the same name in 1843. The younger Parker was a religious and intellectual liberal, who brought to the firm Maurice and the Christian Socialists on the one hand and John Stuart Mill on the other.[3] The Parkers projected 'as a speculation' parallel series of annual volumes of essays by graduates of each of the two universities, 'two yearly volumes like reviews'.[4] The *Oxford* and *Cambridge Essays* were open to all opinions, religious or political, from their respective alumni, with the then unusual feature that all articles were signed, in order that each author could avoid responsibility for the opinions of others by avowing responsibility for his own. Wilson was offered the editorship of *Oxford Essays*, which appeared along with *Cambridge Essays* from 1855 to 1858. His editorship involved merely collecting the articles, with no attempt at editorial control, a procedure later adopted by *Essays and Reviews*. Of the future Essayists and Reviewers, Temple, Baden Powell and Mark Pattison wrote in *Oxford Essays*, to which Wilson contributed his own 'Schemes of Christian Comprehension' in 1857, and Charles Goodwin wrote for *Cambridge Essays*. The volumes excited little comment and no opposition, though Powell and Wilson anticipated their controversial essays of 1860. The series probably came to an end because 'we had no more to say',[5] but Wilson's new interest in a theological review which would combine the religious elements of the two *Essays* may have had something to do with it.[6]

Wilson was drawn into another form of publication in 1855 under the influence of another future Essayist, Mark Pattison. Pattison, fellow of Lincoln

College, Oxford, had been a youthful Tractarian under the personal influence of J. H. Newman; but after Newman's defection in 1845 he gradually abandoned his High Church views 'by the slow process of innutrition of the religious brain and development of the rational faculty'.[7] Becoming a liberal in every sense of the word, he was active in the movement for University reform. He was balked by a cabal from election as rector of Lincoln College in 1851, which left him permanently embittered. He turned to research, becoming a pioneer in the history of ideas, and developed literary ambitions, writing for quarterly reviews. John Chapman, publisher and editor of the radical *Westminster Review,* having lost the services of his assistant Marian Evans (George Eliot) in late 1853, looked about for help in her fields of theology and philosophy. Chapman may have secured some reviews from Pattison for the January 1854 number;[8] he definitely obtained Pattison's acceptance of the theology and philosophy section of short reviews of 'Contemporary Literature' in late 1854.[9] Pattison did the section for the January 1855 number but found himself unwilling to continue it regularly. He therefore introduced Wilson to Chapman, and Wilson became editor of the theology and philosophy section with the April 1855 issue, thereby obtaining a position in which he could comment anonymously on the range of issues that concerned him.[10]

Pattison and Wilson almost succeeded in capturing the *Westminster Review* as the organ of the Broad Church (the only religious movement which lacked a periodical organ),[11] but they were only a part of Chapman's assorted collection of radicals. In October of 1857 Pattison urged Chapman to turn the *Westminster* entirely into a review that 'can lead thinking men in Theology and Religion'.[12] But Chapman knew that only a general review had any commercial chance of success, and he shunted Pattison into editing the section on history and biography. Then Wilson was offended when Chapman, against his advice, published in the January 1858 number Francis Newman's article on 'The Religious Weakness of Protestantism', hostile to all organized forms of Christianity. Wilson 'could not reconcile myself to a continued cooperation … with other persons whose ultimate object is to destroy Xty root and branch'. He therefore submitted his resignation of the theological section. In the end Wilson continued to edit the section; but the affair had drawn his thought to finding a more suitable organ for the Broad Church: 'if theological and kindred subjects are to receive a free treatment and yet to be approached … in a reverent spirit, it must be done by an organ in the hands of those who have been "hewn out of our own pit"'.[13]

At first the plan was for a theological quarterly, about which Wilson had already been speaking to others. Wilson soon found that 'a new Quarterly is probably beyond our means', both as to finances and contributors, and began to think in terms of 'an annual Volume of Essays with Appendix'. At this juncture he was approached by 'Mr. Sanders', who told him 'that J. W. Parker might perhaps be disposed to merge the Oxford and Cam. Essays in a new Theological organ'.[14] The plan of a volume was adopted at a meeting in London of Wilson,

Pattison and Rowland Williams, Wilson's Cambridge contact, on March 26, 1858. Wilson was to edit or assemble the volume on the model of *Oxford Essays*, and the device of signed articles was again adopted. Parker would publish what was projected as the first of an annual series devoted to religious subjects.

Rowland Williams, who was thus introduced into the scheme, was already known as an individualistic Broad Churchman. A Welshman, fellow of King's College, Cambridge, Williams became in 1850 vice-principal and professor of Hebrew at St David's College, Lampeter. In 1854 he was select preacher at Cambridge and published his sermons in 1855 as *Rational Godliness*. He developed his characteristic views, that the human element in the Bible must be acknowledged, that revelation was progressive and not confined to Jews and Christians, and that prophecy was not merely predictive. This especially provoked evangelicals: Bishop Ollivant of Llandaff asked Williams to resign as his chaplain, and 70 clergymen demanded his removal from Lampeter. Thirlwall, bishop of St David's, saw no reason to exercise his jurisdiction, but privately suggested to Williams that he ought to resign in view of the state of clerical feeling. Williams declined to resign and published *Lampeter Theology* in 1856 to vindicate his teaching. Thirlwall's triennial Charge appeared in 1857 and was mostly devoted to the Williams affair. He found Williams' theology not unorthodox but criticized his obscure style and harsh tone; but 'the man is better than the work'. Thirlwall's main concern was 'to protect that freedom of thought, word, and action, which the Church has hitherto granted to her ministers and members' from 'aggression on the rights of conscience'.[15] Williams regarded this as a 'masterly evasion of the real points at issue',[16] and his embitterment explains his willingness to enter into *Essays and Reviews*.

Williams continued to be controversial. In 1857 he published a prize-winning essay on *Christianity and Hinduism*, a pioneering effort in comparative religion which treated the Hindu scriptures with as much respect as the Bible.[17] In 1858 he was presented to the college living of Broad Chalke (Wilts), but he did not leave Lampeter until 1862. His irritation with Thirlwall continued, for he thought that the bishop really agreed with him but would not speak out. In early 1860 Williams published *An Earnestly Respectful Letter ... On the Difficulties of Bringing Theological Questions to an Issue*, addressed to Thirlwall, hoping to force him to declare himself. Thirlwall easily caricatured Williams' posing as a victim and satirized 'the mastery which you have attained in the art of putting questions, so as most effectually to prevent the possibility of an answer'.[18] But Thirlwall refused to bring the substantive questions to an issue. Nor did he say anything on biblical subjects in his 1860 Charge, although by then *Essays and Reviews* had appeared.

Williams was expected to find other Cambridge contributors to *Essays and Reviews*, but he was only able to find one, the only layman in a volume largely clerical and Oxonian, Charles Wycliffe Goodwin. The brother of a future dean and bishop, Goodwin was an unhappy barrister who returned to Cambridge as

fellow of St Catherine's College, resigning in 1847 when he refused to be
ordained 'as he could no longer conscientiously subscribe to the tenets that were
required of him'.[19] He returned to London and the law, engaged in literary
pursuits, studied Hebrew and geology and became a leading Egyptologist: his
essay on 'Hieratic Papyri' in the 1858 *Cambridge Essays* 'marks an epoch in
Egyptology'.[20]

Pattison was expected to recruit Jowett for the volume. Jowett saw this as an
opportunity to publish the essay on interpretation which he had been unable to
finish for his 1859 commentary. Jowett in turn recruited Temple, recently
appointed headmaster of Rugby. Temple came to believe that the scheme had
originated with Jowett and himself in conversations some years earlier 'on the
great amount of reticence in every class of society in regard to religious views'
and the need to 'encourage free and honest discussion of biblical topics'.[21] He
elaborated on this theme in 1869:

> I liked particularly the opportunity that it would give for speaking out. It
> appeared to me that at that time there was prevalent amongst the clergy a
> most unwholesome reticence. I believed that this publication might serve
> to break through it. I knew that startling things would be said; but I
> believed that it would be worth while that they should be said ... strictly
> within the limits allowed by the Church of England.[22]

Temple was not a major scholar, being occupied with practical problems of
education, but he was open-minded and in favour of open-mindedness. He was
to preach at Oxford in 1860 during the meeting of the British Association for
the Advancement of Science (at which T. H. Huxley had his confrontation with
Samuel Wilberforce over evolution):

> The student of science now feels himself bound by the interests of truth,
> and can admit no other obligation. And if he be a religious man, he
> believes that both books, the book of nature and the book of Revelation,
> alike come from God, and that he has no more right to refuse to accept
> what he finds in one than what he finds in the other.[23]

Jowett also sought to recruit Stanley. His description of the project to Stanley
indicates the new dimension which he and Temple had given it.

> The object is to say what we think freely within the limits of the C[hurch]
> of England.. ... We do not wish to do anything rash or irritating to the
> Public or the University, but we are determined not to submit to this
> abominable system of terrorism, which prevents the statement of the
> plainest facts and makes true theology or theological education impossi-
> ble. Pusey and his friends are perfectly aware of your opinions ... but they
> are determined to prevent your expressing them. I do not deny that in the
> present state of the world the expression of them is a matter of great nicety
> and care, but is it possible to do any good by a system of reticence? ... I
> want to point out that the object is not to be attained by any anonymous
> writing.[24]

But Stanley, whether through caution or the press of other business, would not take part. He urged his 'prior obligations' to the *Quarterly* and *Edinburgh Reviews*, and added that 'we certainly should not conciliate public attention more, from advancing to charge the public in a body'. He preferred the counsel of Dean Milman of St Paul's (who had startled the public in 1829 with a critical *History of the Jews* which described Abraham as a Bedouin sheik) that each writer should publish separately, 'saying all that is peculiarly his own in his own books, and saying all that he thinks can be better said elsewhere thro' the established Reviews'.[25] So Stanley did not join in the greatest venture of the 'Stanleyites'.

Others were expected to join in. When Jowett wrote to Stanley, they had secured the Scot Sir Alexander Grant and the philologist Max Müller 'if he has time'.[26] But Müller did not have time, and Grant was prevented by an appointment to India. William Thomson (later archbishop of York) and G. D. (later Dean) Boyle are reported to have agreed to join but to have failed to send their papers to the printer in time.[27] This seems doubtful: it was practically impossible to be too late.

The chief omission from the list of authors was the 'Cambridge three', Lightfoot, Westcott and Hort, New Testament critics and (except for Jowett) the only constructive biblical scholars in the Church of England. Williams did approach F. J. A. Hort through a mutual friend, but Hort declined:

> The chief impediment is a wide difference of principles and opinions from the body of your coadjutors. I can go all lengths with them in maintaining absolute freedom of criticism, science, and speculation ... But I fear that in our own positive theology we should diverge widely ... There are, I fear, still more serious differences between us on the subject of authority, and especially the authority of the Bible ... It is surely likely to bring on a crisis ... The errors and prejudices, which we agree in wishing to remove, can surely be more wholesomely and also more effectually reached by individual efforts of an indirect kind than by combined open assault. At present very many orthodox but rational men are being unawares acted upon by influences which will assuredly bear good fruit in time, if the process is allowed to go on quietly; but I cannot help fearing that a premature crisis would frighten many back into the merest traditionalism. And as a mere matter of prudence, it seems to me questionable to set up a single broad conspicuous target for the Philistines to shoot at, unless there is some decided advantage to be gained. Moreover I must confess a strong repugnance to any measure likely to promote anything like a party organisation.[28]

Hort took no public part in the controversy over *Essays and Reviews*, but his private letters provide some of the sagest commentary on it.

With the defections and refusals, it seemed that there might not be enough material to make a book, and a late decision was made to invite the Savilian professor of mathematics at Oxford, Baden Powell. Powell had been born into the pre-Tractarian High Church and passed easily into the circle of the 'Noetics', a liberal and critical orthodoxy of the 1820s. He took it upon himself to monitor developments in science on behalf of Anglican apologetics. But science conquered its watchdog, and Powell's constantly evolving attitude became increasingly radical, though he remained a devoted Anglican. As early as 1833, in *Revelation and Science*, he was prepared to concede that science must follow evidence to its conclusion, even if this conflicts with the Bible. By the 1850s, Powell came to his final position, which he enunciated in a series of works from *Essays on the Spirit of Inductive Philosophy* (1855) to *The Order of Nature* (1859), including an article on Christian evidences in the 1857 *Oxford Essays*. The order of nature is absolutely uniform; therefore miracles, as violations of the uniform laws of nature, cannot occur. Christianity must be separated from all relation with physical things; as a purely spiritual religion, it will triumph by its moral effects.[29] Powell was already being bracketed with some of the future Essayists by orthodox alarmists, but he had pursued his course in isolation and so was not a first choice. But he was so full of his subject, which was in effect a summary of *The Order of Nature*, that, though he joined late, his essay was the second to be submitted.

Thus were assembled the seven Essayists and Reviewers. 'There was neither plan nor editorial policy. Nor was there an agreed theological perspective. It was a typical Broad Church production. Every man spoke for himself'.[30] Only then did Wilson undertake his editorial duties, chiefly to prod the contributors into producing their articles. He so impressed Temple with the urgency of the situation that Temple hastily revised a sermon he had recently delivered, which became his essay. Powell, Williams, Goodwin and Wilson himself delivered their articles in time, and Parker advertised the forthcoming volume in February 1859, exactly a year after the last of the superseded *Oxford* and *Cambridge Essays*.

The last two papers delayed publication by a year. Pattison traveled to Germany in 1858 and 1859, and Jowett was working on the second edition of his commentary well into 1859 and then was unable to work for personal reasons.[31] Publication was postponed until October. Had *Essays and Reviews* been published then, it would have been the major book of 1859, rather than Darwin's *Origin of Species*, published in November. Pattison finally responded to Wilson's urgent appeals and began to write in November,[32] and Jowett got seriously to work over the Christmas vacation. Pattison sent in his essay in January 1860,[33] and Parker set the articles in print for revision by the authors.[34] Jowett's article, which expanded as did everything he wrote, came in at the last possible moment before publication on March 21, 1860.

CHAPTER FOUR

The Essays

The book opened with a simple title page, containing only the words *Essays and Reviews* at the top and publication data at the bottom. The title was precise: two contributions (Williams and Wilson) were 'reviews' as that term was used in periodicals, and the rest were essays. There followed a prefatory note 'To the Reader' which became important in the debate:

> It will readily be understood that the Authors of the ensuing Essays are responsible for their respective articles only. They have written in entire independence of each other, and without concert or comparison.
>
> The Volume, it is hoped, will be received as an attempt to illustrate the advantage derivable to the cause of religious and moral truth, from a free handling, in a becoming spirit, of subjects peculiarly liable to suffer by the repetition of conventional language, and from traditional methods of treatment.

The first paragraph was based on the prefaces to the *Oxford* and *Cambridge Essays*, which made similar disclaimers of joint responsibility. If Wilson thought that this would 'readily be understood', he miscalculated, an error compounded by the terse wording, which compares unfavourably with the earlier volumes.[1] The second paragraph was also terse, a bare statement capable of being read as a manifesto and seeming to contradict the denial of concert by stating a common purpose. Thus the preface, though a valid statement of the character and purpose of the book, had a negative effect.

In keeping with the assertion of individual responsibility, the table of contents listed, with each essay, the name, degree, and title of its author.[2] The essays were printed in the order in which Wilson received them.[3]

Temple's essay, 'The Education of the World', was a warmed-over sermon, having first been preached in Rugby school chapel and then more elaborately before the University of Oxford 'without provoking much adverse comment'.[4] Temple sent it promptly to Wilson, having spent no more than ten hours working on it. Its sermonic origin was evident in its use of 'one of those elaborately false analogies which are the bane of pulpit oratory',[5] the analogy of the life of the individual and the growth of mankind. Its theme, the progressive education of the human race, 'had from the time of Lessing formed part of the ordinary consciousness of the educated world',[6] and Lessing indeed supplied the title; but the immediate influence was that of Arnold.[7] The novelty lay in the application of this theme to a plea for freedom of biblical scholarship.

Applying his analogy, Temple spoke of the childhood, the youth and the manhood of the world, three stages of training. 'First come Rules, then Examples, then Principles. First comes the Law, then the Son of Man, then the Gift of the Spirit'. These stages applied to the history of the Church, Christ being the supreme Example. In the manhood of the world, the Church had to work out her principles by natural action, finding that many of her early doctrinal decisions were 'practically obsolete' or 'plainly unfitted for permanent use'. In modern times the Church had been taught the lessons of toleration– 'to modify the early dogmatism by substituting the spirit for the letter, and practical reason for precise definitions of truth' –and of science, the revelation of nature. The firm spot on which the Church stood was the Bible, because of its indefiniteness of dogmatic statement, which served 'to evoke the voice of conscience'. The current flowed 'to the identification of the Bible with the voice of conscience … by virtue of the principle of private judgment, which puts conscience between us and the Bible, making conscience the supreme interpreter'. Thus Temple argued that the manhood of the world required the free study of the Bible.

> He is guilty of high treason against the faith who fears the result of any investigation … If geology proves to us that we must not interpret the first chapters of Genesis literally; if historical investigations shall show us that inspiration, however it may protect the doctrine, yet was not empowered to protect the narrative of the inspired writers from occasional inaccuracy; if careful criticism shall prove that there have been occasionally interpolations and forgeries in that Book, as in many others, the results should still be welcome. Even the mistakes of careful and reverent students are more valuable now than truth held in unthinking acquiescence.[8]

Temple's essay would, under other circumstances, have passed unnoticed. He engaged in no biblical criticism of his own; his suggestions of its results were hypothetical. Those who criticized his essay condemned it on the ground of its 'tendency', its omission of the Fall and Atonement, its denial of doctrinal definiteness in the Bible and its substitution of conscience for authority. Thirlwall was to criticize it in 1863 for opening 'the broadest room for an assault upon the foundations of an historical Christianity, without setting up any defence against it'.[9] A later writer hailed it as 'the most significant indication of the immanentist trend to be found in *Essays and Reviews*'.[10] Both comments centre upon the progression from precept to example to inner religion,[11] which left no external point of fixity. To Temple, however, conscience was not arbitrary but the product of spiritual discipline and religious life; he did not renounce authority but relocated it from the text to the spirit. His intention would have been clearer if he had retained the title of his sermon, 'The Fulness of Time', with its reference to Galatians 4:4, which supplied his three stages. His essay, itself of little importance, was inadvertently an appropriate introduction to *Essays and Reviews*, the recurring theme of which was the separation of the substance of the Christian faith from the encrustations of past interpretations.

Williams' review of 'Bunsen's Biblical Researches' was as interesting for its subject as its ideas. When the project of a theological review was suggested,

Williams offered to review either Bunsen or Renan (then known only as a philologist).[12] The choice of Bunsen was appropriate, since Williams' purpose was to introduce German biblical criticism to England. Married to an English-woman, known to touring Englishmen for his *soirées* in Rome, Bunsen became Prussian minister to Britain from 1842 to 1854, when he won a place unique for a foreigner in English life. The Anglo-Prussian bishopric of Jerusalem was a product of his ecumenical enthusiasm, and he was largely responsible for the vogue of philology in Victorian England, introducing Max Müller to Oxford.[13] He was a conduit of German scholarship to Broad Churchmen such as Arnold, Hare and Williams. Bunsen, known as a devout Christian, seemed to provide assurance that biblical criticism was compatible with real faith. As a critic he was an amateur, isolated from the mainstream of academic criticism and idiosyn-cratic in his views. At once the most reverent and reckless of critics, Bunsen enjoyed a reputation in England which had no counterpart in Germany; in the histories of biblical criticism, he is disregarded.[14]

Williams' article was a 'review' of the totality of Bunsen's work. As a reviewer, Williams had a difficult task in distinguishing his description of Bunsen's views from his own generally favourable evaluation of them. Williams was fiercely independent, never fully agreeing with anybody and proud of his originality. 'I both hail his concurrence and quote him as a shield; but I do not count myself as his pupil'.[15] Williams felt that 'the reviewer's selection of an author implies sympathy, but not identification'.[16] He explicated this in his article: 'Passing over some specialities of Lutheranism, we may meet in the field of research which is common to scholars; while even here, the sympathy, which justifies respectful exposition, need not imply entire agreement'.[17] But the distinction was less clear to readers, and Williams did not always make it explicit when he was speaking for Bunsen and when he spoke for himself.

The rambling opening of the essay argued that questions about the extent of divine intervention in Revelation, as in geology, 'include inquiries into evidence, and must abide by verdicts on the age of records'.[18] 'We cannot encourage a remorseless criticism of Gentile histories and escape its contagion when we approach Hebrew annals; nor acknowledge a Providence in Jewry without own-ing that it may have comprehended sanctities elsewhere'. Ideas of revelation had been widened, and reason and conscience must be regarded as more fundamen-tal than the revelatory element. Conventional opinions must be revised 'if we are to retain the old Anglican foundations of research and fair statement'. Williams introduced Bunsen, whose 'enduring glory is ... to have brought a vast erudition, in the light of a Christian conscience, to unroll tangled records ... No living author's works could furnish so pregnant a text for a discourse on Biblical criticism'.[19]

Bunsen's works were discussed. *Egypt's Place in Universal History*, using philo-logical evidence, showed that 'our Biblical chronology was too narrow in its limits'.[20] Oriental traditions modified our interpretation of Genesis. 'Our del-

uge takes its place among geological phenomena, no longer a disturbance of law
from which science shrinks ... In the half ideal half traditional notices of the
beginnings of our race, we are bid notice the combination of documents, and
the recurrence of barely consistent genealogies'.[21] In *Gott in der Geschichte*,
Bunsen turned to the religious element of the Bible, rejecting literalism for a
faith in God's reason apprehended by man's conscience: 'the Bible, as an expression of devout reason, and therefore to be read with reason in freedom'.[22]
Williams illustrated such a reading:

> When the fierce ritual of Syria, with the awe of a Divine voice, bade
> Abraham slay his son, he did not reflect that he had no perfect theory of
> the absolute to justify him from departing from traditional revelation, but
> trusted that the FATHER, whose voice from heaven he heard at heart, was
> better pleased with mercy than with sacrifice; and this trust was his salva-
> tion ... So in each case we trace principles of reason and right, to which
> our heart perpetually responds, and our response to which is a truer sign
> of faith than such deference to a supposed external authority as would
> quench those principles themselves.[23]

Williams expected Bunsen's *Bible for the People* (in progress) to show 'that
there was a Bible before our Bible, and that some of our present books, as
certainly Genesis and Joshua, and perhaps Job, Jonah, Daniel, are expanded
from simpler elements'.[24] Bunsen showed the moral lessons of the Bible and
spiritualized the prophecies. Even in England the predictive element in prophecy was losing ground.[25] 'But in Germany there has been a pathway streaming
with light, from Eichhorn to Ewald ... throughout which the value of the moral
element in prophecy has been progressively raised, and that of the directly
predictive, whether secular or Messianic, has been lowered'.[26] Bunsen recognized such conclusions as the composite authorship of Isaiah; the 'servant' of
Isaiah lviii was not a prediction of Jesus; and the late date of Daniel, which
'contains no predictions, except by analogy and type'.[27] The recognition of such
things

> is not inconsistent with the notion that Almighty God has been pleased to
> educate men and nations, employing imagination no less than conscience,
> and suffering His lessons to play freely within the limits of humanity ...
> The great result is to vindicate the work of the Eternal Spirit ... If such a
> Spirit did not dwell in the Church the Bible would not be inspired, for the
> Bible is, before all things, the written voice of the congregation.[28]

Some might feel that Bunsen used biblical language in a 'philosophical'
sense. Williams suggested Bunsen's answer:

> In reply he would ask, what proof is there that the reasonable sense of St.
> Paul's words was not the one which the Apostle intended? Why may not
> justification by faith have meant the peace of mind, or sense of Divine
> approval, which comes of trust in a righteous God, rather than a fiction of
> merit by transfer? ...

> ... Justification would be neither an arbitrary ground of confidence, nor a
> reward upon condition of our disclaiming merit, but rather a verdict of
> forgiveness upon our repentance, and of acceptance upon the offering of
> our hearts ... Propitiation would be the recovery of that peace, which
> cannot be while sin divides us from the Searcher of hearts.[29]

To estimate the truth of such views, we should not confine ourselves to one
particular moment of revelation, or to early Christian writings inadequate 'to
guarantee narrative inherently incredible, or precepts evidently wrong. Hence
we are obliged to assume in ourselves a verifying faculty, not unlike the discre-
tion which a mathematician would use in weighing a treatise on geometry, or
the liberty which a musician would reserve in reporting a law of harmony'.[30]

Concluding, Williams acknowledged that some might reasonably disagree
with Bunsen. When Bunsen asked, 'How long shall we bear this fiction of an
external revelation', some might think his language too strong.

> Others will think burning words needed by the disease of our time. They
> will not quarrel on points of taste with a man who in our darkest perplex-
> ity has reared again the banner of truth, and uttered thoughts which give
> courage to the weak, and sight to the blind. If Protestant Europe is to
> escape those shadows of the twelfth century, which with ominous recur-
> rence are closing round us, to Baron Bunsen will belong a foremost place
> among the champions of light and right.[31]

Williams advanced no views in his essay that he had not suggested in his
earlier works: the human element in Scripture, a progressive revelation not
limited to the Jews, and (his favourite theme) the non-predictive nature of
prophecy. But there seemed to be an aggressiveness in the way in which he flung
out opinions, an arrogant confidence and a casualness verging on flippancy. He
assembled a century of German criticism and treated it as accepted truth by
which both Bunsen and English theologians must be judged. Nothing could be
more offensive to pious ears than this confident assertion of startling propositions, coupled with frequent hits at the obscurantism of orthodoxy. Williams
seemed to challenge the very concept of orthodoxy, substituting for authority an
open-ended 'verifying faculty', carrying private judgement to an extreme. Williams
remarked that the Essays were written 'rather with a view to awakening the
formalist than of confirming the doubtful or converting the sceptic'.[32] He could
not have been surprised that his essay provoked a reaction. What surprised him
was the confusion as to the extent to which Williams as a reviewer identified
himself with Bunsen's views. This was partly the fault of hostile reviewers:
Williams had warned that 'respectful exposition need not imply entire agreement', and the most offensive sentences, on justification and propitiation, were
prefaced by 'in reply he would ask'. But Williams' insouciance of style encouraged the assumption that he entered fully into everything; and in fact he largely
agreed with Bunsen. The confusion revealed a widespread uncertainty as to the
extent of a reviewer's responsibility.[33]

Williams' eccentricity obscured some merits of his essay. Biblical criticism was a German product, and Williams' essay was the only one to give an extended account of German criticism. He chose as his subject a German as eccentric as himself, but he referred frequently to other Germans, more than any other Essayist. Williams was the most perceptive of the Essayists in his treatment of the literary element of the Bible. This was no accident: it was integral to his studies of prophecy. Above all, Williams preached an openness to 'the Spirit'. The freedom of reason and conscience which he sought was a freedom to respond to 'the Spirit', however it should manifest itself. He preached this awkwardly and with a passion easily discounted as 'Celtic'; but had he not been a Welshman, he might now be numbered, like Maurice, among the prophets. Amid the rationality of *Essays and Reviews*, Williams alone raised the voice of prophecy.

Baden Powell's essay 'On the Study of the Evidences of Christianity' was a recapitulation of much that he had published earlier. His confidently assertive essay left no room for nuances. Powell began by calling for a judicial rather than advocatory approach to the question of Christian evidences, which, insofar as it was a question of external fact, must be dealt with solely by reason and intellect. The discourse with unbelievers had been conducted so far entirely in terms of external evidences which validated the Christian revelation, particularly the evidence of miracles, to which Powell addressed his 'purely contemplative and theoretical'[34] discussion.

Those acquainted with the uniformity of nature portrayed by modern science must find miracles antecedently incredible, notwithstanding any testimony in their favour: 'no testimony can reach to the supernatural; testimony can only apply to apparent sensible facts'. Such facts must bear rational investigation and are subject to 'that vast series of dependent causation which constitutes the legitimate field for the investigations of science, whose constancy is the sole warrant for its generalizations, while it forms the substantial basis for the grand conclusions of natural theology'. Powell asserted that 'the evidential force of miracles' was 'wholly *relative* to the apprehension of the parties addressed'.[35] The Christian miracles had evidential value only at the time they occurred, and Paley had overvalued them.[36] In the present stage of scientific knowledge, miracles supplied no evidence for Christianity and were in fact an embarrassment to its advocates. The absolute uniformity of nature was a better argument for the 'supreme intelligence' which governs it. Powell sketched his own apologetic:

> All reason and science conspire to the conclusion that beyond the domain of physical causation and the possible conceptions of *intellect* and *knowledge*, there lies open the boundless region of spiritual things, which is the sole dominion of *faith*. And while intellect and philosophy are compelled to disown the recognition of anything in the world of matter at variance with the first principle of the laws of matter – the universal order and indissoluble unity of physical causes – they are the more ready to admit

the higher claims of divine mysteries in the invisible and spiritual world. Advancing knowledge, while it asserts the dominion of science in physical things, confirms that of faith in spiritual; we thus ... admit that what is not a subject for a problem may hold its place in a creed. The more knowledge advances, the more it has been, and will be, acknowledged that Christianity, as a real religion, must be viewed apart from connexion with physical things.[37]

This separation of faith from science was Powell's contribution to theology. He reviewed and refuted the Paleyan evidences (praising, in passing, the recent work of Darwin),[38] concluding that miracles had ceased to support and instead become one of the difficulties of Christianity, objects rather than evidences of faith: 'we neither have nor can possibly have any evidence of a *Deity working miracles*; – for that, we must go out of nature and beyond reason'. He concluded by rejoicing that 'the strength of Christianity lies in the *variety* of its evidences, suited to all varieties of apprehension',[39] not limited to external signs and ultimately relying on faith, for 'by faith we stand' not 'in the wisdom of man, but in the power of God'.[40]

Powell's essay could have subjected him to prosecution for heresy had not his death on June 11, 1860, removed him 'to a higher tribunal'. In the calmest possible manner, he had wiped out a century of apologetics and eliminated the core of the 'evidences of Christianity'. He had not denied miracles absolutely; he had denied the possibility of miracles as external physical or historical facts, allowing them as objects of faith in the spiritual realm, but denying them value as evidence. To most Englishmen, this was the same as outright denial; and the calmness of his tone gave an impression of a coldness still more repellent. The counterpart of his scientific detachment was a faith so profound that it was untroubled by the collapse of external supports. Powell tried to eliminate at a stroke the conflict of science and religion by showing that 'there was no common ground between them'.[41] This positive element in his religion, separating science from faith, allowed faith to survive the abandonment of untenable external 'evidences'. But this radical fideism was only implied, not developed; no grounds for faith were offered to replace those which were given up. The English public was frightened by a *sola fide* that really stood alone. Hence Thirlwall regarded Powell's essay as the most dangerous in the volume,[42] voiding Christianity of its character as an historical revelation and leaving only an ineffable spirituality. Powell was the most thoroughgoing of the Essayists in jettisoning the accidental elements of Christianity to save the essential, sacrificing the indefensible to make the faith invulnerable.

Wilson's essay on 'The Natural Church', like the two previous, was the summation of the teachings of a lifetime. But unlike Powell, Wilson had no passion for order or clear dominant principle. His essay was diffuse and disorganized, one idea leading to another in a sort of theological stream of consciousness. It was a 'review' of the Macaulay sort, in which a book was used as a peg on which to hang an essay. The peg was a series of lectures in Geneva, *Séances Historiques de Genève*, or rather a statement in one of them by a M. Bungener praising the idea of a national or 'multitudinist' church, composed of individuals of differing sorts, opinions and characters – rather like the Church of England.

Wilson was disturbed by 'a very wide-spread alienation, both of educated and uneducated persons, from the Christianity which is ordinarily presented in our churches and chapels'.[43] This alienation was due, not to German speculation or criticism, but to English observation and thought. Modern Englishmen knew, for instance, that there were nations to whom the Gospel had never been preached; if belief in Christ was necessary to salvation, must Christians hold that these multitudes were damned? This question was open to the moral sense, which recognized no 'fine distinctions between covenanted and uncovenanted mercies'[44] and could find words of Christ 'declaring that the conditions of men in another world will be determined by their moral characters in this, and not by their traditional or hereditary creeds'. The teaching of Jesus was primarily moral, not doctrinal. The Apostolical Churches were multitudinist, comprising persons who differed doctrinally and morally, as would naturally be the case 'except upon the Calvinistic theory of conversion'. The national tendency is more natural than the individualist in Christianity, addressing itself to 'the spiritual progress of the nation and of the individuals of which it is composed, in their several states and stages'. It must define itself by its nationality, not by its peculiarity; it could not do this 'if while the civil side of the nation is fluid, the ecclesiastical side of it is fixed; if thought and speech are free among all other classes, and not free among those who hold the office of leaders and teachers of the rest in higher things'.[45]

This led Wilson to discuss clerical subscription to the Thirty-Nine Articles, particularly the sixth,[46] 'the pivot Article of the Church', which 'contains no declaration of the Bible being throughout supernaturally suggested ... not the least hint of the relation between the divine and human elements in the composition of the Biblical books'.[47] The Article did not require everything in Scripture to be believed, and it allowed the idea that 'the Word of God is contained in Scripture, whence it does not follow that it is co-extensive with it'.[48] 'Under the terms of the sixth Article one may accept literally, or allegorically, or as parable, or poetry, or legend', the various miraculous stories in the Bible. Anglicans were thus able to avoid literalism and penetrate beneath the 'dark patches of human passion and error' to the 'bright centre of spiritual truth within'.[49] This 'freedom of opinion which belongs to the English citizen should be conceded to the English Churchman',[50] clergy as well as laity.

Was subscription a restraint upon the clergy? Wilson, arguing that 'the strictly legal obligation is the measure of the moral one', found the obligation of subscription quite vague, amounting only to 'an acceptance of the Articles of the Church as the formal law to which the subscriber is in some sense subject'.[51]

The nature of the subjection was deduced from two canons of 1603 and a statute of Elizabeth, which Wilson analysed so as to minimize their definite content, allowing modern forms of expression 'without directly contradicting, or refusing assent to [the Articles], but passing by the side of them'.[52] While the Articles ought to be left as 'the ultimate law of the Church, not to be contradicted', the requirement of subscription and declaration of assent ought to be abolished. Thus 'there would disappear the invidious distinction between the clergy and laity of the same communion, as if there were separate standards for each of belief and morals'.[53] The nation needed strong-minded men in the clergy, and it must have no artificial barriers of professed belief to deter their entry.

> A national Church must be concerned with the ethical development of its members. And the wrong of supposing it to be otherwise, is participated by those of the clericalty who consider the church of Christ to be founded, as a society, on the possession of an abstractedly true and supernaturally communicated speculation concerning God, rather than upon the manifestation of a divine life in man.[54]

Wilson then dealt with the variety of allowable interpretations of the Bible, contrasting the literalist with the 'idealist', who disregards the historical factuality of biblical narratives and seeks their 'ideological' content. All these interpretations were permissible, for

> Jesus Christ has not revealed his religion as a theology of the intellect, nor as an historical faith; and it is a stifling of the true Christian life, both in the individual and the Church, to require of many men a unanimity in speculative doctrine, which is unattainable, and a uniformity of historical belief, which can never exist. The true Christian life is the consciousness of bearing a part in a great moral order, of which the highest agency upon earth has been committed to the Church.[55]

Wilson concluded by noting that few men even began to develop the moral potential which the Church fosters. The multitude were of a 'neutral character', to whom neither salvation nor damnation seemed suitable. He indulged in speculation about further spiritual development in the next life, with the possibility of progress to universal salvation:

> we must rather entertain a hope that there shall be found, after the great adjudication, receptacles for those who shall be infants, not as to years of terrestrial life, but as to spiritual development – nurseries as it were and seed-grounds, where the undeveloped may grow up under new conditions – the stunted may become strong, and the perverted be restored. And when the Christian Church, in all its branches, shall have fulfilled its sublunary office, and its Founder shall have surrendered His kingdom to the Great Father – all, both small and great, shall find a refuge in the bosom of the Universal Parent, to repose, or be quickened into higher life, in the ages to come, according to His Will.[56]

Wilson's essay was the most Coleridgian[57] in the volume, animated by the ideas that religious truth must be ascertained by the moral sense and that the Church must be comprehensively national. Both led Wilson to a strongly anti-dogmatic position in which the function of religion was exclusively the cultivation of the moral life. Although Wilson recognized biblical criticism as the key issue of freedom within the Church, it was a characteristically English criticism of common-sense inquiry. The essay's main point was that the Church must be kept truly national by having a clergy free to respond to the concerns and beliefs of the entire nation. The clergy must not be bound by formal statements of doctrine that fix them to the concepts of past ages rather than the light of their own. Wilson argued both that existing formularies imposed no effective limitation and that they nonetheless ought to be removed.

Many things were bound to give offence. Wilson denied the principle of no salvation outside the faith. He asserted the provisional character of doctrinal statements. He denied that the entire Bible was the 'Word of God' and held that parts of it could be treated as myth. He employed a casuistical method in dealing with subscription which was reminiscent of Newman in that Tract 90 which Wilson himself had denounced in 1841. Wilson's method allowed subscription in a sense which was, if not 'non-natural', substantially meaningless. Denying that the Church was concerned with speculative doctrine, he implied that there was no doctrinal element in revelation. Most shocking was his conclusion, which allowed the possibility of salvation to the damned. These were points on which Wilson could be charged with formal heresy. But he did more to offend the orthodox parties in the Church, evangelical and Puseyite; he threw out gratuitous hits at Calvinism and at the concept of religious authority. Even Stanley, who sympathized with everyone, criticized 'the unpardonable rashness of throwing out statements, without a grain of proof, which can have no other effect than to terrify and irritate'.[58]

There were three primary heads of offence. The most obvious was the off-hand suggestion of salvation outside Christianity and of the ultimate redemption of the reprobate. This secondary aspect of Wilson's essay aroused more concern than his basic ideas.[59] The second was the minimization of subscription to the Articles, which was regarded not merely as destructive of Church order but as dishonest and casuistical, incompatible with Wilson's part in the Tract 90 affair. The third was the effective elimination of all definite doctrinal content in Christianity, leaving only a 'bright centre of spiritual truth' undefined but apprehensible by the moral sense. This notion of 'ideology' was Coleridgianism pushed to extremes. Yet in his clumsy way Wilson came to grips, more than any Essayist or opponent, with the spiritual alienation of many ordinary Englishmen, the 'spontaneous recoil, on the part of large numbers of the more acute of our population, from some of the doctrines which are to be heard at church and chapel ... misgivings as to the authority, or the extent of the authority, of the Scriptures'.[60] He sought to enable the Church to deal with the 'negative theology' of the many doubters who had quietly dropped out of religious life. But his cure proved more troublesome than the disease. 'To preach comprehensiveness to a Church already divided ... was only to divide it further'.[61]

The layman Goodwin devoted his essay, 'Mosaic Cosmogony', to the creation account in Genesis. He had devoted his long vacations since 1851 to geological researches.[62] In the past 30 years, after discoveries in geology and paleontology which required a much longer time-span of creation than the six days of Genesis, there had developed an extensive literature designed to 'harmonize' the biblical narrative with modern geology, showing that the Bible was true, that is, not false, even by the lights of science.[63] The often tortuous reasoning of the 'theological geologists'[64] offered a tempting target to Goodwin.

Goodwin began with an allusion to the case of Galileo, when the attempt to resist astronomical science on biblical grounds had failed. 'It would have been well if theologians had made up their minds to accept frankly the principle that those things for the discovery of which man has faculties specially provided are not fit objects for a divine revelation.' But theologians regarded the first chapters of Genesis as revelations which must be harmonized with the discoveries of geology. Goodwin would examine these efforts, believing 'that if the value of the Bible as a book of religious instruction is to be maintained, it must be not by striving to prove it scientifically exact, at the expense of every sound principle of interpretation, and in defiance of common sense, but by the frank recognition of the erroneous view of nature which it contains'.[65] He analysed minutely the opening chapters of Genesis,[66] pointing out that the style is narrative, not poetical or mystical, that its *prima facie* meaning is directly opposed to modern astronomy and geology, and 'that the order of things as we now know them to be, is to a great extent reversed'.[67]

Goodwin dealt with the two main lines of 'harmonizing'. The first was represented by Dean Buckland's Bridgewater treatise of 1836,[68] which argued that 'In the beginning' covered an indefinite period of time, sufficient for all the changes recorded by geology, so that the six days of Genesis were only a final restructuring of the world for mankind after a brief chaos. Goodwin had no difficulty in showing how this argument did violence to 'the grand and simple words of the Hebrew writer'. Further, Buckland was refuted by the other leading 'harmonizer', the popular geologist Hugh Miller, who argued instead that the 'days' of creation represent geological eras. Goodwin pointed out that the order of the days of creation does not match the order in which species are found in geological strata. Both theories treated the 'Mosaic' account as a riddle, not to be interpreted according to the plain meaning of the words, but rather to be made to fit the current state of geological thought. It would be more honest to acknowledge the fallibility of the Mosaic account, 'the speculation of some Hebrew Descartes or Newton', giving his theories in factual language, imperfect but sufficient, for 'the plan of Providence for the education of man is a progressive one' and uses imperfect men as its agents. The Mosaic account was to be revered for its role in laying the foundation of religion, but it need no longer be defended as factual: 'we recognize in it, not an authentic utterance of Divine knowledge, but a human utterance, which it has pleased Providence to use in a special way for the education of mankind'.[69]

In one sense Goodwin's essay was the most successful of the seven, for the 'harmonizing' school soon vanished from the scene: 'the argument has died of its own victory'.[70] But Goodwin deserves little credit for this: 'harmonizing' would anyhow have been superseded by the debate over evolution,[71] which covered the ground in a more fundamental manner than Goodwin, who disproved the 'harmonies' only by showing that they contradicted each other. Goodwin was flogging a dying horse. He was undoubtedly correct. 'But the arguments men cannot answer are those which arouse their deepest resentment'.[72] Goodwin's pedantically sarcastic style made his essay unpleasant to read. More than any other, it may be faulted for its 'negative tone'.[73] The only positive element lay in the conception of a divine plan for the 'education of mankind', a notion similar to Temple's. But Goodwin's task was a negative one, to demolish fallacious rationalizations of a fallible Genesis, clearing the field for an appreciation of the real revelatory elements in the Bible.

Pattison's essay, 'Tendencies of Religious Thought in England, 1688–1750', is the one truly original and enduring contribution to *Essays and Reviews*. He had been working on the problem of the rise and decline of deism[74] for two years; but the essay almost cries out for a sequel, such a work as, under its influence, Leslie Stephen was to write.[75] Pattison's essay was a pioneering work in the history of ideas, doubly so in that it applied history to religious ideas regarded as products of the culture of their age. 'We have not yet learnt, in this country, to write our ecclesiastical history on any better footing than that of praising up the party, in or out of the Church, to which we happen to belong. Still further are we from any attempt to apply the laws of thought, and of the succession of opinion, to the course of English theology'.[76]

The eighteenth century was despised as a period of religious barrenness; Pattison opened with an apology for treating it seriously. 'The facts of history cannot be disposed of by forgetting them. Both the Church and the world of to-day are what they are as the result of the whole of their antecedents'. To understand the present situation of the Church, one must understand the agencies which produced it. Pattison cited three: the growth of toleration, the Methodist and evangelical revival, and the rise and diffusion of that mode of thought known as rationalism. He found rationalism, 'the assumption of the supremacy of reason in matters of religion', common to all groups, Christian and anti-Christian, 'a habit of thought ruling all minds'. The thought of the entire century was devoted to proving the truth of Christianity by reason, but it can be divided, about 1750, into two periods, the first dealing with the internal, the second with the external, evidences of Christianity. He concentrated on the first period, occupied with the controversy with the deists. However, he offered a brief but severe critique of the writers of the second period, dominated by Paley, whose external evidences were only ingenious intellectual exercises, avoiding the real problems of the historical study of the origins of Christianity. The current 'unwholesome state of theological feeling among us, is perhaps traceable in part to the falsetto of the evidential method of the last generation', which 'professes that its religious belief rests on historical evidence' but 'refuses to allow that evidence to be examined in open court'. Both parts of the century were liable to the common censure that the study of the evidences of Christianity is philosophy rather than theology, an argument for religion rather than religious knowledge itself. 'When an age is found occupied in proving its creed, this is but a token that the age has ceased to have a proper belief in it'.[77]

Most of Pattison's essay is a study of the deistical controversy, a debate characterized by the appeal to common-sense reason by all sides. Its result was a religion which amounted to an ethical code reinforced by divine sanctions but devoid of the supernatural. 'The defect of the eighteenth century was not in having too much good sense, but in having nothing else besides'. The evidential method was an inadequate instrument of theological inquiry; but Pattison suggested that the test of common sense might not be entirely useless 'in the present day when a godless orthodoxy threatens ... to extinguish religious thought altogether, and nothing is allowed in the Church of England but the formulae of past thinkings ... As poetry is not for the critics, so religion is not for the theologians'. The vice bequeathed by the religious thought of the eighteenth century to the nineteenth was the habit of advocacy rather than inquiry, the obsession with defending the faith. Eventually, the failure of prudential ethics led to the rise of the evangelical movement, which replaced 'legal' with Gospel preaching; but even the evangelicals felt the temper of the time and sought to rationalize an atonement-centred doctrine. Pattison concluded ironically.

> ... whoever would take the religious literature of the present day as a whole, and endeavour to make out clearly on what basis Revelation is supposed by it to rest, whether on Authority, on the Inward Light, on Reason, on self-evidencing Scriptures, or on the combination of the four, or some of them, and in what proportions, would probably find that he had undertaken a perplexing but not altogether profitless inquiry.[78]

Pattison's article, original both in method and substance, is 'the best single study in the book',[79] serving still as one of the finest surveys of eighteenth-century religious thought.[80] It was, with few exceptions, purely historical; it offered no occasion for objection on doctrinal grounds; even the inevitable criticism of its 'negative tone' and 'coldness' meant only that readers in 1860 were unable to appreciate an objective study of religious history. In fact, Pattison's objectivity concealed some polemics. He threw out occasional remarks against High Church obscurantism; he showed that the evangelicals fell into the rationalist trap; his critique of the evidential method struck at the foundations of current apologetics; and, by showing that religious ideas had a history, he implied that nineteenth-century orthodoxy was also subject to change. Basil Willey found Pattison's 'oblique strategy'[81] more subversive than any other essay. Contemporary readers were more likely to be repelled by Pattison's icy impartiality, to find an aura of menace in his pitiless dissection of all views and in his open-ended conclusion. The feature which makes the essay valuable in the twentieth century, historical objectivity, was a fault in the nineteenth: the failure of the author to state his own position seemed a dishonest evasion of responsibility.[82] Pattison suggested his own creed only in hints: his separation of religious philosophy from theology, his recognition of the need for a supernatural element lacking in rational religion, and his demand for that truthfulness and fact-facing which could not be found in existing parties in the Church.

Jowett's tremendous though wayward essay 'On the Interpretation of Scripture' was the longest in the volume. It was the product of more than a decade's thought. Conceived in 1857, it was intended as an appendix to the second edition of the commentary on St Paul (1859), but Jowett could not finish it in time. Wilson's proposal of *Essays and Reviews* provided an occasion to complete the essay. Much of it was written during the winter vacation of 1859–60 on a visit to Tennyson.[83] Yet readers might have thought it specially written for the volume, so easily does it seem to incorporate and sum up themes from other essays, to bring them round again to the theme of 'the education of the world',[84] and to raise the discussion to a reverential atmosphere.

Jowett began by noting that there was a greater variety of interpretation of the Bible than of any other book. Yet the Bible remained unchanged in its meaning: 'The office of the interpreter is not to add another, but to recover the original one; the meaning, that is, of the words as they first struck on the ears or flashed before the eyes of those who heard and read them'. The interpreter must transfer himself in thought to the biblical age, 'disengage himself from all that follows', including 'all the after-thoughts of theology',[85] and see things as they then were. The apologetic tendency of much writing on Scripture obscured this, but the recent development of the critical spirit in Germany led educated persons to ask 'not what Scripture may be made to mean, but what it does'. Charges of deism or atheism against such inquirers 'are inconsistent with the freedom of the truth and the moral character of the Gospel'.

The first question for reasonable criticism was that of inspiration, a vague term for many of whose uses there was little warrant in Scripture. Our only knowledge of inspiration is that which we have from Scripture, with all its variations, inaccuracies and partial presentations of truth; yet 'a principle of progressive revelation admits them all'. A true concept of inspiration must conform to established facts of history and science. The question of inspiration was largely irrelevant to that of interpretation: it was more important to find the meaning than the proofs. Scripture had been selectively interpreted, some portions given undue weight and others neglected. Jowett cited eight doctrines which had uncertain Scriptural warrant: divorce, marriage with deceased wife's sister, inspiration, the personality of the Holy Spirit, infant baptism, episcopacy, divine right of kings, and original sin. 'To avoid misconception' he stated that many of these 'have sufficient grounds; the weakness is the attempt to derive them from Scripture'.[86] Jowett showed the difficulties of 'proving' doctrines from Scriptural passages and the danger of using creedal or liturgical language to interpret Scripture.[87] His object was not to determine any of these questions but to point out that they needed to be determined before progress and agreement can be achieved in interpretation. Only critical principles could overcome the present licence of interpretation, the use of Scripture as a vehicle for current opinions. 'The book in which we believe all religious truth to be contained, is the most uncertain of all books, because interpreted by arbitrary and uncertain methods'.

Some might feel the exposure of the difficulties of Scripture to be dangerous, and the third and greatest section of the essay responded to this concern. The difficulties were well known to educated people and inherent in current tendencies of thought; 'reticence' led to 'a sort of smouldering scepticism ... Doubt comes in at the window, when Inquiry is denied at the door'. Since the Gospel must not be opposed to the love of truth, 'as the time has come when it is no longer possible to ignore the results of criticism, it is of importance that Christianity should be seen to be in harmony with them ... The Christian religion is in a false position when all the tendencies of knowledge are opposed to it'. Those who seek to avert 'the withdrawal of the educated classes from the influence of religion' must disengage Christianity from all suspicion of dishonesty:

> They are willing to take away some of the external supports, because they are not needed and do harm; also, because they interfere with the meaning ... When interpreted like any other book, by the same rules of evidence and the same canons of criticism, the Bible will still remain unlike any other book ... it will create a new interest and make for itself a new kind of authority by the life which is in it.[88]

A few simple precepts provided sufficient guidance; above all, '*Interpret the Scripture like any other book*'.[89] The meaning must be ascertained by an 'inductive' process. Each text has but one meaning: that which it had to the original prophet or evangelist and his audience, into whose world the interpreter must be reborn, and which admitted of no hidden or mysterious meanings. Scripture must be interpreted from itself, only the works of one age or writer being compared with themselves, avoiding indiscriminate use of random parallel passages. 'Scripture is a world by itself, from which we must exclude foreign influences, whether theological or classical.' The soul of Scripture is the growing revelation of the Old and New Testaments; its body is language, which must be truly understood.

> Of what has been said, this is the sum; – 'That Scripture, like other books, has one meaning, which is to be gathered from itself without reference to

the adaptations of Fathers and Divines; and without regard to *a priori* notions about its nature and origin. It is to be interpreted like other books, with attention to the character of its authors, and the prevailing state of civilization and knowledge, and modes of thought and figures of speech. Yet not without a sense that as we read there grows upon us the witness of God in the world, anticipating in a rude and primitive age the truth that was to be, shining more and more unto the perfect day in the life of Christ, which again is reflected from different points of view in the teaching of His Apostles.'[90]

Jowett, distinguishing the interpretation from the application of Scripture, devoted the rest of his essay to applications, encouraging 'a more truthful use of Scripture in practice'. Criticism was for the educated, not the multitude, yet it contributed to all by opening the original meaning and universal truth of Scripture. As criticism put an end to traditional controversies about the Bible, its moral power would grow. For those clergymen who found criticism difficult, there was other pastoral work; but those who renounced inquiry must not condemn the inquirers. 'Criticism is not only negative; if it creates some difficulties, it does away others. It throws us back upon the conviction that religion is a personal thing, in which certainty is to be slowly won and not assumed as the result of evidence or testimony'. He who undertakes the work of criticism, despite public opinion or church parties, 'has by a divine help been able to plant his foot beyond the waves of time ... not without a sure hope that the love of truth, which men of saintly lives often seem to slight, is, nevertheless, accepted before God'.[91]

Jowett's essay towers above the others, simmering with intense but restrained passion, reverent yet intellectual, and readable and worth reading a century later. Purely as literature, it was 'a masterpiece of cool, but not cold, English writing upon a hot and explosive topic'.[92] The religious sentiment and reverence for the Bible tended to make it palatable to the religious public and difficult to assail,[93] even by those who were shocked by its easy disclosure of difficulties in orthodox interpretations. Jowett argued for a renewal of that Reformation spirit which opened the Bible to the people, purifying religion by clearing away false ideas and returning to the sources. In its aspirations if not its results, his essay was the most constructive in the volume. His immediate task was destructive, removing obstructions to the direct hearing of the Word of God. Trusting that the Word would speak for itself when its meaning was made evident, Jowett felt no need to propose his own reconstruction of the Christian faith.

The essay was not without faults. Jowett's canon that each text of the Bible bore only one meaning was simplistic and inadequate even from a literary point of view. His literary criticism was little more than mere philology, 'a static view of literature'.[94] Jowett was deficient in his view of history: he insisted on a progressive revelation but denied progress or development in the growth of theology. Thus he appeared to deny a legitimate place for definite theological statements in the work of religion. His main fault was a failure to perceive that the word 'interpretation' concealed two distinct operations, the analysis of the text and the search for the meaning.

> For inside Jowett two persons strove for the mastery. One was the Platonic philosopher, the other the textual critic of Greek. The Platonic philosopher wanted to see the ideal truth embodied behind the external word, and desired men not to look to the letter but the spirit. The textual critic wanted to go straight to the text of Scripture, strip it of traditional interpretations, see it in its historical context, and discover a single meaning. The critic took men to the letter, the philosopher urged them to rise above it. In consequence this long and powerful essay, for all its fragmentary beauty, left the reader in doubt how he ought to pursue the truth of religion.[95]

Jowett's achievement was not his biblical criticism but his effort to avert the 'withdrawal of the educated classes from the influence of religion' by bridging the gap between Christian teaching and the intellect of the age. It must be shown that Christianity was not only true but truthful, that it could honestly face up to the results of science and criticism. 'His object was to reconcile intellectual persons to Christianity, and to exhort the clergy to the love of Truth'.[96] His essay was a plea, rising to impassioned eloquence, for the freedom of scholarship necessary to find that truth which unites reason to faith. In the literature of human freedom, Jowett's essay deserves a place beside Milton's *Areopagitica*.

The seven essays and reviews were uneven in their quality, diverse in their subjects, and diffuse in their effects. Had they been published separately or anonymously,[97] none would have occasioned a controversy. It was the conjunction of them in one volume, implying a common theme, and signed by persons of important clerical status, that drew attention. The orthodox regarded this as a conspiracy. The historian is more likely to be struck by the lack of coordination, the accidental factors that drew these writers to publish together in this format, and the unplanned coincidence of views and cumulative effect of such disparate writings.

In this volume, the English religious public was exposed, seemingly for the first time,[98] to a concentrated dose of biblical criticism, with the suggestion that its results should transform received theological views. The achievements of German scholarship were presented in English by approving English clergymen. The 'Germanism' of *Essays and Reviews* struck contemporaries more forcibly than it should have. It was not particularly advanced or radical: the approved Germans were moderates such as Ewald or De Wette; Baur was slighted and Strauss disapproved.[99] The essays varied in their Germanism: Wilson and Pattison pursued peculiarly English themes; Goodwin cited no Germans; Powell went his own way.[100] Only Temple, taking his title from Lessing, Williams, who intended to introduce English readers to German thought, and Jowett, who confidently assumed its results, show clear German influence. In any case, no German could have written as the Essayists did. Ieuan Ellis, who argues that 'the essayists' "Germanism" is the most important element in their book', concedes that it was 'qualified and conditioned' by the fact that 'the essayists used the German teachers for their own purposes'.[101] Even in its 'Germanism', *Essays and Reviews* is a very English book.

More significant was the influence of Coleridge; but even this was neither dominant nor uniform. Perhaps the only Coleridgian concept accepted by all the Essayists was the rejection of the external evidences of religion. Goodwin was otherwise immune to Coleridge, and Powell, who quoted him once, was largely opposed. The two most explicitly Coleridgian Essayists were Williams with his 'verifying faculty' and Wilson with his 'National Church'.

Although the book brought biblical criticism to English readers, it made no contribution to biblical studies. Only Pattison broke new ground, in the field of history; Jowett's efforts were limited to methodology. The function of the Essayists was to clear the way for a work which they themselves did nothing to advance.[102] The Essays were prolegomena to a prolegomenon. They were never followed up.

Certain leading ideas were common to most Essayists,[103] and the tentative outlines of a common theology may be discerned. It appeared most evidently as a negative theology, seeking to destroy false ideas and attitudes; only in hints and implications can its positive elements be found. The implications were those of a new Reformation, with the goal of allowing the inner essence of the Bible and faith to manifest itself without interference. The two cornerstones of the new Reformation were truth and conscience.

The conventional teachings of orthodoxy were regarded as obstacles to the truth of Christianity and the truthfulness of its professors. Orthodox theology had rested the truth of revelation on the external evidences of miracles and prophecies; it had treated revelation as isolated statements of facts accepted as given; it had rejected scientific, historical or literary criticism which differed from prejudged conclusions. The common sense of educated laymen was beginning to recognize the falsity of many orthodox positions, and a gap was opening between professed faith and real belief. Dishonest maintenance of false interpretations was breeding an unnecessary rejection of the truth of Christianity. (The most passionate expressions of the Essayists came when they denounced the dishonesty by which faith was defended.) The gap between Christianity and modern society, between faith and reason, must be bridged. This could only be done by a fearless acceptance of all truth and a scrupulous truthfulness on the part of the defenders of Christianity. They must be ready to abandon all untenable positions and to recognize that the faith was not dependent either on the factual accuracy of the Bible or on an evidential apologetic.

The positive theology was less fully developed. Revelation must be recognized as having been progressive. Its truth was not factual but spiritual, the 'bright centre of spiritual truth' which remained even when its evidential props were removed. It could be ascertained by a 'verifying faculty' in the moral sense. The Christian revelation consists not of doctrinal propositions but of moral principles, and doctrines must conform to the standards of conscience. The ultimate revelation was in conscience itself, awakened by the Church and instructed by the Bible.

Such a theology has beauties never adequately appreciated and difficulties all too easily recognized. On the negative side it was reductionist, seeking to place Christianity beyond challenge by avoiding vulnerability to the results of scientific inquiry. But the spiritual truth that remained was as indefinable as it was invulnerable. It seemed to consist of a pure ethicality surrounded by an ineffable glow of spirituality, a will to believe rather than the substance of belief. Among intellectuals, morality touched with emotion might be viable; but it was a rather thin religion for the multitude. Yet this criticism is not entirely just to the Essayists. They were in fact anti-intellectualist. They confined the role of the intellect to the negative operations of clearing away false interpretations, leaving revelation and conscience to conduct their dialogue undisturbed. To this dialogue the intellect had nothing to contribute; hence the Essayists denigrated doctrinal theology as 'scholastic'. They had faith in the ability of the conscience to respond to Christian truth when that truth was presented in its nakedness. Hence they exposed the nakedness of Victorian Christianity, and they met the predictable Victorian reaction – shock.[104]

The shock was all the greater because *Essays and Reviews* challenged precisely those positions upon which orthodoxy had chosen to fall back at this particular moment.[105] When Mansel rested the case for revelation solely on the external evidences of miracles and prophecies, when Archbishop Whately of Dublin thought it a sufficient defence of the faith to republish Paley's works,[106] English theology had confidently exposed its most vulnerable points to a criticism which, even if inadequate by German standards, would nonetheless be withering. Seeking to lance the boils of error and deceit, the Essayists had touched the rawest nerves of Victorian orthodoxy.

CHAPTER FIVE

Early Responses

Unlike Darwin's *Origin of Species*, *Essays and Reviews* did not obtain instant notoriety. It seemed that the book received little notice. The usual account is that the debate began in October, with Frederic Harrison's review in the *Westminster Review*, followed in January by Samuel Wilberforce in the *Quarterly* and in April by Stanley in the *Edinburgh*. But there was a prehistory of the debate before the three great quarterlies placed it in the public domain.[1]

The volume appears not to have been reviewed by the daily newspapers, certainly not by *The Times*. A few general weeklies noticed it. The *Spectator* published the first review on April 7, 1860, praising the 'noble precedent' of the Essayists as champions of free speech for the clergy.[2] The *Literary Gazette* had an unfavourable review on April 14.[3] A substantial hostile review appeared on April 21 in the *Press*, a Tory journal.[4]

It was the religious press that carried the debate, which started slowly. A periodical that missed the early debate, the nonconformist *Evangelical Review*, explained that, although 'we' had read the volume, 'we saw no need of calling attention to it, as from its contents it appeared unfitted for general reading'.[5] The first notice came in the High Church weekly, the *Guardian*, on April 4, as 'a slight sketch', sarcastically noting 'a book which is likely to create a sensation'.[6] Williams called this 'a satirical but ignorant mention of the existence of *Essays and Reviews*, with the promise of more hereafter'.[7] The more extensive review did not appear until late in May.

The first reviews in religious monthlies appeared in May. A long article entitled 'Broad Church Theology' was published in the evangelical *Christian Observer*. After criticizing the essays *seriatim*, it concluded: 'This volume of *Essays and Reviews* is the "Tract No. XC" of the Broad Church School ... meant to establish the principle, that a man may retain the orders and benefices of the Church, *without believing the Bible* ... the church must cleanse itself from this shame, or find its existence endangered'.[8] This was the first call for action against the Essayists. Another theme which reappeared in the debate was sounded at the same time by the High Church *Ecclesiastic*. Calling *Essays and Reviews* the inauguration of a 'New Gospel', it suggested conspiracy and joint responsibility:

> if there was not concert, there was, at least, community of purpose and ... some kind of prearrangement. This strengthens the indignation which must be felt at the moral obtuseness of cowardice ... which makes one of the parties to an onslaught against revealed religion, shrink from the responsibilities of his fellow-worker.[9]

The article concentrated on Temple as the first essayist; a sequel, on 'Dr. Williams and Others', appeared in the next issue.[10]

Notices of *Essays and Reviews* appeared in the Anglican evangelical newspaper, the *Record*, in May. Covering the May meetings at Exeter Hall, it reported a speech on May 2 by Canon Miller to the Bible Society, alluding to 'a volume of essays, recently published by clergymen of eminence connected with Oxford, which was a sign of the times'.[11] On May 21 a Presbyterian asked in a letter why such men were permitted to remain clergymen: 'Can nothing be done to revive the discipline of the Church of England?'[12] That day the *Record* spoke for itself in a leading article. *Essays and Reviews*, 'if unchallenged, will produce more evil than anything which has issued from the press for a long period ... their direct and necessary tendency is to subvert all faith'.[13]

On May 23 the *Guardian* published its review, severe yet judicious. It discriminated between the inoffensive essays of Temple and Pattison and the objectionable essays of the others. Each of the offending five was dealt with in detail, with a special tractarian cut at Wilson, who had protested against Newman in 1841: 'the famous "Tract 90" contained no special pleading if these articles do not'. The *Essays* were 'fraught with dangerous error, and even utterly subversive of revealed religion'.[14] Their 'chief influence will be with minds naturally of a speculative and sceptical turn; and, with them, it will tend to a confirmation of doubts, and the shaking of their faith ... And thus the Church may lose ... some few, yet those few not the least able, of those whose best and freshest energies ought to have been dedicated to her'.[15]

In June the *Record* established itself as the most inveterate opponent of *Essays and Reviews*. On June 1, it published a critical review of Temple's essay, drawing attention to Temple's personal position as a Doctor of Divinity, chaplain to the Queen and headmaster of Rugby.[16] A leading article on June 8 discussed the position of the Essayists as clergymen of the Church of England. Clergymen do not have the same 'freedom of thought' as laymen:

> ... they are bound by the ties of honour and morality not to transgress the margin indicated by the Church. Should they do so, it becomes the duty of all who have authority to testify their disapprobation in the strongest possible manner ... It is peremptorily necessary that the heterodox sentiments put forth in the volume ... should be publicly condemned ... Unless this cancerous development be eradicated from amongst us, and that quickly, there will be a general defection from the truth.[17]

On June 18 the *Record* reported an incident at the Middle Class Examinations at Birmingham at which the chairman, Rev. W. Cockin, interjected some comments hostile to the volume, apropos of Temple, an originator of the Examinations: 'It would be an evil day for this country when the unsanctified intellect was made the idol which all men were to worship'.[18]

Whether due to the reviews or to the publisher's advertising,[19] the first edition of *Essays and Reviews* was exhausted in June and a second edition, also of

1000 copies, was published. At the end of the month the book received un-wanted praise when it was favourably noticed by the atheist *National Reformer*.[20]

In July the High Church *Christian Remembrancer* had a chance to become the first quarterly to deal with *Essays and Reviews*: its article was 'already in type' when an 'accident ... at the last moment postponed' its appearance until Octo-ber.[21] But the *Christian Observer*, which had promised a sequel to its May article, delivered a joint review of *Essays and Reviews* and a life of the Unitarian Theodore Parker, whose views it regarded as identical. The *Christian Observer* stressed the personal positions of the Essayists:

> We have a chaplain to the queen, a head-master of Rugby school, a vice-president of St David's college, a vicar of Broad Chalke, a vicar of Great Staughton, and two Oxford professors, not believing the creeds of the Church, – those very creeds on the profession of which they were admit-ted ... into the possession of all these honours and preferments!

It insisted on the collective liability of the Essayists to censure:

> ... in secular matters, the combination of seven men, to do a certain illegal act, is always taken to involve every one of them in the whole guilt ... If this volume ... is left without censure, it is difficult to see what notice can hereafter be taken of the broadest and plainest declaration of infidelity on the part of any minister of the Church of England.[22]

This article was favourably noticed by the *Record* and the *Church of England Magazine*.[23]

The first reviews in nonconformist journals also appeared in July. The *London Review*, a Methodist organ, reviewing 'The Oxford Essayists', treated them as 'representative ... of the Neologian section of the English Church', with a 'marvellous harmony, more than fortuitous' in its 'desolate strain of an emanci-pated, creedless, semi-mystical Christianity', 'wanting in nothing that the most advanced sections of rational Illuminism could desire'.[24] The Congregationalist *Eclectic Review* also took the orthodox line in a two-part article on 'The Oxford School' in its July and August numbers. It was specifically anti-Anglican and anti-Oxford: 'And this from a Bachelor of Divinity, and a beneficed clergyman of the Church of England! No wonder if, when the Christian ground is cut from beneath their feet, the people should fall back upon Tractarian forms, or into the arms of the Romish Communion'.[25] On the other hand, the Unitarian *Inquirer* was delighted to find in the *Essays* 'the most important confirmation of our most cherished principles'.[26]

August saw the first review in a general magazine, *Fraser's*. Writing as an Anglican layman, W. D. Watson praised the book, saying that 'the educated laity ... will feel deeply grateful to the writers'.[27] But the *North British Review*, the organ of the Scottish Free Kirk, attacked *Essays and Reviews* in a massive review of 'Recent Rationalism in the Church of England', noting that 'what is really new and interesting, is the fact that such a volume should have issued from within the pale of the English Establishment'. In a laboured but reasoned statement of the orthodox position, it argued that the Essayists' method of interpretation was 'inconsistent with the idea that there is present in the Bible a supernatural element, imparting to it the characters of unerring truth and Divine authorship'.[28] The *Christian Observer* published a letter headed 'Religion Without a Creed', complaining that the Essayists denied the ancient creeds without putting anything in their place.[29] The *Record* reappeared with a leader on August 27, noting that *Essays and Reviews* had 'provoked a storm of indignation which will last for some time to come'.[30]

The evangelical journals continued the attack in September. The *Christian Observer* devoted an article to 'Dr. Temple's Place amongst the Oxford Essayists'. Temple was as guilty as any other Essayist and his introductory essay was the 'key-note' of the others. Authoritative censure was demanded:

> Cannot the university, which is alike insulted and injured by such a volume of 'Oxford Essays' ... pronounce an authoritative condemnation? ... then may we not look to our bishops. Can not, and will not, our bishops collectively, as well as individually, pronounce their solemn verdict against Dr. Temple and his compeers? This is the season for visitations and episcopal charges; let the note of warning be clear and lucid.[31]

The *Record* filled the month with articles on *Essays and Reviews*. A leader on September 3 lamented that 'the criticisms which we and others have thought proper to make ourselves responsible for on the late notorious *Essays and Reviews* should, by some of the conductors of the press, be sternly denounced as another attempt to smother liberty of thought and bind the human intellect in the trammels of a self-styled orthodoxy'.[32] This may be a response to the article in *Fraser's* or to a short notice that Wilson had inserted in the July *Westminster Review*.[33] Two articles, on September 12 and 14, dealt with Williams' essay; they were principally intended to demolish Bunsen's reputation but included the usual reflections on Williams' personal position.[34] An article on September 21 reviewed Powell and Pattison, defending the 'external evidences' of the Bible with an original evangelical slant.[35] Wilson's essay was reviewed on September 28, the reviewer accusing all the Essayists of 'the virtual denial of all objective truth' and calling the book 'infidelity with a surplice on'.[36] The series was completed with articles on Goodwin and Jowett in early October, but the *Record* continued to pursue the Essayists intermittently through 1860.[37]

In October this debate, largely confined to the religious press, was taken to a larger audience with Harrison's article in the *Westminster Review*, commencing another stage in the controversy. That month also saw the last of the major religious reviews, the postponed article in the *Christian Remembrancer*, whose author used the postponement to expand a 24-page essay with a 34-page peroration, the first largely devoted to Williams and Wilson and the second to Jowett. The article summed up (with a High Church bias) the main lines of attack on *Essays and Reviews*: the collective responsibility of the authors (with exceptions

for Temple and Pattison), the incompatibility of their doctrines with those of
the Church, the personal dishonesty of retaining Church benefices while holding such doctrines, and the need for authoritative condemnation:

> ... we witness the publication of a volume, six of the authors of which are
> clergymen, which ... impugns either directly or by implication all the
> fundamental doctrines of the Church of England. Not only has this vol-
> ume appeared without a disclaimer from either of the Universities ...
> without the smallest notice on the part of any Bishop ... but it has ...
> been met with no sign of disapproval excepting from the *Christian Ob-
> server*, the organ of a party fast hastening to decay.[38]

But this statement was not quite correct. In the religious press, a fairly
vigorous reaction was well under way by October, which the *Record* felt able to
call 'a storm of indignant criticism'. In fact all the main lines of subsequent
criticism had been laid out in these early reviews, and the demand for action
which they seemed to make in vain was about to meet with response. Controversies, like trains, start slowly, and must first build up a head of steam.

CHAPTER SIX

The Great Reviews

Until October 1860, the controversy over *Essays and Reviews* was effectively confined to the specifically religious press, and the general public knew little of its existence. The medium by which it would reach the public was the great quarterly reviews, the radical *Westminster,* the Tory *Quarterly,* and the liberal *Edinburgh.* Conventional accounts of the controversy ignore the religious press and regard the debate as commencing with the *Westminster Review* in October, followed by the *Quarterly* in January 1861, and the *Edinburgh* in April.[1] The Essayists may have been disappointed at the initial lack of notice. Wilson, who continued to write short notices of theology and philosophy in the *Westminster,* took advantage of his anonymous position to publish a preliminary notice in July 1860, describing 'this thoughtful and fearless volume' as 'a work that in a less pusillanimous age would awaken admiring sympathy as well as provoke open and spirited opposition'.[2] Frederic Harrison's full review in the *Westminster* was suggested by Jowett's Balliol friend William Lambert Newman, who told him that Jowett 'feared it was going to be ignored; and that it was Jowett's desire to have the real character and aim of the book made evident'.[3] Newman chose the wrong man. Harrison, a fellow of Wadham College, had just experienced the collapse of his own faith. He saw the Essayists' claim for freedom of thought within the Church in the light of his own emotions on abandoning the Church and was stimulated to write and offer a review to John Chapman, publisher of the *Westminster,* always glad to obtain gratuitous contributions.

Harrison's article, entitled 'Neo-Christianity', proclaimed its glee at finding the spokesmen of Christianity vindicating the principles of rationalism. But it betrayed an impassioned and barely suppressed bitterness against the equivocations by which orthodoxy defended itself and, still more, against the adaptations and compromises by which men of liberal intellect kept themselves within a Church which, if they were consistent with their principles, they ought to leave. Harrison 'felt deeply the moral evil of all this wriggling and prevaricating' and 'wrote under the influence of strong emotion and tension of mind'.[4] Thus he was concerned less with the ideas of the Essays than with the position of the Essayists, whom he regarded as acting as a body, speaking from within the pale of orthodoxy, removing its intellectual foundations yet claiming to be acting in the interests of faith. By stressing the personal position of the Essayists and raising the question of the morality of remaining in the Church while holding their views, Harrison gave the debate its distinctive *ad hominem* character.

'A book has appeared which may serve to mark an epoch in the history of opinion'. Harrison treated *Essays and Reviews* as 'a manifesto from a body of kindred or associated thinkers'[5] opening a new phase of religion, accepting many of the radical ideas of the *Westminster Review* but failing to reach their proper conclusions. He stressed the joint responsibility of the Essayists, both in their 'virtual unity' of purpose and because 'each writer receives a weight and an authority from all the rest of his associates.' The distinguished positions of the authors in the Church gave the work an official *imprimatur* in that it had not been repudiated by the authorities. Yet it was 'in direct antagonism to the whole system of popular belief' and 'incompatible with the religious belief of the mass of the Christian public'. The Essayists had reworked the entire scheme of faith, abandoning the ordinary and natural sense of traditional doctrines. And yet 'they are the pride, the directors, and the representatives of our ecclesiastical foundations'.[6]

The book was then analysed, with Temple's essay given prominence, perhaps because the idea of 'the education of the world' was taken, Harrison said, from Auguste Comte. Temple 'reduced the national position of the Hebrews to the level of the Romans'; Williams, speaking through Bunsen, 'has reduced the critical authority of the Bible to the level of Livy'; Wilson used Ideology by which 'the facts are eliminated, the ideas remain'; and so on through the Essays except for Pattison's, exempt because of its 'purely historical' character. Throughout,

> facts are idealized; dogmas are transformed; creeds are discredited as human and provisional; the authority of the Church and the Bible to establish any doctrine is discarded … In their ordinary, if not plain sense, there has been discarded the Word of God – the Creation – the Fall – the Redemption – Justification, Regeneration, and Salvation – Miracles, Inspiration, Prophecy – Heaven and Hell – Eternal Punishment and a Day of Judgment – Creeds, Liturgies, and Articles – the truth of the Jewish history, and of Gospel narrative – a sense of doubt thrown over even the Incarnation, the Resurrection, and Ascension – the Divinity of the second Person, and the Personality of the third. It may be that this is a true view of Christianity, but we insist in the name of common sense that it is a new view.[7]

But this 'neo-Christianity' was deficient in the light of its own principle of development. Why did the Essayists, after criticizing the Bible, still assign it a singular place in human religion? This ignored the contributions of the larger part of mankind; it interrupted the regularity of the law of development by an external revelation; it gave the Jewish nation an unwarranted importance. This could only be justified on a supernatural basis, which the Essayists rejected. 'Now we maintain that Scripture, as such, has either a supernatural basis, or none at all.' The Essayists, however they may exalt the Bible, could not make it authoritative Scripture. 'There is little use in denouncing bibliolatry in order to encourage bibliology.' The Essayists were like the 'harmonizers', retreating and shifting positions; they were 'exactly in the Hugh Miller stage of the Bible controversy'[8] and must eventually suffer his fate. They were driven by the force of their concept of development, exemplified by Darwin[9] and Buckle, but their own view of development was narrow. They did not fully accept the implications of progress by determinable laws.

The Essayists undermined all religious doctrine and indeed abandoned the idea of doctrine. Jowett's essay 'brings down all the influence of grand and hallowed phrases upon minds enfeebled by a long training of sentences and words ... It offers them a bright, not too systematic view of human goodness, and it frees them from the thraldom of intellectual convictions'. But this was not enough to make a religion. 'Every religion which ever flourished did so by the strength of a body of doctrine and a system of definite axioms ... The whole teaching and influence of every religion has rested ultimately and entirely on cardinal propositions universally received as true.' The 'residuum' of Christianity left by the Essayists was not enough for a religion. Yet their work seemed to have been accepted by the Church. 'Nowhere has there been seen or heard a sign of official repudiation. These professors, tutors, principals, and masters still hold their chairs and retain their influence. No authorised rebuke has been put forward. They have been left to the bark of the toothless watchdogs of orthodoxy.'[10]

The whole affair showed the 'prevalence of intellectual doubt ... the vague intellectual craving, the waste of moral purpose, the sense of blank indifference' within the Church, affecting its best elements. 'It must be a profound evil that all thinking men should reject a national religion. It is almost worse that they should falsely pretend to accept it.' The only remedy for this 'hypocrisy' was for men to 'bury their dead convictions' and face the conclusions of their own thought. 'Religion, to have strength, must have a doctrine; and a doctrine, to endure now, must embody the outgrowth of human thought.' Such a rational religion could not be attained by the Essayists, 'by subliming religion into an emotion, and making an armistice with science ... of all recent adaptations, the most earnest, and – the most suicidal'.[11]

Harrison's essay instantly established him in the world of letters. It hit home at many points. The rhetorical strategy of the essay was unique. Whole sections were written as if from the standpoint of orthodoxy; they were later to provide staples of orthodox commentary. Only when he had demonstrated that the Essayists taught 'neo-Christianity' did Harrison bring in his own incipiently positivist ideas, which he pointed to as the logical conclusion of their thought. The Essayists were trapped: rationalists were told that they were inadequate, and Churchmen were told that they were unorthodox. By taunting 'the toothless watchdogs of orthodoxy' for not condemning this heresy, Harrison virtually goaded them into doing so. By resting the importance of *Essays and Reviews* on the ecclesiastical positions of the Essayists, Harrison set the tone of the debate, ensuring that it would focus on the persons of the Essayists rather than their ideas.

Harrison's article had an interesting personal sequel. He was both denounced by Stanley for personal malignancy and threatened by an orthodox professor with the loss of his fellowship. To avert the latter he sought help from Stanley and Jowett. Stanley was convinced that his remarks were unjust and removed them from his republished *Edinburgh* essay, though he still felt 'that it was this article which fired the train and gave direction to the subsequent explosion'.[12] Jowett took the young man under his wing, seeking both to prevent Harrison's expulsion and to direct his energies to the removal of subscription to the Articles.[13] But Harrison went on to become the leading positivist in England.

The *Westminster Review* brought *Essays and Reviews* to the attention of the educated public, as the religious periodicals had brought it to the attention of the clergy. So distinct were the two audiences that many clergy might not have known of the article had it not been mentioned in the second act of quarterly reviewing, the January 1861 article in the Tory and Anglican *Quarterly Review* by Samuel Wilberforce, bishop of Oxford. Wilberforce's review was not planned as a response to Harrison.[14] Wilberforce was already engaged in the crusade against *Essays and Reviews*. He had spoken out in his visitation Charge on November 15, 1860, the first bishop to do so.

> When from within our own encampment we hear voices declaring that our whole belief in the atonement wrought for us in the Sacrifice upon the Cross is an ignorant misconception – that the miracles and the prophecies of Scripture are part of an irrational supernaturalism which it is the duty of a remorseless criticism to expose ... that men may sign any Article of the national Church, if it is only their opinions which are at variance with them ... whilst, I say, such words as these are heard from ordained men amongst us, and who still keep their places in the national Church, is it not a time for us ... to combine together in prayer, and trust, and labour, and love, and watching, lest whilst we dispute needlessly about the lesser matters of the law we be robbed unawares of the very foundations of the faith.[15]

Wilberforce's *Quarterly* article was a more massive denunciation. Asking how the volume had excited a degree of interest which far exceeded its merits, Wilberforce found the answer in 'the positions of its writers', the startling novelty that clergymen 'should be the putters forth of doctrines which seem at least to be incompatible with the Bible and the Christian Faith as the Church of England has hitherto received it'. It was a 'painful duty' to point out that 'infidelity, if not Atheism, is the end to which this teaching inevitably tends'.[16]

The first question Wilberforce raised was 'how far it is to be considered as a whole for which all its writers are jointly responsible'. For the purpose and object of the volume, the authors 'admit a unity from which joint responsibility cannot be severed'. This 'common liability ... must extend to the common action of the firm. Any one who undertook to unite in the "free handling" of such subjects in a common volume made himself responsible for the common effect of all the essays as a whole'. Each has the same purpose and 'general tone': 'the free handling of most sacred subjects, the free insinuation of doubts, the freedom of assertion, the free endeavour to defend some shadowy ghost of

Christianity by yielding up all that has hitherto been thought its substance'. Notwithstanding the contrast between 'the pleasing but feeble religious tones of Dr. Temple and the earnest and often loving and plaintive utterances of Mr. Jowett' and 'the scarcely-veiled Atheism of Mr. Baden Powell ... the open scepticism and laxity of Mr. Wilson, and the daring flippancy of Dr. Williams', 'the book must be taken as a whole, and, if condemned, must condemn every writer in it who does not, by some after act, visibly separate himself from the fellowship of opinions to which he is here committed'.[17]

Only after labouring the point of joint responsibility did Wilberforce turn to the substance of the Essays, beginning with Williams, in whose notion of the 'verifying faculty' he found 'the great principle of this school. The idea of this "verifying faculty" – this power of each man of settling what is and what is not true in the Inspired Record – is THE idea of the whole volume'. 'Instead of subjecting man, as to his faith and duty, to an external revelation, he subjects the revelation itself to man's internal consciousness.' Beyond this was Wilson's concept of 'ideology', by which 'the already well-nigh unlimited power of explaining away the letter of the Word of God is increased to the uttermost'. The Creation, the Fall, the Incarnation and the Redemption 'pass away together in the mists of this rationalizing ideology'. Wilberforce especially criticized Williams' denial of predictive prophecy. He summed up the teaching of the Essayists as the acceptance, in a Bible largely legendary or poetical, of a residuum of revelation, determinable by each man's 'verifying faculty', excluding most of the Old Testament, all miracles and predictive prophecy, useful only for moral instruction, not specially inspired by God but merely 'the record of the religious life of past ages'.[18]

'The definite dogmatic teaching of the Church is the object of the essayists' peculiar animosity.' Temple suggested and Jowett developed the 'dissolving in a general halo of goodness all distinct doctrinal truth', and their 'more outspoken brethren' pursue this 'abandonment of all Christian doctrine ... without the aid of that softening haze of Christian sentiment'. In Jowett and Wilson 'there is an absolute lack of perception of what sin is, and so of what atonement is', a repudiation of 'the cardinal doctrine of the Atonement'. Williams 'sublimes into symbol and poetry the Trinity, the Incarnation, man's justification with God through faith in Jesus Christ, and the resurrection of the body'.[19]

Wilberforce then came to his main point:

> ... as honest men and as believers in Christianity, we must pronounce these views as absolutely inconsistent with its Creeds, and must therefore hold that the attempt of the Essayists to combine their advocacy of such doctrines with the retention of the status and emolument of Church of England clergymen is simply moral dishonesty ... It is impossible honestly to combine the maintenance of such a system and the ministry of the English Church.

Wilson's effort to reconcile subscription with lack of assent was dismissed as 'Jesuitry': 'in the name of the God of truth, either let all teaching cease, or let the fraudulent instructor abdicate willingly his office'. Subscription 'is to be considered as binding the conscience of the promiser to the fulfillment of that which he believes the imposer of the obligation to intend'. Wilberforce contrasted Wilson's 1860 position with his condemnation of Newman's loose views of the Articles in 1841. Whether the ideas of the Essayists were right or wrong, 'they are essentially and completely at variance with the doctrinal teaching of the Church of England, and cannot ... be advisedly maintained by honest men who hold her ministry ... Those who hold them are in a position in which it is impossible to remain'.[20]

The position of the Essayists must lead further, to unbelief. 'They believe too much not to believe more, and they disbelieve too much not to disbelieve everything'. Wilberforce noted that 'they are claimed as brethren by infidels of every shade', citing the *National Reformer*[21] and the article in the *Westminster Review*, from which he quoted at length. 'It is not often that we can agree with our outspoken contemporary ... but undoubtedly he is here altogether in the right. It is not indeed a "neo-Christianity", but a new religion, which our Essayists would introduce.' They should do 'as their brother unbelievers invite them to do, renounce the hopeless attempt at preserving Christianity without Christ, without the Holy Ghost, without a Bible, and without a God'. Believers must give them no hearing, but 'guard themselves against the first approach of everything which it can be shown tends to shake their faith in that revelation, the reception of which is so great a part of their probation'. For 'the spiritual child of the Rationalist develops into the Atheist'.

> There can be no religious system which is not founded upon definite teaching as to God, and as to His relations with us ... The attempt to retain the Bible ... as a rule of life; as giving moral precepts; as expressing high and ennobling sentiments; and yet to deprive its voice of the authority of inspiration, and to silence it as to the great doctrines of Christianity, – is to endeavour to maintain unshaken a vast and curiously constructed edifice, when you have deliberately removed all the foundations upon which it is built.[22]

Wilberforce argued that the Essayists' overvaluation of criticism was drawn from 'the German Rationalists', themselves the heirs of eighteenth-century English deists. German criticism had been 'completely refuted' by other Germans. Wilberforce criticized 'the shallow philosophy and indifferent scholarship of the writers'. They had strung together 'the current and already abundantly repelled objections and fallacies of German rationalism'.[23]

Wilberforce concluded by repeating his 'conviction that holding their views, they cannot, consistently with moral honesty, maintain their posts as clergymen of the Established Church'. He did not fear that they would 'exert any widespread influence'. The Church would unite, for 'all the schools ... of theological opinion amongst us are opposed to the Essayists'. His final word was to dismiss the 'craving' for a 'theory of inspiration' to explain the Bible rationally, itself 'a part of the disease we have to treat'. 'Holy Scripture has never laid down any theory of inspiration; the Church has never propounded one; and there are plain and we think sufficient reasons for this reticence.' One must accept 'that there is a mighty and mysterious presence of God in this His Word' and not seek to penetrate the mystery with 'proud curiosity'.[24]

Wilberforce's article created a sensation, sending the January number of the *Quarterly* through five editions.[25] It established the bishop of Oxford as the leader of the crusade against *Essays and Reviews*. Virtually every argument that appeared in the later outpouring of tracts can be found in this much-cited article. It shows 'Soapy Sam's' style at its most effective, sometimes slashing, often clever, full of telling phrases, masking invective with authoritativeness and religious fervour, sometimes personally unfair while assuming the position of one who had been unjustly injured. It was intellectually able, presenting the case for dogmatism explicitly and reasonably. It was sullied by the personalistic element, the stress on joint responsibility before considering the substance of the arguments, and the insistence on the untenability of the personal position of the Essayists as clergymen, which was to dominate the debate. But it was the most effective piece of controversial writing in the entire debate.

Stanley's essay in the April *Edinburgh Review* was deliberately written to complete the series of three great reviews, responding directly to the other two. He began by treating the affair as an episode in 'the history of religious panics'.[26] He traced the origins of *Essays and Reviews*, emphasizing the unconcerted character of the book. Stanley fixed 'the main responsibility of the whole subsequent agitation' on the *Westminster Review* article, 'the first muttering of a coming whirlwind' with its 'unscrupulous misrepresentation' and 'malignant insinuations',[27] after which 'the partisans of the two chief theological schools' took up the issue. 'The first decisive signal that the rising hostility had penetrated into a higher sphere' was the article in the *Quarterly*, which made it 'apparent that a powerful ecclesiastical influence was at work, eager to seize the opportunity of crushing not merely the book, but the writers themselves'. It was 'an elaborate invective aimed at high reputations, and stimulated by the dread lest inquiry into any single part of theological truth should overturn the whole of the popular religious systems of the day'. A month later came the episcopal letter, 'a document we believe without precedent in the history of the English Reformed Church', which involved the bishops 'in a fierce attack on the ecclesiastical position of five distinguished clergymen ... yet brought no precise charges against them ... It was an unqualified censure of a book, of which the varied sentiments and unequal merits required the most discriminating judgment'. Stanley scoffed at the votes in Convocation, 'an indiscriminate censure directed against a book whose contents they claimed the privilege of never having read, and which, having thus condemned, they subsequently proceeded to examine through a committee'.[28]

Turning to *Essays and Reviews*, Stanley began with criticism:

> The project of such a composite work was, as we have thought from the
> very first, a decided blunder ... The joint appearance of the 'Essays' was
> certain to excite the suspicion of an identity of sentiment, when no such
> identity really existed. Combined action is useful only in cases where each
> name in the combination gives strength to every other. But, in this case,
> with perhaps one exception, every name out of the seven, in the eyes of
> those who most needed to be conciliated, added not strength but weakness
> to the rest.

But 'the whole panic is based on a falsehood', the notion of a conspiracy. 'Their
protest against joint liability has been shamefully disregarded; and they cannot,
as it seems to us, add to its force by any further disclaimer.' Stanley criticized the
'negative character' of the book, though acknowledging 'constructive elements'
in the essays of Temple and Jowett. 'Still there is a disparaging tone throughout
the work as a whole which provokes opposition, and excites distrust.' Another
fault was that the book was 'addressed to the public promiscuously'. Its opponents had alarmed the public with misleading quotations, but the Essayists had
'overlooked this natural consequence of such a publication'. Williams and Wilson
were particularly at fault, 'Conclusions arrived at by the life-long labours of a
great German theologian are thrown before the English public, who never heard
of them before, without any argument to support or recommend them.'[29]

All other faults must be attributed to individual writers. Stanley did not
speak of Baden Powell, now dead, whose essay 'stands in no direct relation to
the others, and may be treated as belonging altogether to the past', nor of the
layman Goodwin, whose essay 'may also be considered as practically defunct'
because the irrelevance of Scripture to geology was generally acknowledged. The
other Essayists deserve 'a respectful consideration' for their antecedents and
future position in the Church. Temple 'sits in the chair of Arnold'; Jowett 'is the
only man in the University of Oxford who has exercised a moral or spiritual
influence at all corresponding to that which was once wielded by John Henry
Newman'.[30]

Turning to the essays, Stanley agreed 'that most of them fail in reaching quite
to the level of the reputation of their respective authors, and that the first and
the last stand far above the others'. Temple's essay must be viewed as the sermon
it once was, validated by its text on 'the fulness of time'. Jowett furnished 'a
valuable supplement' to his work on St Paul. 'We do not envy the man who can
read through the Essay, and particularly its closing pages, unimpressed by the
lofty tone which breathes through its expositions of the power of our Lord's
words, and its inculcations of the love of truth as the first of religious duties.'
Pattison's learned essay was a sequel to those he had written in the *Quarterly
Review*. 'No lens less powerful than the microscope for detecting heresies, could
have discovered any dangerous tendencies in it, had it appeared under a brown
instead of a purple cover.' Williams was blamed for his 'flippant and contemptu-

ous tone'. Wilson's 'powerful though often rash defence of the general principle of a national church' led him to make 'extreme statements'.[31]

The volume and its critics raised two general questions, the proper mode of interpreting the Bible and the relative worth of internal and external evidence. On these points,

> it has been a prodigious mistake to suppose that this volume contains anything new ... with the possible exception of Professor Powell's Essay, and a few words of Dr. Williams and Dr. Wilson, there is no statement of doctrine or fact in this volume which has not been repeatedly set forth by divines whose deep and sincere faith in the Christian religion cannot be denied without the worst uncharitableness.

Stanley listed predecessors and contemporaries, German and English, from Coleridge to Westcott, who recognized the same facts and beliefs. 'If there be a conspiracy, it is one far more formidable than that of seven Essayists. For it is a conspiracy in which half the rising generation, one quarter of the Bench of Bishops, the most leading spirits of our clergy, have been, and are, and will be engaged'. On 'the question of Inspiration itself, there is nothing in the present volume which ought to excite surprise beyond what has been said a hundred times before'. Inspiration 'is a question to be solved not by speculating what the Bible ought to be, but by seeing what it actually is', its 'multiform diversity' and mixture of the human and the divine. Was it pious or reverential 'to deny the human in order to exalt the divine? ... It is because we prize the kernel that we are content to break the shell'. On the question of evidences, Stanley cited authorities from Justin Martyr to Dean Trench who prefer internal evidences. The Essayists

> do not deny miracles, but they feel the increasing difficulties which scientific and historical criticism places in the way of the old, unreasoning reception of mere wonders as interferences with natural law, or as absolute proofs of a Divine Revelation ... they have done their best to lessen the collision between the religious belief and the scientific conclusions of mankind ... They have attempted, in short – mistakenly or not – to place Christianity beyond the reach of accidents, whether of science or criticism; to rest its claims on those moral and spiritual truths which, after all, are what have really won an entrance for it into the heart.[32]

The gravest question concerned the right of free discussion of these subjects within the Church of England. 'This common challenge is unquestionably the one common ground between the seven authors. Every one of them by lending his name to the book at least implied that, however much he may differ from the views contained in any other essay than his own, he yet vindicates the lawfulness of holding those views within the English Church.' Their critics, by demanding their withdrawal as clergymen, treat the truth or falsehood of their views 'as a matter almost of indifference', as if 'Truth was made for the laity and Falsehood for the clergy'. 'Against this godless theory of a national Church we solemnly protest. It is a theory tainted with a far deeper unbelief than any that has ever been charged against the Essayists and Reviewers.' A clergyman need only consider 'whether he can sincerely accept as a whole the constitution and worship of the Church of which he is a minister'. But there was no clash with doctrine here.

> The questions raised by the Essayists, with very few exceptions, are of a kind altogether beside and beyond the range over which the Formularies extend ... No passage has ever yet been pointed out in any of the five clerical Essayists which contradicts any of the Formularies of the Church in a degree at all comparable to the direct collision which exists between the High Church party and the Articles, between the Low Church party and the Prayer-book.

Above all, 'there is no Article on Inspiration'. The Church has given to all its members 'free play' in these questions. Nor was there an Article on the relative merits of internal and external evidences. 'There is, after all, no opposition between the Articles and the doctrines of the book', and even its opponents doubt whether it could be challenged legally. Stanley admitted that, while this was the 'general tendency' of the work, occasional passages might contradict the language of the Formularies. 'Let him who agrees with every word and statement of the Formularies cast the first stone at these variations'.[33] No one so believed.

> If the Bishops had been successful in terrifying or driving out of the Church those whom they themselves confess to be among its chief ornaments, not only would the individual loss have been irreparable, but the heavy blow and discouragement to all Biblical study – the breach between religion and science, between devotion and truth – the repulsion ... of the higher intelligences and more generous spirits of the rising generation from the sacred profession – would have gone far to have reduced the National Church to the level of an illiterate sect or a mere satellite of the Church of Rome.

The future was now in the hands of the Essayists. 'It will be theirs to show, not for the first time, that the widest range of inquiry and knowledge is not inconsistent with the most practical usefulness and the purest piety'. For 'if the Church of England is to hold its place as a national institution – if Christianity is to hold its place as the religion of the world – it must be by the fulfilment of hopes such as that which breathes through the chief Essay in this now celebrated volume'.[34]

Stanley's object was to moderate the debate, 'to steer a middle course between the bottomless Charybdis of the "Westminster" and the barking Scylla of the "Quarterly"'.[35] His review failed of its purpose, pleased neither side and mollified nobody. Its tone of calm superiority contrasted with the occasional sharp invective and personal allusions. Its surface impartiality was recognized by all as an effort to shelter the Broad Church, and especially his friends Temple and

Jowett, within the broad comprehensiveness of the national Church. The catenas by which Stanley sought to legitimize their positions and play down their novelty convinced nobody, for many of the names cited (such as Arnold) were equally offensive to the orthodox. Some of his remarks offended friends such as Tait;[36] his favouritism for Jowett and Temple offended other Essayists, especially Williams.[37] Opponents would hardly be mollified by repeated attacks on the High and Low Church parties. The religious press almost unanimously slighted Stanley's article. The *Guardian* summed it up: 'very bad the cause is which seems to admit of no better defence'.[38] The *Saturday Review* attacked Stanley so virulently that three of the staff withdrew from the journal.[39] Yet the article had its merits. On most of the points at issue, it was substantially right. The Essayists were entitled to have their positions stated and treated fairly. Stanley wrote with ability and, especially in his plea for toleration and concern for the educated laity, occasional eloquence. It was a courageous performance: as Stanley's mother foresaw, 'it puts out of the question your ever being a Bishop'.[40] But it hardly merits Basil Willey's rhetoric that 'it falls on the ear with the calming and distancing effect of a Greek chorus'.[41] Stanley's task of moderation and mediation left no room for the sense of urgency, the fire that had made Harrison and Wilberforce so effective.

Stanley's article suffered the additional disadvantage that it came as an anticlimax. By the time it appeared, the bishops had spoken, Convocation had debated, and numerous pamphlets had appeared. More important, the lay public had been drawn into the debate, a result to which the earlier reviews had contributed. This can be seen in the pages of *The Times*, where the report of the bishops' manifesto was followed by the letter of Henry Sidgwick ('A Cambridge Graduate', February 20 1861). But the surest sign that the controversy had entered the general consciousness was its appearance in the pages of *Punch*. At the end of 1860, there was a reference to it in a satire on Disraeli as a champion of the Church: 'When Neology scales e'en the citadel's walls,/ And Heresy whispers in grey College Halls'.[42] Mr Punch took the side of the Essayists in March 1861:

> Those *Essays and Reviews*
> How idle to abuse
> In terms of vague unmeaning condemnation:
> Do you think the people look
> For your censure of the book?
> No, ye Bishops, but expect your refutation.[43]

A clerical debate had clearly got out of hand when the general public appeared as interested spectators.

CHAPTER SEVEN

Censures

The demands in the religious press for official censure or action against the Essayists and Reviewers had been anticipated by Pusey's favourite disciple H. P. Liddon. Liddon had read the book immediately upon publication, alerted the High Church leader John Keble on March 31, 1860, and brought it to the attention of Bishop W. K. Hamilton of Salisbury (Williams' diocesan) by April 10.[1] But Hamilton took no action.[2] No bishop noticed the book until November; indeed Thirlwall remarked in his October Charge that the preceding three years had 'not been signalized ... by any very peculiar agitation of theological controversy'.[3] Wilberforce's Charge on November 15 was the first episcopal response. It is possible that Wilberforce was stimulated by Pusey, who drew Harrison's article in the *Westminster* to his attention on October 31.[4] The only other episcopal action came toward the end of the year, when Bishop Charles Sumner of Winchester, addressing candidates at an ordination, announced his intention of refusing ordination to anyone who held the opinions of the Essayists.[5]

The still uncensured book had acquired a notoriety which made it a publishing success. The first two editions having sold out, Parker published a third edition of 750 copies early in January. But the heart had gone out of the firm when the radical younger Parker died on November 9, 1860. There may also have been some pressure on the elder Parker, with his ecclesiastical connections, to give up *Essays and Reviews*. At any rate, he withdrew in mid-January. The work was immediately taken over by Longmans, who profited from the transaction. Longmans published a fourth edition of 1000 copies later in January, a fifth of 2000 in February and a sixth, seventh, eighth and ninth, each of 3000 copies, during March.[6] Large purchases were made by Mudie's circulating library. The Essayists scored another, though unrelated, success early in 1861, when Pattison was elected rector of Lincoln College on January 25.

The cry for official action against the Essayists, unheeded by the episcopate, was taken up by the lower clergy. An occasion for acting in concert arose in the election of the professor of Sanskrit at Oxford. The candidates were Max Müller, the great philologist, and Monier Williams, competent but less distinguished. Müller, being German, was assumed to be a 'Germanist' in his theology,[7] and hundreds of clergymen streamed into Oxford to vote in defense of orthodoxy. On December 7, 1860, Williams was elected by 833 to 610. The massing of clergymen in Oxford was used (by Pusey, according to Stanley)[8] to hold a meeting at which it was resolved to draw up a petition against the Essayists, addressed to the archbishop of Canterbury, to be signed by a large number of the clergy. A committee was elected which drew up this petition:

> We the undersigned, Clergy of the United Church of England and Ireland, respectfully request your Grace's attention to certain opinions contained in a Volume of 'Essays and Reviews' recently published, the tendency of which, as it appears to us, is to annihilate the authority of the Bible as the Inspired Word of God – to reject all Miracles (not excepting those of our Blessed Lord) as incapable of proof and repugnant to reason – and, in one instance at least, to undermine faith in God as the Creator.
>
> These opinions have been promulgated, with one exception, by Clergymen of our Church, holding positions of great trust, and possessing opportunities favourable in no ordinary degree for the diffusion of error.
>
> We therefore earnestly entreat your Grace to take counsel with the other members of the Episcopate, and to devise such measures as may, with God's blessing, 'banish and drive away' from our Church all such 'erroneous and strange doctrines.'
>
> The opinions against which we protest, as being repugnant to the natural meaning of our formularies and inconsistent with the teaching of the Church of England, are expressed in the accompanying extracts from the Essays to which we refer.[9]

The task of drafting the petition with its accompanying extracts (largely by Archdeacon W. J. Irons and Alexander McCaul, High and Low Church respectively) and of collecting the signatures, ultimately over 8000, took three months.

The clergy could express themselves more immediately in smaller bodies meeting locally. As early as October 11, 1860, a meeting at Derby of the Midland District of the Clerical and Lay Association for the Maintenance of Evangelical Principles discussed *Essays and Reviews* and drew up a protest which called on the bishops and the authorities of universities and schools to take 'such special and determined action as may be most effectual to counteract its pernicious influence'.[10] A meeting of the fellows of Sion College (incumbents of London parishes), on January 24, 1861, adopted a resolution against *Essays and Reviews*, asking their bishop to bring the issue to his colleagues to devise 'such measures as in their piety and wisdom shall to them seem desirable'.[11]

The most common occasion for gatherings which could draw up petitions was the semi-annual meeting of the clergy of a rural deanery. Several meetings in early 1861 addressed the bishops, seeking action against *Essays and Reviews*; after the bishops spoke, other addresses expressed approval. The address to which the bishops chose to respond came from the rural deanery of Dorchester:

> We wish to make known to your Grace and to all the Bishops the alarm we feel at some late indications of the spread of rationalistic and semi-infidel doctrines among the beneficed clergy of the realm. We allude especially to the denial of the atoning efficacy of the Death and Passion of our Blessed Saviour, Jesus Christ, both God and man, for us men and for our salvation, and to the denial of a Divine Inspiration, peculiar to themselves alone, to the Canonical Scriptures of the Old and New Testaments.

We would earnestly beseech your Grace and your Lordships, as faithful stewards over the House of God, to discourage by all means in your power the spread of speculations which would rob our countrymen, more especially the poor and unlearned, of their only sure stay in comfort for time and eternity. And to this end we would more especially and most earnestly beseech you, in your Ordinations, to 'lay hands suddenly on no man' till you have convinced yourself (as far as human precaution can secure it) that each deacon who, in reply to the question, 'Do you unfeignedly believe all the Canonical Scriptures of the Old and New Testament?' answers 'I do believe them,' *speaks the truth* as in the sight of God.[12]

A meeting of most of the bishops was held at Lambeth Palace on February 1, 1861. All that is known of 'the secret history of the episcopal letter'[13] comes from Wilberforce's private memoranda, for the publication of which his biographers were later criticized.[14] The archbishop of Canterbury, John Bird Sumner, brought up to the bishops the addresses, which 'had put us into a difficulty, if we did not answer them it would be most injurious to us'. Bishop R. D. Hampden of Hereford bluntly said 'that this was a question between Infidelity and Christianity, and that we ought to prosecute'. Tait, now bishop of London, sought to ward off action against his friends Temple and Jowett, and proposed a declaration of doctrine. Wilberforce opposed this 'because by such action Bishops would originate, and secondly because it would be condemning the essayists unheard'. Charles Sumner of Winchester supported him, asked 'how are we to stop after a declaration', and wanted legal advice. Thirlwall, who had been trained for the law, observed that a declaration not followed by action would amount to admitting 'that we had no means of repressing prolate heresy'. Tait replied that it was not 'a reflection on the Church of England that her Articles did not meet every form of evil. He thought that false doctrine must be endured'. The meeting took no decision, and Wilberforce retired for the night to Fulham Palace with Tait and the bishops of Rochester and Carlisle. At their request, Wilberforce drew up a reply to the addresses, to relieve the bishops of the immediate difficulty of responding to them. The Dorchester address was selected for response presumably because it did not explicitly mention *Essays and Reviews*, which Wilberforce also did not specify. The reply was unanimously adopted by the two archbishops and 17 bishops on February 2.[15] The absent were asked by Tait for their assent by letter;[16] all agreed except Henry Phillpotts of Exeter, whose name was nonetheless subscribed by Wilberforce,[17] and the unconsecrated Henry Philpott of Worcester.[18] Thus was prepared the 'episcopal manifesto' sent out over the primate's signature.

Reverend sir, – I have taken the opportunity of meeting many of my Episcopal brethren in London to lay your address before them. They unanimously agree with me in expressing the pain it has given them that any clergyman of our Church should have published such opinions as those concerning which you have addressed us. We cannot understand how these opinions can be held consistently with an honest subscription to the formularies of our Church, with many of the fundamental doctrines of which they appear to us essentially at variance.

Whether the language in which these views are expressed is such as to make their publication an act which could be visited in the Ecclesiastical Courts, or to justify the Synodical condemnation of the book which contains them, is still under our gravest consideration. But our main hope is our reliance on the blessing of God, in the continued and increasing earnestness with which we trust that we and the clergy of our several dioceses may be enabled to teach and preach that good deposit of sound doctrine which our Church teaches in its fulness, and which we pray that she may, by God's grace, ever set forth as the uncorrupted Gospel of our Lord Jesus Christ.[19]

The letter was universally taken to be an episcopal condemnation of *Essays and Reviews*, though in fact it was an evasion of that issue, an expedient to ease the minds of the clergy. One reason for this misunderstanding was the manner in which the document was released. It had been intended to publish it along with the address to which it responded. Instead, it appeared in *The Times* on February 16 without that address, having been sent in by W. E. Fremantle without authorization.[20] As printed in *The Times*, it read 'their opinions' instead of 'these opinions', thus appearing to refer to the persons of the Essayists and Reviewers.[21]

The agreement of certain bishops to the episcopal manifesto occasioned surprise. Hampden had been a victim of organized opposition in 1836 and 1847. But Hampden had been a Noetic, never a Broad Churchman, and was orthodox on the points at issue.[22] Thirlwall occasioned more surprise, then and since. G. M. Young remarked: 'Of all the anfractuosities of the Victorian mind, none perplexes me more than Thirlwall's concurrence in the prosecution of the Essayists'.[23] But Thirlwall did not concur in their prosecution, merely in the condemnation of their book, which is consistent with his dissection of it in his Charge of 1863. That he was fiercest against it in these early bishops' meetings is attributed by his biographer to Wilberforce's 'extraordinary charm',[24] but it may have been due to Thirlwall's fascination as a former lawyer with the technical problem of dealing with 'prolate heresy', heresy scattered about through a work, not amenable to specific censure. The only remedy was to condemn the book as a whole. Thirlwall does seem to have been offended by the refusal of unoffending authors to withdraw from such a book.[25]

The other bishop who occasioned surprise was Tait, a Broad Churchman and one-time biblical scholar, and the friend of Jowett and Temple. Tait's line throughout was in fact consistent: he distinguished among the Essayists, finding nothing objectionable in Temple, Pattison and Jowett, but was strictly orthodox in condemning Powell, Williams and Wilson, and censuring as a whole the book which contained them. But this line, which he expressed in the bishops' meeting, was not yet known to the public or his friends. He had in fact entertained both Jowett and Temple at Fulham shortly before the meeting, leaving them with the impression that they were not censurable. He had, however, expressed the desire that they should publicly state 'what is the *positive* Christianity which they hold. It is a poor thing to be pulling down. Let them build up'.[26] His adherence to the episcopal manifesto shook Jowett, Temple and their friend Stanley. Jowett declined to protest to Tait or to speak out publicly: 'in quietness and confidence shall be your strength'.[27] But Temple was furious at what he considered a personal betrayal. He engaged in an agitated correspondence with Tait from February 21 to March 4. Some idea of his indignation may be gleaned from these extracts from one letter:

> Many years ago you urged us from the University pulpit to undertake the critical study of the Bible ... To tell a man to study, and yet bid him, under heavy penalties, come to the same conclusions with those who have not studied, is to mock him. If the conclusions are prescribed, the study is precluded. ... You complain that young men of ability will not take orders. How can you expect it when this is what befalls whoever does not think just as you do? ... I for one joined in writing this book in the hope of breaking through that mischievous reticence which, go where I would, I perpetually found destroying the truthfulness of religion. I wished to encourage men to speak out. I believed that many doubts and difficulties only lived because they were hunted into the dark, and would die in the light ... Having spoken leniently, you were pledged to deal leniently ... What you did had not the intention, but it had all the effect, of treachery.[28]

Tait replied that, as bishops, 'appealed to, I cannot see how they could do otherwise ... What was issued was a condemnation of the book as one whole, leaving individuals each to speak for himself in exculpation ... private friendship should not be interfered with by the necessity for public acts'.[29] But Temple was dissatisfied, and his friendship with Tait was permanently impaired.

Tait had urged Temple to say something to dissociate himself from the offending Essayists; so also had Wilberforce and the master of Balliol, Robert Scott.[30] But Temple refused to separate himself from those he had encouraged to speak out. He found himself in personal difficulties regarding his headmastership at Rugby. The trustees debated whether to dismiss him. Temple 'declined to discuss with them any question but the welfare of the school. It has ended in a great growl, and for the present nothing more'.[31] Temple did not lose his post, but he felt that he had embarrassed the school. Parents were alarmed (in answer to an anxious mother, a sixth-former replied, 'Temple's all right; but if he turns Mahometan, all the school will turn too').[32] He admitted to a blunder in writing in a book 'which would encourage those boys to plunge into critical speculation before their time'. He spoke to the sixth-form boys on February 23, insisting that 'that book ought to have been published', but warning them 'against entering on the speculations contained in that book in a light or cursory way, and against supposing that I agree with all that is said in that book'. He spoke to the assistant masters, explaining the origin and purpose of the volume, acknowledging that 'as Headmaster here I made a mistake in doing so, a great mistake, on account of the boys', and complaining of the injustice of the episcopal letter. 'Although I differ widely from several things in the Essays, I cannot make any public declaration at present, as it would certainly be misconstrued into a condemnation of the book ... that would run directly contrary to the principles of toleration which we advocate.'[33] Finally, Temple arranged to publish a volume of his *Sermons*, to demonstrate his orthodoxy.

Temple's friend Stanley also reacted sharply against Tait's joining the episcopal manifesto, assuming the position of external defender of the Essayists (or at least his Oxford friends). In a correspondence beginning on February 16, he complained that Tait's action went contrary to assurances Tait had given him on an earlier visit to Fulham, 'the contradiction between your acquittal of three of the Essayists to me in private and the sweeping censure of them in public ... you could not have adopted a measure more calculated to injure the cause of Christianity or the Church in this country'.[34] In the correspondence, which continued into July, Tait insisted that the book and not the men had been censured, authorized Stanley to advertise his refusal to censure Temple, Pattison or Jowett, and urged him to persuade Temple to disavow the other Essayists.[35] Writing to a friend, Stanley said: 'It is the excessive inequality and inequity of the Episcopal judgment of which I complain. There is no ... fair distribution of praise and blame'.[36] He began his counter-offensive immediately, with a letter published in *The Times* on February 18, entitled 'The Episcopal Manifesto', under the signature of 'Anglicanus'.

> It is an unqualified condemnation of certain opinions, without any indication of what those opinions severally are, or how widely this condemnation is meant to extend. It attacks ... five living clergymen, of eminent learning but diverse sentiments, in language almost amounting to a libel, without drawing any distinction between the writers, without specifying either the precise charges against them or the formularies of the Church which they are supposed to contradict ... it ventures, without a trial, to pronounce a condemnation which nothing but the clearest legal proof could justify.[37]

An even more powerful criticism of the episcopal manifesto appeared in *The Times* on February 20 in a letter 'on behalf of the thinking laity of England' by the philosopher Henry Sidgwick, signed 'A Cambridge Graduate'.

> What we all want is, briefly, not a condemnation, but a refutation. The age when ecclesiastical censures were sufficient in such cases has passed away. A large portion of the laity now, though unqualified for abstruse theological investigations, are yet competent to hear and decide on theological arguments. These men will not be satisfied by an *ex cathedra* shelving of the question, nor terrified by a deduction of awful consequences from the new speculations. For philosophy and history alike have taught them to seek not what is 'safe', but what is true.[38]

The bishops were not to be allowed to stop with the publication of their letter. While both the *Guardian* and the *Record* expressed their approval, the *Record* 'regretted that the precise charges against the Essayists should not have been more formally specified, but this defect will shortly be supplied ... A memorial from a large number of clergy all over England is in the course of signature, which distinctly specifies the grounds of complaint'.[39] In fact the presentation of the petition originated at Oxford was delayed by the large number of signatures that were being collected. But the bishops were further prompted by a letter from the two Irish archbishops 'to call your attention to it, with a view to your putting your clergy on their guard'.[40]

The focus of activity now shifted to Convocation, the clerical counterpart of Parliament, which had been revived in the 1850s and had previously done little without royal licence, but which nonetheless served as the synod of the province of Canterbury. Convocation, like Parliament, had two houses, an Upper House of bishops and a Lower House of deans, archdeacons, a proctor from each cathedral chapter and two proctors from each diocese, with a prolocutor as its speaker and a somewhat arcane parliamentary procedure. On February 26 the subject of *Essays and Reviews* was raised by R. W. Jelf, principal of King's College, London.[41] Jelf's motion prayed 'the official attention of his Grace and their Lordships to the volume ... with a view to synodical action in reference thereto', appending to his motion nine specific charges of unsound doctrine with extracts from the book to support them.[42] The motion was seconded by the evangelical Alexander McCaul, who had already denounced the Essayists in print. The debate was rather wild; the reverend gentlemen were not yet accustomed to parliamentary procedure. The previous question was moved by way of opposition. Several speakers opposed action to condemn the book, either because of the futility of censures or the unfairness of action against those who were not able to defend themselves. The debate was marked by the first interventions of Archdeacon G. A. Denison, an extreme High Churchman who did not 'hesitate to say it is an infidel book', and of Harvey Goodwin, dean of Ely, brother of the Essayist Charles Goodwin, who disapproved the volume and disagreed with his brother but argued that 'we ought not to give any judgment at all'. Canon Christopher Wordsworth proposed an amended motion which, after the previous question was defeated and Jelf withdrew his own motion, was passed by a large majority:

> That the clergy of the Lower House of Convocation in the province of Canterbury, having agreed to the unanimous censure which has been already pronounced and published by the Archbishops and Bishops of both provinces on certain opinions contained in a book entitled *Essays and Reviews*, entertain an earnest hope that, under the Divine blessing, the faithful zeal of the Christian Church may be enabled to counteract the pernicious influences of the erroneous opinions contained in the said volume.[43]

Denison was 'wholly dissatisfied'[44] with this action, but it threw the ball back into the court of the bishops, who had in fact not condemned *Essays and Reviews* quite so explicitly as the Lower House implied. The Upper House met on February 28, and Wilberforce, who tended to dominate simply by being always ready with an initiative, presented a petition from the High Church English Church Union to 'take measures to arrest the progress of such dangerous doctrines'. Wilberforce was momentarily upstaged by Hamilton of Salisbury, Williams' diocesan, who announced that he had consulted counsel on legal proceedings against him. Tait then made a statement that he was 'the intimate personal friend' of two of the Essayists (Temple and Jowett), that their essays and opinions differed from the others, and that he desired 'that an opportunity should be given to them of doing what I trust they will do – namely, make a declaration satisfactory to the country that they are not responsible for every word that appears in this unfortunate volume'.

Thirlwall responded that a mere general statement of disagreement would not be sufficient; the two must 'enter into a detailed explanation' of those 'statements which they distinctly disclaim and condemn'. Wilberforce, while honouring 'the affectionate courage of the Bishop of London', also insisted on 'an entire retraction of error, and not a vague assertion of holding the truth'. Tait replied to Wilberforce's extracts from *Essays and Reviews* that 'it is impossible to judge of them by extracts' and insisted on separating 'the individuals from their opinions'. John Jackson of Lincoln wished also to except from censure Pattison, whom as Visitor of Lincoln College he had admitted as Rector, but only on condition of explaining his disagreement from the other essays. Other bishops also opposed Tait's moderate proposal. The debate was concluded by Archbishop Sumner, who surprisingly said that the Upper House of the Convocation of Canterbury was not at liberty to take action, because the original episcopal manifesto had emanated from the bishops of both provinces, and the northern bishops were not present.[45]

Tait had made a misstep by trying to save his personal friends, an act which was much criticized.[46] In fact none of the Essayists was willing to save himself by disavowing the others, so Tait's efforts were vain. The most that any Essayist was willing to do was Temple's publication of his *Sermons* and the publication by Jowett's friends of a collection of his *Statements of Christian Faith and Practice*, to demonstrate their soundness.

Tait found one way to speak out personally and yet publicly. He arranged to publish some discourses he had given in 1846 under the title of *The Dangers and Safeguards of Modern Theology*, with an introduction referring to *Essays and Reviews*. Tait urged that controversy be conducted in 'a Christian spirit of forbearing love'. Those who emphasize the human element in the Bible should also reflect on the divine element. 'Scripture is the Word of God.' As for the Essayists, 'it would be unfair to regard the several authors as individually responsible for each other's opinions', but 'they have only themselves to blame' if the public insists on regarding the book as a whole, since they need not have published in that form. They were bound in fairness to say where they stood: 'let each state what his view of Christian truth is'. 'The Church of Christ and His truth will not suffer by free inquiry; but no man has a right to remove the old landmarks of thought and religious feeling, without being prepared to point out others.'[47] In his diary, Tait noted: 'We have had a great duty, – to express our disapproval; a great duty also, I think, to guard the accused from ill-usage; a great duty to the Church to guard its doctrine; and also to watch for its children likely to be led astray by any appearance of persecution'.[48]

Other bishops were finding ways of speaking out against the Essayists, whenever they had occasion to make speeches, especially when responding to the petitions of their clergy. Finally, on March 12, the mass petition of the clergy, now signed by over 8000 clergymen, was presented to the archbishop of Canterbury by Irons and McCaul in a display of High and Low Church unity. Sumner could now express his personal agreement.

> I cannot be surprised that the clergy should unite in desiring to clear themselves from the reproach which may be cast against the Church itself, when some of her members 'holding', as is justly stated, 'positions of great trust,' shall have published a volume the tendency of which is to undermine the very foundations of Christianity.[49]

The petition had been, historically, a powerful political weapon, and this petition proved an effective method of mobilizing the clergy at large. The Essayists stood condemned by the clergy even before official action was taken.

Convocation was to resume on March 14. On the 13th, the bishops held a preliminary private meeting. Bishop Hamilton of Salisbury, having taken legal advice, announced that he had decided to prosecute Williams for heresy. This started two debates, the main one on the preferability of prosecution to synodical condemnation by Convocation, and a second on whether all the bishops should join in the prosecution. Wilberforce favoured prosecution but felt that it acted only against one writer and therefore wanted synodical action as well. Tait opposed both. Several bishops offered to share in Hamilton's expenses, which he declined. By a narrow majority, the bishops decided against a joint prosecution; by nine votes to five, they supported synodical condemnation.[50]

The initiative was taken in the Lower House on March 14. Denison, taking the lead, presented a *gravamen* signed by 20 of the 38 members present, noting that *Essays and Reviews* contained 'doctrines subversive of the inspiration and authority of Holy Scripture' and that six of the seven essays were written by clergymen, and praying that the bishops 'will be pleased to direct the appointment of a committee of this house to make extracts from the said book, and to report thereon to this house', the first formal steps leading to condemnation. The prolocutor, Archdeacon Edward Bickersteth, suggested that the *gravamen* be presented directly to the Upper House as the private petition of Denison and his associates, so that the bishops would originate the instruction. Denison agreed, and Bickersteth carried the petition to the bishops.[51]

Wilberforce, taking the lead among the bishops, asserting that the evil must be met 'by the voice of authority', moved that the archbishop of Canterbury, as president, be requested to issue the requested directive 'in order that the Lower House might communicate to this house its opinion whether there are sufficient grounds for proceeding to a Synodical judgment upon the book'. A. T. Gilbert of Chichester seconded the motion to protect the faithful from disquiet by the absence of a condemnation by the Church. Tait argued strongly against the motion, urging that the bishops had done enough by their original letter, of which the Lower House had already expressed its approval. Even that had drawn more readers to the book than if it had been let alone. Thirlwall held that it 'is absolutely requisite for maintaining the character, I would almost say the very being, of the Church as a Church, that it should have a distinct opinion on these matters', and that the episcopal letter had indicated that the bishops were considering further action. Charles Baring of Gloucester opposed action on the peculiarly Low Church ground that Convocation (whose revival had been pushed by the High Church) was not the voice of the church, though 'some few of the clergy and some few old ladies who are readers of the *Guardian* will say that when the Houses of Convocation have condemned these *Essays and Reviews*, the matter will be settled for ever – that no heretical dog will ever dare to bark again after the utterance of this voice of the Church of England'. The High Church Hamilton of Salisbury, who regarded Convocation 'as a sacred Synod', observed that 'at any rate, it is our only organ'. Having discovered the uncertainties of legal proceedings, it seemed 'the more necessary that we should censure this book, and express our clearest and most deliberate judgment that the doctrines of these writers are such as cannot be taught with impunity by ministers of the Church of England'. The bishops voted by eight to four in favour of Wilberforce's motion, the dissentients being Tait and Baring from their idiosyncratic standpoints and R. J. Eden of Bath and Wells and J. T. Pelham of Norwich on grounds of prudence.[52]

The matter was then brought back to the Lower House which appointed a 15-member committee, including Jelf and McCaul and the prolocutor *ex officio*. The chairman was Denison,[53] by right of having moved the original motion for the committee[54] (he owed his knowledge of procedure to his brother, Speaker of the House of Commons). It would not be for several weeks that the committee could present its report, although Denison tried to speed matters by presenting a draft report as chairman.[55] The committee preferred to work up its own report, which showed the influence of Jelf's *Specific Evidences*, the appendix to his motion of February 26.

The Convocation of the Province of York, for whose concurrence it had been intended to wait, met on March 21. More conservative than its southern counterpart, it did not appoint a committee but proceeded to immediate condemnation, on the motion of Hugh McNeile, the evangelical leader of Liverpool. The motion, passed with no trouble, expressed their 'unfeigned satisfaction' at the condemnation of *Essays and Reviews* in the episcopal manifesto (which the northern bishops had signed) and then specifically denounced the idea of the 'verifying faculty' on the ground that the distinctive Christian doctrines

> are mysteries not to be received by any verifying faculty in man, but only in submission of mind to a reasonably attested revelation from God. And, therefore, we hold it a solemn duty – distinguishing between the evidences for a revelation of which man is fully capable of judging, and the contents of a revelation of many of which man may be wholly incompetent to judge – to record our utter rejection, nay, our unfeigned abhorrence, of the principle referred to, as well as of other kindred principles characteristic of the volume.[56]

Throughout March, April and May clerical addresses kept pouring in to the bishops, now applauding their stand against *Essays and Reviews*, and affording the bishops further opportunities of denouncing the book in their replies. Some of them also began their visitations, which gave them opportunities of denouncing the book in their Charges. Archdeacons, who delivered charges each year, also began charging against the Essayists. One more potent than any bishop, the evangelical lay leader Lord Shaftesbury, spoke out, first at a local meeting in April and then as chairman of the May meeting of the Bible Society, urging to cheers that 'the laity must back up the bishops'. Tait, who as bishop of London was on the platform, responded that 'our attitude ought to be one of calmness, and that nothing could be gained by throwing ourselves into a state of alarm'.[57] His moderation was criticized by the *Record*.[58]

Thirlwall, who had been so unexpectedly ferocious against *Essays and Reviews*, had his troubles. Stanley suggested in his *Edinburgh Review* article, published in April, that ideas similar to the Essayists' were held by some of the bishops, evidently referring to Thirlwall, with whom he was conducting a vigorous correspondence.[59] A pamphlet, *'Essays and Reviews' Anticipated'*, which was attributed (probably wrongly) to George Eliot but came from the *Westminster Review* circle,[60] pointed to Thirlwall's translation of Schleiermacher as the source of the Essayists' rationalism. When the *Spectator* reviewed the pamphlet favourably on April 20, Thirlwall had to publish a letter explaining somewhat lamely that he had been a lawyer, not a clergyman, when he translated Schleiermacher, but concluding 'I am not aware of having refused to others any licence which I ever claimed for myself. And, if it please God, I shall never consent to the narrowing, by a hair's breadth, that latitude of opinion which the Church has hitherto conceded to her Ministers'.[61]

Such latitude of opinion had been narrowed in the case of Wilson, who had been invited by the Rev. John McNaught, himself a notorious liberal, to preach three sermons in his church in Liverpool on May 24. Bishop John Graham of Chester inhibited Wilson, not being a priest of the diocese, from preaching or officiating. Wilson complied by having MacNaught preach his sermons for him.[62] Wilson later published his sermons, which were in his usual line, with a preface upholding the right of the clergy to freedom of thought.[63] Wilson was the only Essayist to reply publicly to the attacks on *Essays and Reviews*.

Jowett suffered in a different fashion. As regius professor of Greek, his salary had been set by Henry VIII at £40 and had never been raised since. The wrongfulness of this was obvious, and Stanley, regius professor of ecclesiastical history since 1858, began a campaign to raise the salary. He was joined in 1860 by Pusey, who detested Jowett's theology but felt as a gentleman that an injustice was being done. But Pusey attached to Stanley's motion an amendment which prevented it from coming to a vote at that time, before *Essays and Reviews* became controversial. When the motion was voted on by the Oxford Convocation in May 1861, clerical feeling against the Essayists combined with opposition to University reformers to cause it to be heavily defeated. The same fate awaited similar proposals in subsequent years, and the issue, which paralleled the controversy over *Essays and Reviews*, was not finally resolved until 1865.

Bishop Hamilton's decision to prosecute Wilson in the ecclesiastical courts was made public at the end of May.[64] It had no immediate effect on the proceedings in Convocation, as Denison's committee continued and completed its assigned work, meeting over 70 hours on 12 days during these weeks. The report was printed for distribution to Convocation when it resumed on June 18. It was a lengthy document, with careful and specific charges documented by extracts from the book. The committee found three leading errors:

> (1) That the present advanced knowledge possessed by the world in its 'manhood' is the standard by which the educated intellect of the individual man, guided and governed by conscience, is to measure and determine the truth of the Bible.
> (2) That where the Bible is assumed to be at variance with the conclusions of such educated intellect, the Bible must be taken in such cases to have no divine authority, but to be only 'a human utterance'.
> (3) That the principles of interpretation of the Bible, hitherto universally received in the Christian church, are untenable; and that new principles of interpretation are now to be substituted if the credit and authority of the holy Scriptures are to be maintained.

The report concluded that 'the general tendency and effect of the volume is unduly to exalt the authority of human reason; to lower the authority of Revelation in regard to things divine and spiritual; to unsettle faith; and to consign the reader to a helpless scepticism'.[65]

Denison presented the report to a thin Convocation on June 18 and gave notice of a motion 'that in the opinion of this house there are sufficient grounds for proceeding to a Synodical judgment on the book entitled *Essays and Reviews*'. Harvey Goodwin protested 'against the principle of condemning a book by extracts' and insisted on a delay while members could read the book and compare it with the report. Christopher Wordsworth, no supporter of the

Essayists, wished that they should be enabled to express themselves. Denison agreed to postpone his motion to June 21 and moved only that the report be received, which was carried by 28 to 14.[66]

On June 21 Denison, in his individual capacity, made his motion. 'We are asked to give a specific answer to a specific question put to us by the Upper House.' He was seconded by McCaul in a lengthy speech, which treated the question as one of 'public morality' which 'could not be maintained if clergymen holding these opinions were to maintain their position'. Wordsworth, who felt that 'it is one of the worst books ever published since the Reformation', nonetheless opposed proceeding to 'a judicial act', noting that many who sat in Convocation had disqualified themselves as judges by signing the clergy petition. He raised the legal question: 'we are not entitled to deliberate with a view of proceeding to a Synodical judgment, without the licence of the Crown'. The debate became disorderly when seven amendments were introduced. Archdeacon William Hony, a supporter of Hamilton's prosecution of Williams, moved to amend Denison's motion by adding 'but at the same time it is not expedient to revive the power of Synodical action under the existing circumstances of the Church'. Harvey Goodwin opposed both Denison's and Hony's motions, saying that the committee report 'does appear to me to be a most unfair representation of the book'. Canon William Selwyn also opposed 'a sweeping condemnation of the whole book', and several speakers feared that a condemnation might turn public opinion against Convocation. Professor James Heaviside denounced 'the new doctrine of joint responsibility' and opposed condemnation 'in the name of the young men of England'. But there was much support for action against what Denison called 'this most fatal, this most pernicious, this most wretched book … What was important was, not that Christianity should be brought into harmony with the deductions of human reason, but that the deductions of human reason should not be assumed to be … more true and more certain than the Bible'. Hony's amendment was defeated by 29 to 10, and the other amendments were defeated by similar margins. Finally, Denison's original motion was passed by 31 to 8.[67]

The vote in the Lower House, coupled with the widely signed petition of the clergy, signalled that a majority of the clergy of England condemned *Essays and Reviews*. Action by the Upper House was necessary to make this condemnation official, and the episcopal manifesto had shown that they were so inclined. But at this juncture Archbishop Sumner hesitated. An old man (he died a year later), his spirit had perhaps been broken by criticism of his conduct as visitor of All Souls College in a case recently decided.[68] Hamilton's prosecution of Williams placed him in an awkward legal position. If the case should go to the final court of appeal, the Judicial Committee of the Privy Council, the archbishops and the bishop of London would sit as judges, and they might be disqualified if they had already passed judgment on the book in Convocation. At any rate, this problem provided Sumner with an excuse for avoiding involvement in another legal proceeding.[69] When the Upper House received the report of the Lower on July 9, Gilbert of Chichester raised the question that, as prospective judges, the archbishop and bishop would either have to absent themselves from Convocation or compromise their future positions, and moved therefore that 'it is expedient to adjourn the further consideration of this subject pending the course of such suit'. The motion passed,[70] and the synodical condemnation, on the verge of passage in 1861, was held in abeyance until 1864.

The result was a blow to Wilberforce, who had taken the lead in pressing for condemnation. It showed that his relative Sumner was no 'rubber stamp'[71] for him. He complained to a fellow bishop that they were failing in their 'duty ... by some *public* and *official* act' of clearing the Church 'from complicity with those who teaching in her name, teach men to give up God's word, Creation, Redemption and the Work of God the Holy Ghost'. He pointed out that 'we are not proposing in Synod to act against the *men* but to condemn the book', and therefore there was no relation between the synodical judgment and the legal case against one man.[72]

Denison, who had led the Lower House, was also bitterly disappointed by 'the delay in recovering the Catholic position of the Church of England in respect of spiritual censure of heretical books'. He felt that Hamilton should not have gone into court but should have proceeded against Williams by excommunication.[73] In the absence of synodical action against *Essays and Reviews*, he took his own. He published his original draft report of the committee as a pamphlet, and organized a series of tracts against *Essays and Reviews* under the title *Faith and Peace*. Thus the official proceedings against *Essays and Reviews* melded into the pamphlet war which was already under way.

Before the year was out, the ecclesiastical censures had drawn in one politician. Benjamin Disraeli, speaking at Oxford in November, criticized the Essayists for publishing views inconsistent with their 'engagements with the people of this country' and (to cheers and laughter) satirized German philosophy: 'No religious creed was ever destroyed by a philosophical theory; philosophers destroy themselves'. He combined praise of the ecclesiastical censures with veiled criticism of Hamilton's prosecution: 'It denounced what it deemed pestilent heresies but it did not counsel the prosecution of the heretics ... I wish this frank and reasonable course had been followed in high places ... the nineteenth century appears to me a season when the Church should confute error, not punish it'.[74]

CHAPTER EIGHT

The War of the Pamphlets

Of the approximately 150 pamphlets directed against *Essays and Reviews*, the largest number appeared in the first half of 1861.[1] In 1860 the controversy had been largely confined to the periodicals, but some pamphlets began to appear. What was probably the first was preached as a visitation sermon at Derby on June 12 by S. A. Pears, headmaster of Repton school, and 'Published by Request' as *The Weapons of our Warfare*.[2] *Essays and Reviews*, with which Pears' auditors were then unfamiliar, is not explicitly mentioned in the text of his attack on those who undermined doctrine, especially the doctrine of the atonement, but it was copiously cited in Pears' footnotes.

The first full critique of the Essayists was Prebendary William Gresley's *Idealism Considered*, published before October. Gresley took his title theme from Wilson's notion of 'ideology', and Wilson was the chief target of his attack on those who sought to make a 'revolution' in doctrine, but he critiqued each of the Essayists except Pattison. Gresley linked the Essayists with the 'ultra-ideologist' Darwin.[3]

Another type of attack on the Essayists was pioneered by George Moberly, who republished his *Sermons on the Beatitudes* with a preface directed against *Essays and Reviews*, written before Harrison's article and revised after it.[4] This technique of republishing an earlier work with a preface relating it to the present controversy was followed in 1861 by Archdeacon Pratt, who published a fourth edition of his *Scripture and Science Not at Variance* with additions relating to Goodwin;[5] by Tait with his *Dangers and Safeguards of Modern Theology*; and by Archbishop Sumner who, in April 1861, published a new edition of his *Evidence of Christianity* with preface and appendices directed against the Essayists.[6]

The link between the sporadic pamphleteering of 1860 and the furious pace of 1861 was supplied by Alexander McCaul, the evangelical active in the clergy petition and in Convocation, who published three letters in the *Record* on December 31, 1860, and January 7 and 16, 1861, which were printed as a pamphlet, *Rationalism and Deistic Infidelity*. The learned McCaul had stationed himself as a sentinel to monitor German biblical scholarship, and he assured his English readers that the 'rationalism' of the Essayists was not a product of German learning but a reprise of the deism and infidelity of the eighteenth century originated in England and later carried to Germany.[7] In a later pamphlet McCaul defended the Mosaic account of Creation.[8]

The numerous publications of 1861 may best be dealt with by categories. One such, illustrating a characteristic of religious controversy, consists of ongoing controversies into which *Essays and Reviews* could be drawn. Thus, evangelicals who were pressing for revision of the liturgy found the 'Negative Theology' of the Essayists an additional reason for their cause.[9] A controversialist already engaged in debate with one of Maurice's disciples extended his controversy to include *Essays and Reviews*.[10] The Rev. R. P. Blakeney and the Presbyterian John Cumming, veteran anti-Catholic polemicists under the aegis of the Protestant Reformation Society, found the Essayists 'decidedly Romanistic in their tendency' because they subverted the authority of the Bible and thus 'are calculated to make infidels of some and Romanists of many more'.[11] They published a series of 16 Protestant Reformation Society tracts,[12] subsequently combined in a volume, *Modern Infidelity and Rationalism Exposed and Refuted*.

Another category consists of statements on official occasions, which, when published, add to the pamphlet literature. Bishops visited their dioceses triennially, delivering Charges; six of these were published.[13] Archdeacons visited and charged annually, and these were occasionally published.[14] There were also the by-products of the Convocation debates, Jelf's speech on February 26 with its appendix and Denison's draft report.[15]

Published lectures form another category of pamphlets. An address at the opening of classes in Dublin in November 1860 was dusted off to become a pamphlet in 1861.[16] Occasional lectures at meetings were 'published by request' of the audience.[17] More important was an address by the Rev. B. M. Cowie to the fellows of Sion College, a fair treatment of 'neology', an avowed plea for 'moderation', rejecting the 'verbal' inspiration of the Bible and allowing its infallibility only in matters affecting salvation, but insistent on miracles and the control of private judgment by 'the voice of the Church'.[18] Still more important were the annual Boyle Lectures, founded by Robert Boyle for proving the Christian religion against 'notorious infidels'. The lecturer in 1861, nominated by Tait as bishop of London, was Edward Garbett, editor of the *Record*, who through that newspaper and his own monthly *Christian Advocate* (founded in 1861 for the purpose) was a constant adversary of *Essays and Reviews*. Garbett's lectures, *The Bible and its Critics*, were an extended and detailed reply to the 'infidelity' of *Essays and Reviews*, upholding the evidential argument 'to assert the objective reality of revealed truths', and asserting that 'there is no middle course between the absolute acceptance, and the absolute rejection, of revelation'.[19]

Innumerable sermons were preached on topics related to *Essays and Reviews*, and many of these were published. When the preachers were unbeneficed, one suspects ambition as a motive, displaying orthodoxy in the hope of attracting a patron.[20] Other sermons came in the regular course of preaching.[21] Some courses of sermons were of more than passing importance. Moses Margoliouth, a converted Jew who stationed himself to keep up with Old Testament scholarship, published two sermons and a letter which learnedly refuted the several Essayists.[22] Christopher Wordsworth preached two courses of five sermons each in Westminster Abbey, published respectively as *The Inspiration of the Bible* and

The Interpretation of the Bible. The Bible was throughout free from error: 'the Bible, the whole Bible, and nothing but the Bible is the written word of God'.[23] Wordsworth's High Church bias was shown in his blaming of private judgment for the growth of rationalism. Faith in Scripture is part of 'the trial of our faith'.[24]

The pulpit of Oxford University was particularly used to attack *Essays and Reviews.* Charles Heurtley, Lady Margaret professor of divinity, printed a recent uncontroversial sermon in order to find an occasion to publish with it an older sermon on the inspiration of Scripture.[25] Edward Hawkins, provost of Oriel College and the last of the Noetics, preached on *The Province of Private Judgment,* denying that either reason or conscience can judge revelation: 'the critical study even of the Scriptures is subordinate to the moral, devotional, religious study'.[26] Sermons were preached against *Essays and Reviews* on Easter Sunday and Tuesday.[27] Two courses of sermons occasioned secondary controversies.

Samuel Wilberforce preached two university sermons early in 1861 whose combined title, *The Revelation of God the Probation of Man,* expresses its underlying thesis. Warning against the pride of the intellect, he urged the avoidance of doubt, a temptation leading to sin. 'Once let the mind, instead of receiving humbly, begin to doubt, and doubt will be everywhere.' He gave a lugubrious account of 'the doubter's death'. The Christian should fling doubt 'from him as if it were a loaded shell shot into the fortress of the soul'.[28] Goldwin Smith, regius professor of modern history and a religious radical, responded with an open letter to Wilberforce entitled *The Suppression of Doubt is not Faith.* Arguing 'the case of conscientious doubt', Smith urged that 'inquiry necessarily begins in doubt, and without free inquiry, we can have no assurance of the truth … It is the suppression of conscientious doubt, my Lord, not the fair admission of it, that is really "subversive of all true faith"'.[29] 'A Clergyman' replied to Smith with a pamphlet *Concerning Doubt,*[30] to which Smith responded with another pamphlet, objecting to 'the enforcement of a pretended belief in doctrines which no human being can pretend to understand'.[31] Smith's objective was the abolition of all religious tests and formularies, but he had been provoked by Wilberforce's incomprehension of religious doubt. This mini-controversy is an example of the way in which the great controversy spawned lesser ones.

J. W. Burgon was an eccentric High Churchman, the most extreme and consistent opponent of all change. Burgon was a select preacher to the university for 1860–61, and he published his sermons as *Inspiration and Interpretation* with a preface and lengthy 'preliminary remarks' denouncing *Essays and Reviews.* The sermons were blusteringly assertive of the literal inerrancy of Scripture: 'The Bible, from the Alpha to the Omega of it, is filled to overflowing with the Holy Spirit of GOD: the Books of it, and the sentences of it, and the words of it, and the syllables of it, – aye, and the very letters of it'. This apparently evoked some laughter, and Burgon expanded upon it in his next sermon:

... we see not how with logical consistency we can avoid believing the words as well as the sentences of it; the syllables as well as the words; the letters as well as the syllables; every 'jot' and every 'tittle' of it, (to use our LORD's expression) to be divinely inspired ... no misapprehension or misstatement, no error or blot of any kind, can possibly exist within its pages ... as the very utterance of the *Holy Ghost,* we cannot *but* think that it must be absolute, faultless, unerring, supreme.[32]

The preface and especially the preliminary remarks were slashing and unmeasured attacks on the Essayists for their '*conspiracy* against the Faith'. These 'immoral characters' deserved no consideration. 'This infamous book' was 'an insult, the grossest imaginable, offered to the Majesty of Heaven'.[33] Burgon was offended by 'the *un*manly trick' of the Essayists 'of insinuating what they dare not openly avow', a 'cloudy shuffling art' of which Jowett was the 'great master'. 'They *must* either recall their words or resign their stations.' Burgon dealt with the Essayists serially, calling Williams 'vulgar' and Wilson 'one whom in the common concerns of life I would not trust' for his 'playing tricks with plain language,' and calling Jowett's plaintive concluding passage 'the piteous whine of a school-boy who knows that he *deserves* chastisement, and perceives that he is about to experience his deserts'. But his repeated concern was the clerical position of the Essayists. 'It is simply dishonest in a man to hold a commission in the Church of England, and yet to deny her doctrines. An Officer in the Army who should pursue a similar line of action, would be dismissed the Service, – or worse'.[34] Even High Church reviewers were troubled by Burgon's style of attack. While the *Literary Churchman* excused Burgon's 'startling' language because he was dealing with 'monstrous' heresies, the *Ecclesiastic* lamented that 'his work is so sadly disfigured by its style ... young men will not be sneered and bullied into orthodoxy'. The *Guardian,* ever judicious, found it 'scarcely possible to overestimate the mischief which Mr. Burgon's style of handling this subject may cause ... this kind of terrorism will tend to secure for the Essayists some generous, though certainly grievously misplaced, sympathy'. It concluded that 'Sermons are always a somewhat unsatisfactory mode of conducting a controversy'.[35]

Perhaps a more satisfactory mode might be the publication of letters. Letters might be addressed to a 'friend' or to students in universities where their faith might be endangered.[36] But the most important letter was one sent by Pusey to the *Guardian* and later reprinted. Correspondents had asked for answers to be written to *Essays and Reviews* by persons in appropriate positions, such as professors. Pusey argued that the 'random dogmatic scepticism' scattered through the essays afforded nothing definite to answer. 'The writers ... rarely affirm anything, attempt to prove nothing and throw a doubt upon everything ... how can such an undigested heap of errors receive a systematic answer in a brief space, or in any one treatise or volume?' Only by tracing them back to their German sources could they be defined and answered, and the conservative German scholars such as Tholuck and Hengstenberg had in fact answered them. 'The difficulties lie, not in Holy Scripture itself, but in the dispositions with which men approach it.'[37]

Some pamphlets were republications of articles which had first appeared in periodicals. John Cairns republished four articles in the Deal weekly newspaper as *Oxford Rationalism and English Christianity*, blaming rationalism on the recoil from the Oxford Movement.[38] A High Churchman, W. J. Irons, reprinted an article from the *Literary Churchman* in which he argued that the Essayists were the fruit of evangelical opposition to the Oxford Movement.[39] The evangelical dean of Carlisle, Francis Close, republished an article against the American edition of the Essays from the *American Quarterly Review.*[40]

Two other categories of replies to *Essays and Reviews* may be briefly noted. One was the 'popular exposition', written for ordinary people not familiar with theology.[41] Another took the form of poetry (or poetastering), a couple of satirical squibs.[42]

After all these categories are disposed of, there remains half the literature, simply tracts or pamphlets. Aside from a few only incidentally related to *Essays and Reviews*,[43] these can be divided into those that treat particular topics, those that purport to be responses to the work as a whole, and those that reply to a particular Essayist.

Of the topical pamphleteers, the Plumian professor of astronomy at Cambridge justified the first chapter of Genesis, and a provincial writer upheld predictive prophecy.[44] The topic that received the most attention was the central but most difficult issue of the whole controversy, the nature and extent of the inspiration of the Bible. Three pamphlets discussed it, agreeing that divine inspiration was not mechanical but 'dynamical' and that it extended to all the writers and to all doctrinal content, but one differed from the others in allowing that it did not extend to non-doctrinal statements of facts.[45]

Of the general pamphlets, some were the work of regular religious controversialists.[46] Others professed to be written by ordinary men, not necessarily clergymen.[47] Some were professedly High Church, blaming the evangelicals for provoking a reaction;[48] but an avowed evangelical blamed the tractarians.[49] A large number simply defy categorization.[50] There were tracts issued serially, dealing with the work as a whole by taking up the Essayists or their subjects one by one.[51]

It has been possible to deal thus summarily with the general pamphlets (and, indeed, with most of the pamphlet literature of Anglican orthodoxy) because of the essential sameness of their argument. Indeed, the common orthodoxy of Anglicanism may be said to have explicated itself in its argument against *Essays and Reviews.*[52] The replies generally began with a personal attack on the Essayists in their capacity as clergymen in a 'false position' for retaining their posts in the Church whose doctrines they abandoned. It was repeatedly emphasized that they were jointly responsible for the statements of each of them. They were frequently called the *Septem Contra Christum*, seven against Christ. Their arguments were not new, but rather repetitions of German criticism derived from eighteenth-century deism which had led to infidelity. In their own day the deists had been refuted by Butler and Paley. The Germans were confused and mutually contradictory, and recent German scholars such as Hengstenberg[53] had refuted the other Germans. Biblical criticism was inherently dangerous, leading to loss of faith. The Anglican replies would then discuss the several Essayists in detail, pointing out their specific errors. Two errors were regarded as fundamental and common to all. The first was based on Williams' 'verifying faculty', which allowed conscience to pick and choose within Scripture for those parts which it would accept as divine revelation, thus denying the inspiration of Scripture as a whole, the authority of the Bible and any objective standard of doctrine. The other was the attack on the 'evidences' of revelation as laid down by Butler and Paley, miracles and prophecy. The orthodox reliance on the evidential argument was total. The evidences validated the message of God delivered by the authors of the Bible; reason could only examine the evidences of revelation but must never inquire into its contents, to which it must submit with absolute faith.

The relevant features of this common line of argument can be found in those pamphlets which dealt with individual Essayists. Temple, though acknowledged to be the least objectionable, received the most replies, presumably because he came first.[54] Baden Powell followed close behind; the subject of miracles was both important and relatively easy to deal with.[55] Goodwin received several attacks; the controversy over Genesis and geology was still unexhausted.[56] There was one reply to Pattison.[57] Jowett attracted three, two by the same controversialist.[58]

The pamphlet literature was regularly followed and reviewed by the religious press, particularly the weekly *Record* and *Guardian*, the fortnightly *Literary Churchman* and *Clerical Journal*, and the quarterly learned journal, the *Journal of Sacred Literature*. From their reviews we may obtain a notion of the quantity of pamphlets, including some titles not now available.[59] The journals (except the 'factual' *Clerical Journal*) also spoke out for themselves. The *Literary Churchman's* eight reviews of *Essays and Reviews* between January and May were republished as *The Reviewers Reviewed and the Essayists Criticised*, having meanwhile evoked a protest from Rowland Williams that he had been unfairly treated.[60] In a summary article, the journal found the position of the Essayists 'wicked and dangerous' but was disappointed in some of the replies: 'bad defences are worse than none'.[61] The non-denominational *Journal of Sacred Literature* turned some heavy artillery on the essays. An article probably by Samuel Tregelles, a distinguished practitioner of the 'lower' or textual criticism, denied the learning as well as the philosophy of the Essayists, whose 'chief characteristic is a reckless audacity in advancing things which have often been advanced before by inferior minds'.[62] Other articles dealt with particular Essayists.[63]

The Essayists were also criticized in some lay periodicals. Harvey Goodwin reviewed *Essays and Reviews* in a temperate article in *Macmillan's Magazine*, deploring 'the existence of the volume as a volume' but fearing still more that the reaction against it would 'overshoot its mark' and discourage serious inquiry into what were serious questions.[64] The *Saturday Review*, which gave *Essays and Reviews* a balanced review on March 2,[65] dealt so harshly with Stanley's defence of it on May 4 that three of its regular contributors resigned from the staff. There were especially nasty comments on Jowett: 'he seems almost to have erected infirmity into an ideal, and to have persuaded himself that where certainty is truth cannot be'.[66] But the severest blow was dealt by *The Times*, in a leading article on July 1, calling the volume 'the great religious scandal of the day'. Speaking as a layman, the writer complained that the Essayists were in 'collision with the religious creed of the laity' who believe firmly in the authority of the Bible.

> Does not the relation of a clergyman to his parishioners require an identity of belief in the main? ... This is the test of his suitableness for his post. Would he venture to *preach* his views to his own flock in his own church? ... is not their belief essentially and vitally bound up with certain definite doctrines and attested facts ... there is one authority on which they do stand, and that is the authority of Scripture ... such a theory does appear to unfit a clergyman from the practical duties of a parish priest ... if he preaches openly what he thinks, there is no parish in England in which he could stay a week.[67]

In the face of such strong and numerous attacks on the Essayists, they themselves were virtually silent. The volume had originally been intended as the first of an annual series, and in mid-1860 Wilson was hopeful of getting out a second volume at least in 1862; but Parker's defection put an end to such plans. When Longmans determined to issue the tenth edition in a cheaper small octavo, which necessitated resetting the type, Wilson mooted the possibility of the authors making alterations and additions. Temple's strong objection scotched such notions: 'He considers the book as a starting point with which we must now be content'.[68] Temple would neither withdraw from nor change the volume, which must be left to work out its effects. No other Essayist chose to make any statement, except for the outburst from Williams in the *Literary Churchman*. It was left to Wilson himself to speak out, which he did with his printed Liverpool sermons, his anonymous quarterly reviews of current literature in the *Westminster Review*, and a signed introduction to a pamphlet by a layman.[69]

A former pupil of Wilson, R. B. Kennard, beneficed in Hamilton's diocese, felt compelled to protest formally to Hamilton against the episcopal manifesto, suggesting that other clergymen in the diocese felt the same way.[70] He published his protest in the *Dorset County Chronicle* and later, expanded, as a pamphlet.[71] Numerous diocesan clergy, organized by rural deaneries, signed letters of protest against Kennard's imputation that they supported *Essays and Reviews*.[72] Undaunted, Kennard was later to publish two further pamphlets in defense of the Essayists.[73]

Another sub-controversy was provoked when a Worcestershire vicar, Dr George J. Wild, protested against the clergy petition, arguing that doctrines similar to the Essayists' had been held by many eminent divines.[74] A neighbouring clergyman, provoked by seeing Wild cited in Stanley's *Edinburgh* article, published a reply to Wild.[75]

Wilberforce's *Quarterly* article prompted a London pastor associated with Maurice, Harry Jones, to publish a powerful plea for fair play for the Essayists.[76] Two short pamphlets defended the Essayists generally, and Robert Ainslie gave nine discourses in a Brighton church printed in the *Brighton Observer* and reprinted as a pamphlet.[77] An Oxford professor of science published an apology for Baden Powell.[78]

The most important defence of the Essayists was one that was not published. A number of eminent scientists and writers drew up an address directed to Temple as the author of the first article, an expression of their 'sympathy and thanks' for the Essayists' inquiries. 'Feeling, as we do, that the discoveries of science and the general progress of thought have necessitated some modification of the views generally held in religious matters, we welcome these attempts to establish religious teaching on a firmer and broader foundation.'[79] But the letter was never sent. Lay sympathy for the Essayists was expressed in an article in *Fraser's Magazine* deploring clerical intolerance.[80]

Reactions to *Essays and Reviews* were also expressed outside the Church of England. Evangelical dissent was as committed as evangelical Anglicanism to a biblical faith, though it might add concerns of its own such as the establishment of a church that could not guarantee an orthodox clergy. Three of the lions of dissent took part against the Essayists: John Cumming of the Protestant Truth Society; John Campbell, editor of the *British Standard* and other Congregationalist journals; and Edward Miall, leader of the disestablishmentarians and editor of the *Nonconformist* (which, with its sister journal the *Liberator*, joined in the campaign).[81] Less eminent writers also took part, one of them in verse.[82] Some minor denominations joined in, with lengthy tracts by a minister of the New Jerusalem (Swedenborgian) Church and by J. N. Darby, leader of the Plymouth Brethren and a former Anglican clergyman.[83] North of the border, where the controversy was followed with great interest, a Free Church professor contributed a lengthy pamphlet.[84]

The periodicals of these denominations were an integral part of their onslaught. The Congregationalist-dominated *Eclectic Review, British Quarterly Review* and *Evangelical Magazine* each had several critical articles. The Scottish Free Church's *North British Review* contributed several weighty articles.[85] The Methodists expressed themselves extensively in their periodicals, the *London Review* (better known as the *London Quarterly Review*) and the *Wesleyan Methodist Magazine*. The able series of five articles in the latter might have been Anglican, defending orthodox theology with the orthodox rationale.[86]

From a rather different standpoint, Roman Catholic periodicals exploited the controversy. Cardinal Wiseman's organ, the *Dublin Review,* condemned the Essayists but derided 'the efficiency of the Anglican Church as a guardian of the foundations of faith'.[87] A convert, H. N. Oxenham, published in the liberal Catholic *Rambler* one of the ablest articles, arguing that biblical criticism necessarily corroded Protestant faith, and that only Catholicism could defend religion against rationalism and scepticism.[88]

The Essayists found some support on the left of the religious spectrum, or beyond it. The Friends were still dominated by evangelicals, but a Quaker merchant, David Duncan, gave a lecture at the Manchester Friends' Institute in favour of the Essayists, 'as a protest against the intolerant spirit with which they have been assailed in some quarters; as a recognition of the Testimony which the writers bear to an "Inward Guide" superior to the Outward Testimony'.[89] Duncan was severely criticized by the leadership, but he found some supporters, and Manchester Friends continued to produce controversies over subsequent years.[90]

Unitarians provided support to the Essayists in the name of freedom of religious thought.[91] This support was often turned against the Essayists by their orthodox opponents, as were the bemused comments of a Jew who found in the Essayists support for the Jewish reading of the Old Testament.[92] There was also a supportive pamphlet by a deist.[93] Most embarrassing to the Essayists, however, was the apparent endorsement they seemed to receive from avowed freethinkers ('infidels' to the religious world).[94] In addition to their pamphlets, freethinking lecturers frequently cited *Essays and Reviews*.

In July 1861, the *Guardian* felt able to say that 'the era of pamphlets on "Essays and Reviews" is evidently passing away at last'. This was somewhat premature, as pamphlets continued to be produced on the original theme in 1862 and after, and further developments produced new sub-controversies and further pamphlets. However, the *Guardian* was right to discern that the pamphlet was 'an outlet for roused feelings' hastily expressed, typically in the early stages of a controversy, and that this ephemeral genre would be succeeded by 'treatises ... of a more lengthy, laboured, and reflective character'.[95]

CHAPTER NINE

Tracts into Tomes

The latter part of 1861 and the first half of 1862 saw the appearance of large-scale multi-author books or series of tracts, weightier responses to *Essays and Reviews* than most of the pamphlet literature. What might have been the best of these, however, was never published. The 'Cambridge Three', Hort, Westcott and Lightfoot, watched the growing controversy with growing alarm. Hort, whose observations provide the best running commentary on the debate, was annoyed by the carelessness of the Essayists but much more alarmed that the reaction against them might endanger all biblical scholarship. 'They happen at this moment to represent the cause of freedom of thought and criticism.'[1] Hort's initial response to the clerical petition was to propose a counter-declaration:

> We, the undersigned clergymen of the Church of England, desire to protest publicly against the violent and indiscriminate agitation now being directed against a book called Essays and Reviews, and against the authors of it. Believing that the suppression of free criticism must ultimately be injurious to the cause of truth and religion, we especially regret the adoption of a harsh and intolerant policy, which tends to deter men of thought and learning from entering the ministry of the Church, and to impel generous minds into antagonism to the Christian faith.[2]

But Westcott thought that they could not get enough signatures to counter the larger memorial, and Hort's declaration was abandoned.

Westcott instead proposed a 'mediating volume'[3] which would demonstrate both the values which Jowett and his friends had proclaimed and the truths which they had neglected. In *Revelation and History*, Lightfoot would write on 'the preparation of the Gospel', the Jewish history; Westcott would take 'the witness of God in his Son', the Incarnation as revelation; and Hort would deal with the development of doctrine in the New Testament.[4] Hort was willing, but Lightfoot declined, ostensibly 'as beyond his time and present powers',[5] but perhaps for reasons of prudence. *Revelation and History* might have been the one product of the controversy of lasting value.

A mediating effort of a quite different sort did produce a major series of tracts. Maurice, who was to a side of all parties, was disappointed by *Essays and Reviews* but dismayed by an orthodox reaction which adhered to texts and formularies but contained no living faith. 'The orthodoxy which covers our Atheism must be broken through'.[6] In March 1861, he proposed to his friend Thomas Hughes a statement of reasons for not joining in the address to the archbishops. This was quickly abandoned in favour of a series of tracts to set out the positive position of the Mauricians, both clerical and lay. A draft prospectus for *Tracts for Priests and People* was prepared by J. M. Ludlow:

> It is proposed that a set of papers be issued bearing upon the religious questions treated of in 'Essays and Reviews' but considered from a strictly positive point of view ... Upon a mere denial of a negation nothing whatever can be built ... the fact of the incarnation ... Looking at the Bible as the authoritative and inspired exponent of that fact, they wish to assert strongly its right to be treated, not in the bondage of the letter, but in the freedom of the spirit ... they are one and all convinced that nothing is so likely to check the spread of a hearty Christian spirit among the educated and still more the half-educated classes of English society, as any disposition to shrink from free inquiry into God's truth.[7]

Maurice objected to some of the negative elements in this statement, and the eventual preface to the bound series said simply: 'They are suggested by the present condition of religious feeling in England. They will not be confined to the topics which are treated in any particular volume. The writers will express frankly their differences from each other, but they do not shrink from the responsibilities which are involved in a joint publication'.[8]

The first of the *Tracts for Priests and People* was Hughes' *Religio Laici*, acknowledging that the Essayists, while wrong in method, has revealed an underlying doubt 'whether a living, personal God ... has ever revealed himself to man', and arguing for faith by stating his own Incarnation-centred faith.[9] This served to introduce Maurice's main effort, *The Mote and the Beam*. Not the Essayists but 'all of us' have created this state of doubt 'so far as we have substituted arguments against opponents for belief in a living God and charity to living men'. After discussing the Oxford Essayists, Maurice denounced the 'opinion-worship' of both liberalism and orthodoxy and demanded the preaching of 'a Will of God which is above all theories and all men ... a Person, not a Theory'. He advocated a return to the creeds, for 'fixed Creeds, just so far as they deliver us from the worship of opinion, are the protectors of toleration'. He concluded with a criticism of Wilberforce's *Quarterly* article: 'there is no such promoter of strange doctrines as he who merely contradicts them'.[10] It was vintage Maurice, prophetic but not precise, not meeting arguments but transcending them, 'a tract which probably failed to convince anyone as a piece of argument but which lifted the issues onto a higher plane'.[11]

The series continued with tracts by two clergymen, Francis Garden and J. Llewelyn Davies.[12] Then followed an unsought contribution by C. Kegan Paul, a radical clergyman not in the Maurician circle, which Maurice did not like because of its views on the Athanasian creed, but which he was willing to publish with remarks by another clergyman, J. N. Langley.[13] Ludlow and Maurice, as layman and clergyman, then engaged in a dialogue on Wilberforce's sermon on revelation and probation.[14] Ludlow concluded the series with *Two Lay Dialogues* on natural law and positive philosophy.[15]

Most of the reviews in the press were either confused or condemnatory, or both.[16] But the Maurician efforts brought about the first intervention in the debate of the greatest religious journalist of the age, R. H. Hutton. Hutton, at this time a Unitarian and an editor of the *National Review*, had just been appointed literary editor of the *Spectator*, and he began his service in this chair with a review of the first two tracts on June 1, 1861, rejoicing 'that the Seven Essayists and their critics have drawn forth the avowal of so much deep, hearty, and deliberate faith which is entirely untainted by any narrow, dogmatic, or cowardly spirit'.[17] Reviews of successive tracts were in the same friendly spirit, and by 1862 Hutton was prepared to contribute a tract of his own, and shortly thereafter to convert to Maurician Anglicanism.

The second series of tracts was more diffuse, continuing well into 1862 and outlasting the original concern with *Essays and Reviews*. C. P. Chrétien, an erstwhile supporter of Mansel who had been converted by Maurice's arguments, opened with a serious tract on the *Evidences* as a method which 'we have happily outgrown'.[18] Then came a pair of dialogues, Ludlow and Garden on *Dissent and the Creeds* and Maurice and Sir Edward Strachey on *Politics Ancient and Modern*, the latter unrelated to the original controversy.[19] Davies followed with a tract on the Holy Spirit.[20] W. H. Lyttleton, not otherwise connected with the Mauricians, contributed a very liberal tract on *The Testimony of Scripture to the Authority of Conscience and of Reason*.[21] By this time other composite volumes had appeared, and one of them, *Aids to Faith*, contained an attack on Garden's tract; Davies and Garden responded to this with a double tract on *The Death of Christ*.[22] Hutton, still a Unitarian, contributed his tract on *The Incarnation and Principles of Evidence*, 'a vindication of ... the fundamental principle of the English Church, by one who is not a member of it', which Maurice would only publish when joined by his own response.[23] The series petered out with a supplementary number on an unrelated question.[24]

These were the only tracts with irenic intentions; the rest belong in the category of replies to *Essays and Reviews*. The first of these composite replies was the work of Denison, who would rather have condemned the Essays by authority but who temporarily settled for refuting them by argument. He did not write himself, but he found five respectable controversialists, all High Church.[25] He arranged for them to publish their tracts separately in 1861 so as to be able to claim separate responsibility and then published the series as a volume in 1862 with a preface by himself.[26] The first tract was a reply to Temple by Jelf, person-ally sympathetic, charging no formal heresy in Temple's article but condemning its implication of the supremacy of reason over Scripture.[27] The second was a reply to Wilson by James Wayland Joyce, criticizing 'ideology' and upholding doctrinal limits and formularies of subscription.[28] James Fendall, who was to be Wilson's prosecutor, wrote perhaps the most important of the tracts in reply to Jowett, asserting the authority of Scripture as the actual revelation from God and therefore to be received with submission at the command of the Church.[29]

William Lee, a professor at Trinity College Dublin, upheld miracles against Baden Powell with a lengthy argument based upon Butler.[30] Edgar Huxtable wrote a curious reply to Goodwin, conceding that the harmonizers were fallacious and that Genesis 1 was not historical, but then explaining it as a parable designed to convey the religious truth that God was the Creator.[31] *Faith and Peace*, as the series was named, aimed high for quality and contained some solid though tendentious contributions; its partisan origin explains why it was not considered one of the major replies to *Essays and Reviews*.

Denison found a vehicle in which to express himself directly in the *Church and State Review*, a monthly which he founded and edited from mid-1862 as his 'last attempt ... to promote the placing of the relations of Church to State, and State to Church, upon a truer footing', i.e. to ensure the freedom of the Church to condemn works such as *Essays and Reviews*. Although he claimed that the review 'was written chiefly by great hands',[32] its consistently combative style and its regular demand for synodical condemnation suggest that much of it was written by Denison himself.[33]

Two composite volumes were announced in 1861 as the major, quasi-official replies to *Essays and Reviews*, but circumstances prevented their appearance during that year. When they both were published on January 1, 1862 there also appeared the most complete single-author work on the subject, J. N. Griffin's *Seven Answers to the Seven Essays and Reviews*. Expressly evangelical in his stance, competent but pedestrian, Griffin restated the evidential argument based on Butler and Paley.[34] He had the misfortune to appear at the same time as the two major book-length replies, so his book was slighted in the press as an example of a genre now rendered superfluous. In fact, pamphlets, some of them large, continued to appear throughout 1862.[35]

The two composite volumes which appeared on the first day of 1862 were generally regarded as the major quasi-official responses to *Essays and Reviews*. Significantly, they adopted the Essayists' format of independent signed essays, showing that *Essays and Reviews* had shaped a *genre* of volumes of essays by several hands.[36] The first, simply entitled *Replies to 'Essays and Reviews'*, purported to be the product of its publisher, John Henry and James Parker of Oxford; but the guiding spirit was Samuel Wilberforce. Contributions were invited from seven authors, each to reply to a specific essay or review. There was no editorial control; the essays were written 'without concert or comparison', each author taking individual responsibility for his signed contribution. The publisher explained in a tortuous 'advertisement' that he did not accept the principle of individual responsibility but sought to put the *Essays* and the *Replies* on an equal footing: 'otherwise, it might be objected that the latter volume was written under advantages which did not belong to the former, and therefore be refused the possession of the same weight as that volume'.[37] The volume also contained two letters from scientists at Oxford, denying that either astronomy or geology contradicted Genesis.[38]

Wilberforce's preface, written before he had read any of the articles, asserted that the objections of *Essays and Reviews* were not new and required only a restatement of old arguments for the faith, and characterized them as 'pantheism' which was 'but a tricked-out Atheism. The dissolution of Revelation is the denial of God'. Two courses of action were required:

> First, the distinct, solemn, and if need be, severe decision of authority that assertions such as these cannot be put forward as possibly true, or even advanced as admitting of question, by honest men, who are bound by voluntary obligations to teach the Christian revelation as the truth of God ... First, then, and even before argument, our disorders need the firm, unflinching action of authority.
>
> Secondly, we need the calm, comprehensive, scholar-like declaration of positive truth upon all the matters in dispute.[39]

The first 'scholar-like declaration' was a review of Temple by his predecessor as headmaster of Rugby, Canon E. M. Goulburn. The education of the world, Goulburn argued temperately, terminated with the coming of Christ: '*the education (if we are to call it so) of the church is all wrapped up in the rudiments*; – it is simply an expansion of "the faith once delivered to the saints"'. Temple confused 'the progress of the species by civilization with the progress of the Church in divine knowledge'. Temple's statement that 'the faculty of faith has turned inwards' and could no longer accept miracles was 'unphilosophical and unscriptural ... it *is* a law of the mind to expect that a divine message will be accredited by miracles'. Goulburn criticized Temple's identification of the Bible with 'the voice of conscience' as a confusion of conscience with understanding.[40]

The reply to Williams was written by Henry John Rose, an early High Churchman. After first dismissing Bunsen as a rash speculator rejected even by Germans, Rose blamed Williams for writing '*ad populum* rather than *ad clerum*', thereby endangering the faith of the ignorant. Williams had misrepresented the state of biblical scholarship in Germany, implying a unanimity among critics which did not exist and disregarding orthodox writers such as Keil, Hävernick and Hengstenberg. 'The tide has turned ... the prevailing tone is conservative, and that in a degree which is constantly increasing'. Williams also falsely stated that English theologians were abandoning the concept of predictive prophecy. Williams was an unreliable interpreter of key sections of the Bible, particularly of Isaiah liii as a messianic prophecy and on the historicity of Daniel. 'We have ... on the one hand, Christ and His apostles, who assure us that the prophecies are predictions; on the other, we have Dr. Williams and the critical school, who assure us they are not. The question is simply this – Will you believe Christ and His apostles, or will you believe the critical school?' Rose said that Williams was 'entirely disqualified' as a guide to the Bible, whose work could only 'mislead the ignorant'. He concluded with an attack on the book generally, regretting 'the certain infidelity and immorality which must result from principles like these being disseminated among the half-educated and the ignorant'.[41] In an appendix, Rose criticized Stanley's *Edinburgh* review for his suggestion that clergymen were prevented from speaking the truth. 'The simple question before us is this, Whether it is reputable for men to profess one set of principles and teach another?'[42]

The reply to Powell, a straightforward defence of miracles, was written by the evangelical C. A. Heurtley. He asserted that believers 'cannot approach the subject but with a foregone conclusion in favour of the reality of the Christian miracles ... If the Christian miracles were not real miracles, what becomes of our Lord's truthfulness?' Heurtley defined miracles, not as violations of law, but as supersessions of natural law by a higher power acting according to its own law. He upheld the credibility of the Christian miracles by asserting that they were *sui generis*: 'the analogy of the ordinary course of nature affords no suffi- cient ground for doubting the reality of miracles, said to have been wrought in attestation of a revelation which has nothing analogous to it in nature'. The reality of miraculous facts was proven by adequate testimony and explicitly appealed to by Christ and the apostles. Heurtley demonstrated their evidential value with a Paleyan argument built up cumulatively and reinforced by proph- ecy, showing that they were fundamental in establishing the credentials of the founders of Christianity.[43]

Wilson's essay was responded to by W. J. Irons, a High Churchman. Irons contrasted Wilson's 'Multitudinism', which aimed 'to divert attention from the distinctive hope of "salvation" hereafter', with orthodox 'Individualism', which 'makes its appeal to each separate conscience; (because men's future condition will not be determined in masses, but in accordance with individual character)'. Wilson preached a 'Generalized Christianity' without doctrines, a 'Christianity without *certainty of a single fact of the Gospel*', which could not be sustained. 'Christianity, according to the Scriptures, *has a doctrine*, – has a strict *Moral* system, – asks to include *none* who will not rise to its standard of truth and purity, anticipates frequently *narrow results*, aims always at the *individual* con- science, and points, primarily, to an *"eternal life"* beyond the grave.' Multitudinism subverts 'Individual Responsibility' by disregarding the soul and its future. Irons held that the true solution of church–state problems was for the state to leave the Church alone, with corporate freedom to 'reform her convocation, reform her spiritual laws, and regulate her internal Discipline'. It was wrong to see to make the Church less exclusive: 'Christianity aims at *each Conscience*, – and must be left to do its own work'.[44]

Goodwin's essay received a curious reply from a Scottish Episcopalian priest, G. Rorison, whose rambling article began with a literary analysis of the poetic structure of the creation account (Gen. 1:1–2:3), showing that God created matter out of nothing; that all life 'came into being, not by the blind operation of natural law, but by acts of divine volition'; that man is a non-evolved creature *sui generis*. Both astronomy and geology confirm the need of a Final Cause and the uniqueness of man. The inspired record is not contradicted by the discoveries of science, but neither does it anticipate them: 'the chief wonder is how it ever was possible to extract from the oldest and sublimest poem in the world the attributes of narrative prose'. The creation account is a psalm, organized in parallel triads around the mystic number seven: 'thus the "days" themselves are transfigured from registers of time into definitives of strophes or stanzas'.[45] Rorison was unusual in employing literary criticism in defence of orthodoxy.

Pattison's essay received a courteous reply from A. W. Haddan, a High Church rector. Haddan freely acknowledged that Pattison 'must in fairness be exonerated from any intentional participation in the furtherance of scepticism'; his essay was literary, not theological, and 'it is a libel to accuse it of containing either wanton or formal unbelief', although it might be faulted for its tone, some observations on particular authors, and its depreciation of objective standards of religious truth. The Church of England had such a standard in 'Scripture interpreted by Catholic consent'.[46]

Jowett's essay was assigned to Christopher Wordsworth, nephew of the poet, a strong High Churchman. Wordsworth treated Jowett's principle of interpretation as ludicrous. What Jowett called 'the after-thoughts of theology' were really 'the workings of the Holy Spirit in the Church'. Scripture asserts its own inspiration and supplies, along with church history, the interpretation of its prophecies and messages. The 'root of the evil' was that 'the Essayist does not believe in the Inspiration of Holy Scripture, according to the ordinary acceptation of that term'. The proof of that inspiration depended on incontrovertible external evidences: 'whatever the universal Church of Christ has received as divinely inspired Scripture, is the unerring Word of God'. It can be correctly interpreted only by those who understand it as the word of God; we must not lay aside the question of inspiration and treat it as any other book. Jowett's essay 'teems with insinuations. It is a whispering-gallery of indistinct sounds muttering evil'. This approach is dangerous to faith: 'it behoves us to consider well, whether Almighty God, who has given us the Scriptures, has not also given us external as well as internal evidence of their Inspiration; and whether He has not also afforded us sure guidance for their right Interpretation, in the consentient faith and practice of the Universal Church of Christ'.[47]

Replies to 'Essays and Reviews' was a work purely of religious controversy; several of the *Replies* were competent examples of this *genre*, and Heurtley's (the strongest) was a solid restatement of the orthodox position on miracles, but none made a lasting contribution. The High Church tendencies of most of the authors[48] contrasted with the evangelicalism of one or two; Rorison's literary treatment of Genesis jarred with the denunciation by others of Williams' and Wilson's 'free handling'; and Haddan's fairness to Pattison was so great as to place Wordsworth's slashing attack on Jowett in unfavourable relief. The work as a whole could only convince those already disposed to be convinced; it reasserted old principles, but was incapable of entering into new difficulties. But it fulfilled its main purpose. It was produced to still the objection that *Essays and*

Reviews had met no rebuttal of equal length, labour and learning. Such a work could now be cited. The fact of the rebuttal was greater than its merits.

The other major composite reply, *Aids to Faith*, was a more ambitious undertaking representing a broader orthodoxy. Its editor, William Thomson, was an evangelical notable for his moderation. His Bampton Lectures of 1853 had been 'the first to be particularly aimed at systems of unbelief originated in foreign literature'; yet he 'had identified himself with the liberal school of Benjamin Jowett' in matters of university reform.[49] In January, 1861, Canon A. W. Thorold, on behalf of 'some men of influence in London',[50] invited Thomson to contribute to a projected volume of answers to *Essays and Reviews*. By February, Thomson was functioning as editor, inviting Dean Ellicott of Exeter to contribute; Ellicott later advised Thomson on other contributors.[51] The original deadlines were not met (Thomson, becoming bishop of Gloucester and Bristol in August, was the slowest) and the book only appeared in January 1862.

Aids to Faith differed from *Replies* in that it was not intended as direct responses to the several *Essays* but was a professedly non-controversial work designed to provide reassurance and assistance to those puzzled by the Essayists and disturbed in their faith.

> The Essays in this volume are intended to offer aid to those whose faith may have been shaken by recent assaults. The writers ... desire to set forth their reasons for believing the Bible, out of which they teach, to be the inspired Word of God, and for exhorting others still to cherish it as the only message of salvation from God to man ... They have avoided, rather than sought, direct controversy.[52]

A contributor, Harold Browne, wrote 'to aid weak faith, to help doubting and distressed minds ... We were not fighting against the heresies and infidelity of *Essays and Reviews*, but trying to help those who were puzzled'.[53] The nine essays did not all correspond with specific *Essays and Reviews*, nor did they follow its order; the first three dealt with the evidences of Christianity and the last five with aspects of biblical studies. The only imitative element was the disclaimer of joint responsibility.[54]

Notwithstanding these pacific intentions, the first essay, 'On Miracles as Evidences of Christianity', was a direct reply to Baden Powell by the most controversial H. L. Mansel. It was typical of Mansel's either–or logic that he offered his readers 'only the choice between a deeper faith and a bolder unbelief; between accepting the sacred narrative as a true account of miracles actually performed, and rejecting it as wholly fictitious and incredible'. Belief in the reality of miracles was necessary to the entire system of Christianity. It was no mere external accessory, for essential doctrines, notably the Resurrection, involved miracles, and Christ and his apostles had explicitly stated their reliance on miracles to prove their divine commission. The argument against miracles rested on a denial of the possibility of the supernatural; 'but if a single true miracle be admitted as established by sufficient evidence, the entire history to which it belongs is at once removed from the ordinary calculation of more or less probability'. Miracles do not violate the laws of nature but rather introduce a new agent not included within them. Therefore

> the question concerning the possibility or probability of a miracle is to be judged, not merely from physical, but also, and principally, from moral grounds ... The very conception of a *revealed* as distinguished from a *natural* religion implies a manifestation of God different from that which is exhibited by the ordinary course of nature; and the question of the probability of a miraculous interposition is simply that of the probability of a revelation being given at all.

As for the evidential value of miracles, 'it is not *the truth of the doctrines*, but *the authority of the teacher*, that miracles are employed to prove; and the authority being established, the truth of the doctrine follows from it'.[55] This was pure Mansel: ingenious, seemingly irrefutable, ultimately unconvincing but leaving the reader feeling that he ought to have been convinced.

The next essay, 'On the Study of the Evidences of Christianity', by William Fitzgerald, bishop of Cork, was less pointed. Taking as his text (for refutation) Coleridge's strictures on 'evidences of Christianity', Fitzgerald upheld the value of the factual evidences of the reliability of Revelation as against those who stripped Christianity of its historical foundations and reduced it to a matter of sentiment. 'Indeed, if we steadily retain in our minds the *historical* view of Christianity which is presented in the New Testament, and the primitive creeds, as a religion of FACTS, it will be hard to grasp Mr. Coleridge's *dictum* even as a comprehensible utterance.' Man's needs are no measure of religious truth, but even by that test 'we *need* a basis of fact, an historical basis, for our religious belief'. Christianity is 'an historical religion – a religion made up of matters of fact, and propounded on the evidence of matters of fact'; hence the factual evidences of its origin are worthy of study.[56]

The second of the evidences, 'Prophecy', was defended by Alexander McCaul, already involved in the debate. His target was Williams' denial of predictive prophecy (and some remarks by Jowett on unfulfilled prophecies). With an impressive if one-sided display of learning, McCaul upheld the divine mission of the prophets, their power of prediction and the applicability of their predictions to Christ. The real question was 'whether the New Testament or German critics are to be our guides in interpreting prophecy'. Christ and his apostles had explicitly relied on Old Testament prophecies to validate their mission; 'if we give up the prophetic interpretations of Christ and the Apostles, we must prepare also to part with our Christianity'.[57] In particular, McCaul defended the genuineness of Daniel[58] and the messianic interpretation of Isaiah 53.

Between these discussions of the evidences and the remaining essays on biblical questions came an essay on 'Ideology and Subscription', a reply to Wilson, by F. C. Cook, royal chaplain and inspector of schools. Cook traced 'ideology', the rejection of the miraculous facts of Christianity while retaining a belief in its ideal truths, to its German origins, especially Strauss' *Leben Jesu*. This 'un-English and Jesuitical' system is repugnant to conscience and to Englishmen's love of truth. Cook roundly condemned Wilson's reduction of subscription to its legal obligations: subscription imposed a moral obligation, binding not belief but action, giving the laity 'a means of ascertaining what truths a man holds, and what he holds himself bound to teach'.[59]

McCaul's second essay, 'The Mosaic Record of Creation', attacked Goodwin. He concentrated on some of Goodwin's *obiter dicta*, such as the claim that Genesis contains two conflicting accounts of creation; he rejected the Jehovist–Elohist hypothesis on the ground that its proponents differed from and thereby refuted each other. McCaul's main criticism was directed at the argument that the Mosaic cosmogony had been superseded by the progress of science. Comparing the statements of Moses (in a learned analysis of the Hebrew words) with 'the discoveries and conclusions of modern science', McCaul found proof of an astounding 'scientific accuracy' in Moses: 'The ages required for geological development, the infinity of worlds and the immensity of space revealed by astronomy, illustrate, as no other note has ever done, the Scripture doctrines of the eternity, the omnipotence, the wisdom of the Creator'.[60]

This defence of Genesis was followed by a defence of the Mosaic authorship of the entire Pentateuch by George Rawlinson, who had upheld 'The Historical Evidences of the Truth of the Scripture Records' in his 1859 Bampton Lectures. The burden of proof, Rawlinson asserted, lay with those who denied 'the fact of reputed authorship', and they had failed. Rawlinson defended the Pentateuch against criticism on grounds of chronology, the universality of the Flood, ethnology, genealogy, the longevity of the patriarchs and the duration of the sojourn in Egypt. 'Whatever may be the scientific difficulties in the way of a literal reception of some portions, historical difficulties of any real magnitude, there are none.'[61]

This rather specious essay was followed by one quite different, the most judicious and perhaps the most important, on 'Inspiration', by Harold Browne, Norrisian professor of divinity at Cambridge. The nature and degree of the divine inspiration of the Bible was the fundamental question underlying the controversy; yet the Essayists had touched the subject only obliquely, and few of their opponents articulated a full position. Browne's statement was less full than it might have been: he felt 'no call to define dogmatically'[62] but rather sought to soothe troubled pious souls; he advanced no theory of inspiration but instead sought to place the subject in perspective. There was both a human and a divine element in the writing of Scripture; the problem was, how did they co-exist? Browne observed that neither the Gospel doctrines nor the evidences of Christianity depended on any particular theory of inspiration: 'the questions of verbal inspiration, mechanical inspiration, dynamical inspiration, and the like are all questions on which persons believing in the Gospels may differ'. 'Definite theories of inspiration', Browne warned, were 'doubtful and dangerous'. Miracles, predictive prophecies, and types and antitypes in the Old and New Testaments indicate a divine element, 'something more than the inspiration of genius, or than the exalting of their intuitional consciousness', something which makes the books of the Bible the word of God.

> Whatever conclusion, then, may be arrived at as to the infallibility of the writers on matters of science or of history, still the whole collection of the books will be really the oracles of God, the Scriptures of God, the record and depository of God's supernatural revelations in early times to man ... We want to be assured that we have an *infallible* depository of *religious* truth.

'Patience,' Browne concluded, 'is the proper temper fore an age like our own, which is in many ways an age of transition.'[63] His essay was almost a manifesto of moderation, incomplete as a definition but at least reassuring and rallying. If anything, it was perhaps too judicious.[64]

The next essay was the editor's own contribution, 'The Death of Christ', directed not against *Essays and Reviews* but against Jowett's treatment of the Atonement in his 1855 work on St Paul. Thomson recognized that Jowett's critique of the substitutionary theory had a powerful moral appeal and directed his essay 'to those who profess to attach to the sufferings of the Redeemer some preternatural efficacy, beyond that of mere example, yet who would substitute for the received account of their effect some other doctrine'. Most of the essay argued that the New Testament was consistent in treating Christ's death as a sacrifice and that the theory of vicarious Atonement was not invented by Anselm. Then Thomson turned to the moral objection, the repugnance felt against the notions of a wrathful God and of the punishment of an innocent person for the sins of others. He argued that 'imputed sin' corresponded to the commonly observed fact that persons do not have absolutely separate moral responsibility, being affected by environment and heredity; if they become guilty because of others, it is no more contrary to God's justice that another should bear their guilt. The mystery of an innocent Jesus suffering for others is related to the mystery of sin itself: 'a disease so utterly past our comprehension may require means to cure it that shock the ordinary conclusions of our conscience'. Thomson acknowledged that the Atonement had been given a one-sided treatment by friends as well as foes: 'Let us not so exalt the justice of God that we seem to record the harshness of a tyrant, and not the device of a Father seeking to bring His children back. Let us not so dwell on the love of Christ as to forget that one great moral purpose of this sacrifice was to set the mark of God's indignation upon sin'.[65]

The final essay, 'Scripture, and its Interpretation', was written by the evangelical C. J. Ellicott. This essay, much the longest, was a direct reply, section by section, to Jowett's essay; it was expressly controversial ('The believer of the present day must put himself in the attitude of an opponent'). Ellicott first attacked Jowett's remarks about the variety of interpretations, arguing that the

Church had consistently recognized 'the literal and historical method' as the one sound principle. Admitting much diversity of interpretation of particular passages, he accounted for this by the fact that the Bible is different in kind from any other book, that its words often have more than one meaning, and that it is inspired. He offered his definition of inspiration: 'the Holy Ghost was so breathed into the mind of the writer, so illumined his spirit and pervaded his thoughts, that, while nothing that individualized him as man was taken away, everything that was necessary to enable him to declare Divine Truth in all its fulness was bestowed and superadded'. Ellicott considered this definition a 'guarded view'; he refused to commit himself to an absolute infallibility of the Bible: 'viewed on its human side, *and in its reference to matters previously admitted to have no bearing on Divine truth*', one may admit 'imperfections' though not falsehood or conscious error. Ellicott then offered his rules for the interpretation of Scripture to demonstrate his 'literal and historical' method, 'that method which not only concerns itself with the simple and grammatical meaning of the words, but also with that meaning under what may be termed … its historical relations'. The basic rules – '*Interpret grammatically, historically, contextually, and minutely*' – were, he admitted, common to Scripture and other books; but the most important rule was unique: 'Interpret according to the analogy of Faith', considering not only the text in question but the rest of the Bible and the guidance afforded by the Creeds. This was a principle of interpretation directly contrary to Jowett's.[66]

Aids to Faith was more substantial and satisfactory than *Replies*, making the best case that could be made for a reasonable orthodoxy. *Essays and Reviews* had at least received a full-scale response. It was not, however, entirely successful: Fitzgerald's article was lightweight; Rawlinson's 'historical' defence of Moses was a disgrace to history. Despite the editor's intentions, controversy was not avoided; Mansel was a natural controversialist, and Ellicott wrote controversially. But the chief defect of *Aids to Faith* was that common to the best of the orthodox writings: they were incapable of advancing the subject, but could only restate a closed intellectual system. They could not rise above the controversy. All they could do was to offer a reasoned presentation of the orthodox position and indicate that that position remained intact after the onslaught of *Essays and Reviews*.

CHAPTER TEN

The Case in Court

The controversy in the courts, which in early 1862 supplanted the literary controversy as the focus of attention, had its origin a year earlier in the troubled conscience of Bishop W. K. Hamilton of Salisbury. Hamilton was the only tractarian on the bench of bishops.[1] His was a pastoral High Churchmanship, 'a dogmatism wonderfully free from intolerance',[2] and extremely scrupulous. He had scruples in 1858 about instituting Williams to Broad Chalke, which he overcame only after taking legal advice. His concern was for the parishioners who should be protected from heresy. As early as February 28, 1861, he had alerted his colleagues that he was taking legal advice about prosecuting Williams in the ecclesiastical courts for heresy. His legal advisor was his college friend and diocesan chancellor R. J. Phillimore, who as Queen's Advocate was the leading practitioner at the civil law bar (and incidentally Denison's brother-in-law). By March 8 he had put formal questions to Phillimore, who replied on March 11 that Williams was subject to 'canonical punishment' for teachings 'irreconcilable with the teachings of the Church of England' and expressed in 'distinct propositions not only adverse to but subversive of this teaching'.[3] This was a clear recommendation of prosecution, which could have been conducted, under the inquisitorial procedure of canon law, in Hamilton's diocesan court presided over by Phillimore as chancellor. Such unsuitable *ex officio* proceedings were obviated by Hamilton's scruple that he might be deemed to have prejudged the case by signing the episcopal manifesto. The case was therefore to be brought in what would otherwise have been the court of first appeal, the Archbishop's court known as the Court of Arches.

Hamilton's scruples and doubts were not finally overcome until May, by which time he had also consulted a rising barrister at the common law, J. D. Coleridge, Keble's godson and great-nephew of the poet. Authority for prosecution was supplied by the Clergy Discipline Act, 1840, but there was a question whether the prosecution should be under a statute of Elizabeth for contradicting the Thirty-Nine Articles or under the general canon law 'for contradicting the faith'.[4] Hamilton accepted Phillimore's advice to proceed under the latter, which allowed less severe penalties than the deprivation mandated by the former. Hamilton's decision to prosecute was known locally by mid-May, but it was formally announced in a published letter to one of his archdeacons on May 23.[5] Hamilton refused financial assistance from other bishops, but a guarantee fund was quickly organized by his diocesan clergy. The prosecution was formally commenced on June 1, when Letters of Request (to accept the case) were sent to the Court of Arches; and Williams was served with his citation on June 16.

Several persons, including some warmly attached to Hamilton, remonstrated with him for choosing to prosecute.[6] Hamilton found an occasion to explain himself publicly when he delivered his Charge in August 1861. Williams, uncomfortable amid the clergy and people of Salisbury,[7] was in the audience. Hamilton acknowledged that *Essays and Reviews* was not powerful enough to do lasting harm and expressed doubts that 'the constitution of our Courts of Judicature is as well fitted, as I could desire, for weighing in the fine balance of Truth' many questions of religion; but he felt it his duty not to let the book pass unnoticed, which might 'allow the conclusion that such teaching ... was, in 1861, admitted to be not unlawful'. 'The case was beyond the bounds of Toleration.'[8] The Charge was published, the first sign that the legal controversy would generate a pamphlet literature of its own.

Williams was subject to diocesan prosecution because he held a benefice. Of the other Essayists, Powell had been 'removed to a higher tribunal' by death but in any case held no clerical position; like Jowett, he was a professor at Oxford and was subject only to academic jurisdiction. Pattison's post as rector of Lincoln College was a 'donative' not subject to a bishop; Temple as a royal chaplain was immune from any jurisdiction and as headmaster of Rugby had survived the scrutiny of the trustees; Goodwin was a layman and no longer a college fellow. But Wilson was beneficed in the diocese of Ely as vicar of Great Staughton and was also liable to prosecution. His bishop, Thomas Turton, was not willing to institute a prosecution, but he allowed one of his clergy, James Fendall, to commence a private prosecution. Counselled by Wilberforce, who helped to organize a subscription to defray his expenses,[9] Fendall formally commenced his prosecution on December 16.

The cases of Bishop of Salisbury *v.* Williams and Fendall *v.* Wilson were conducted together for the convenience of the court, much to the disgust of the defendants who wished to make distinct defences to the distinct heresies with which they were charged.[10] Williams' supporters had already formed a committee to obtain subscriptions towards his expenses; when the cases were joined, this was superseded by a Williams and Wilson Appeal Fund organized by Stanley, to which the other Essayists contributed.[11] Williams had already selected his legal counsel, who were adopted by Wilson. J. Parker Deane, a leading civil lawyer, led for the defendants; but more important was his junior from the common law, James Fitzjames Stephen, for whom the case was a labour of love, and who was personally committed to the opinions he expressed.[12] Phillimore led for the prosecution, with Coleridge as his common-law junior and his usual civilian junior, Maurice Swabey, as an extra counsel.

The case now entered the world of the civil law, little studied by historians more familiar with the common law. Civil law dealt with maritime cases in the Admiralty Court and with ecclesiastical and probate cases in the ecclesiastical courts. It had its own bar, two dozen advocates with doctorates in civil law, and a body of proctors corresponding to solicitors, although in 1857 common and

civil law bars had been assimilated, and the leading civilians were Queen's
Counsel. The archbishop's court for the province of Canterbury was the Court
of Arches (archly named for its former site in Bow Church) and its judge, Dr
Stephen Lushington, was styled dean of arches. Lushington had been a political
radical; but the professional pecking order was based on merit, and as the
undoubted leader the octogenarian Lushington was both admiralty judge and
dean of arches. Through his son at Oxford he had been drawn into the Jowett
circle,[13] and his ecclesiastical sympathies may be presumed to have been liberal,
but his decision showed the effects of an education in the evidential apologetic.[14]

Even with the fairest of judges, the atmosphere of an ecclesiastical court is
forbidding to defendants. Though the presumption of innocence was imported
by Lushington from the common law, it was not inherent in the ecclesiastical, in
which the prosecution is called 'promoting the office of the Judge' – the office of
the judge being to condemn. The long list of articles of indictment, presented
against Williams in mid-1861, consisted of extracts from his essay set against the
formulary (Thirty-Nine Articles, creed, liturgy or canons) or passage of the
Bible which they allegedly contradicted. Jowett thought the articles were 'con-
cocted in the most monstrous spirit'.[15] Williams was concerned that the legalism
which dealt with isolated passages out of context would not do justice to his
theology.[16] He therefore prepared in October a tract, *Hints to my Counsel in the
Court of Arches*, which he intended to publish but was persuaded merely to print
for private circulation. It is a remarkable document, illustrative both of his
consistency and his combativeness.

> Dr. Rowland Williams, Defendant, leaves the technical part of his case to
> his Counsel, with this remark – No legal subterfuge … The Defendant
> accepts the Articles as they are, and claims to teach them with a fidelity
> and clearness unsurpassed by living man … The general ideas for the
> defence are that a floating tradition of error, especially on the matter of
> Prophecy, is enforced on the clergy by violence, and on the laity by
> disguises … he is the only man for three hundred years in England,
> against whom the law has been invoked, on no ground, and on no sincere
> suspicion, of any ecclesiastical heresy, but with a prosecution directed
> against the principle of free inquiry, and against the public avowal of facts
> … He aims at reconciling the old argument between Science and Faith,
> and thinks such reconciliation impossible, so long as men oppose Faith to
> Reason; but that it would become most easy, if men would only reflect
> that, as Inspiration is a communication between God and Man, it must
> unite the immutable character of Divine Verity with the fluctuating range
> of human knowledge … He thinks it possible, that Christianity may yet
> be destined to attain by purely moral instruments a wider domination
> than it has hitherto enjoyed, and our Church to embrace alienated bodies
> in a larger and manifold unity. But he conceives such destiny can neither
> be wrought out by articles of special pleading, nor by obscuring the moral
> analogies of the Gospel in history and Man's living conscience, in order to
> ground our faith exclusively on an isolated history … The Church, as an

> embodiment of Christ's living spirit, is not a tyranny, but a spiritual commonwealth. Our moral instincts are so tempered by our Maker, that they ever answer through faith to the true doctrine of Christ ... Rather should our Church ... entering upon all knowledge, accept frankly whatever fresh views of literature and science, and whatever tendencies to a larger comprehension may be born, not of human will, but of the will of Him who is not weary of creating and renewing, and who leads us, as we are able to bear it, into the entire Truth.[17]

Following Williams' expressed wish, defence counsel raised no technical objections, as Phillimore had feared. The case against Williams began on December 16, 1861, and lasted over ten days ending on January 16, 1862; the briefer case against Williams followed between February 22 and March 3. The proceedings were of a preliminary or 'interlocutory' kind in which Phillimore presented the articles (or charges) against Williams and the defence argued against their admissibility. Of the 22 articles, the first and last few were formal, but articles VII–XVII were substantive. Article XVII summed them up:

> ... the manifest tendency, scope, object and design of the whole Essay is to inculcate a disbelief in the Divine inspiration and authority of the Holy Scripture, contained in the Old and New Testaments; to reduce the said Holy Scriptures to the level of a mere human composition, such as the writings of Luther and of Milton; to deny that the Old Testament contains prophecies or predictions of our Saviour, and other persons and events; to deny that the Prophets, speaking under the special inspiration of the Holy Spirit, foretold human events; to deny altogether, or greatly discredit, the truth and genuineness of the historical portions of the Old Testament, and the truth and genuineness of certain parts of the New Testament, and the truth and reality of the miracles recorded as facts in the Old and New Testaments; to deny, or interpret by a meaning at variance with that of the Church, the doctrines of Original Sin, of Infant Baptism, of Justification by Faith, Atonement, and Propitiation by the death of our Saviour, and the Incarnation of our Saviour.[18]

Deane, in objecting to the admission of the articles, had to refer to two previous decisions as governing the court's consideration of them. The first was the Gorham judgment of 1850, in which the Judicial Committee of the Privy Council (with Lushington sitting as a member), on appeal from the Court of Arches, held that it was not the duty of the court to rule on the doctrinal soundness of the defendant's statements but only to find whether they were contrary to the Articles and formularies of the Church of England. If those formularies were silent, ambiguous, or admitted of different interpretations, any plausible interpretation was allowable; and in interpreting them, they must be construed by 'the same rules which have long been established and are by law applicable to the construction of all written instruments',[19] the rules of common law. The second case was one on which Lushington had only recently ruled, Burder *v.* Heath, in which a vicar had been convicted for publishing sermons with obscure but provable heresies (such as that saving faith is not faith in

Christ but the faith of Christ himself). In his ruling Lushington had cited the Gordham decision as limiting his duty to 'the ascertainment of the plain grammatical meaning of the Book of Common Prayer and the Articles'. He held that a doctrine which had 'been held without offence by eminent divines of the Church' ought not to be condemned: 'That which has been allowed or tolerated in the Church ought not to be questioned by this Court ... fully recognize the position of the Judicial Committee that there are many matters of Doctrine dehors both the Articles of Religion and the Book of Common Prayer and as to which entire freedom of opinion is allowed'.[20] Deane made use of these rulings, although Burder *v.* Heath was still being appealed.

Deane first objected to one of the general articles which referred to the preface to the volume, complaining that it made the defendant liable for statements in other essays. He then dealt with the specific charges in Articles VII through XVII, pointing out that Williams' article was a review of Bunsen in which he had to state Bunsen's views; a reviewer was not liable for his subject's opinions. The prosecution had extracted passages without regard to their context, and Deane attempted to show their innocence in the context of a review, suggesting that the real question was rather literary than doctrinal. The prosecution had cited the Bible as an authority against the impugned passages, and Deane cited Burder *v.* Heath to the effect that it was not allowable to argue from the Bible itself in a court of law. Deane cited numerous eminent divines who held the impugned doctrines; Lushington allowed the argument but pointed out that he would not be drawn into questions of divinity. Deane turned to the general charge of Article XVII against the 'tendency, scope, object and design' of the essay, objecting that only distinct acts, not tendencies, were liable to condemnation. 'This is a criminal proceeding – let us have criminal justice. Let us have no constructive heresy.'[21] Deane concluded with a plea that ministers of the Church be allowed the use of reason.

Stephen began by stating that the issue was, simply, 'does the Law of England forbid the clergy of the Church of England to use their minds?' The court in a criminal proceeding was required to give the defendant the benefit of the doubt, and was bound by the Gorham judgment to confine itself to the meaning of the Prayer-Book and formularies. The prosecution had attempted to subvert the Gorham judgment by citing passages from the Bible included in the lessons of the Prayer-Book, and Stephen urged that all scriptural references be stricken from the charges. 'The whole authority of the Bible in this court is derived from the law.' Williams had a right to say what he had said, a right left open by the Church. He had never impugned the authority and inspiration of the Bible. Stephen broke new ground by asserting that the Bible contains but does not constitute revelation and may contain other things besides. Canonicity, which Williams had not impugned, is not the same thing as inspiration. 'The church designedly left open all questions concerned with the inspiration, interpretation, and criticism of the Bible.' The church had not declared that every part of the

Bible was the word of God, and the absence of such an explicit declaration was decisive. The question and answer in the ordination service of deacons imposed no legal obligation and does not restrain inquiry. Not only were these questions open, but they had designedly been left open. 'The Church of England is a church by Act of Parliament – it is part of the law and constitution of the land.' Stephen then cited the eighteenth-century theologians who had been content to assert 'not that the Bible was infallible, but that its contents were substantially true ... the Bible contains Christianity, but it does not constitute Christianity'. Divines have held to the principle of Hooker 'that the Bible is perfect for the end for which it was designed, and that that end is the communication of religious truth, from which they have inferred that it is not pledged to scientific or historical accuracy'.[22] He cited two dozen divines, from Hooker to Sumner, Thirlwall and Tait, to prove that the Church was not bound to the literal infallibility of the Bible.

Stephen then turned to the specific articles against Williams. His argument against the first five substantive articles was 'that all questions relating to the mode, the extent, the nature, and the effect on the books of the Bible of the inspiration of those books; all questions of criticism; and all questions of interpretation; are by law open questions, which the clergy were bound to consider.[23] The doctrine 'that the Bible is the word of God, containing a special revelation of his truth', was not in the Articles or the Prayer-Book, but rested on a 'metaphor' which had no dogmatic force. The remaining charges were ascribed to statements which were properly Bunsen's and to which Williams, as a reviewer, did not necessarily subscribe. The phrases 'expression of devout reason' and 'written voice of the congregation' did not deny divine inspiration but affirmed inspiration acting through reason and the church. Inspiration, the interpretation of prophecy and the authorship of particular books were open questions in the absence of explicit declarations in the Articles and formularies. Questioning the authenticity of the text is not questioning the canonicity of the books. The prosecution's objection 'to any interpretation which is providential and not miraculous' was an attempt to tie down the clergy to the outdated evidential theology. The remaining charges were unfair attempts to trip up Williams on vague points, calling upon him to answer for Bunsen's views. Stephen cited the practice of reviewers and argued that the clergy should not be bound not to cite unorthodox opinions except to condemn them. The phrase 'verifying faculty' meant nothing else than reason. Williams was prosecuted because 'he insists that these subjects shall be discussed, and that an appeal shall be made to reason and conscience upon them'. He explained away Williams' statements on propitiation and justification and complained that 'to ascribe heresy ... upon the strength of an indirect reference consisting of a line and a half, is really the most extraordinary perversion of criminal law'.[24] The general charge against the 'tendency' of the essay reflected party differences within the

Church, between those who rest Christianity on reason and conscience and those who rely solely on miracles.

Stephen concluded by arguing that only legislation could restrict the liberty of the clergy. The Articles 'are a protection as well as a restraint, for they authorize what they do not forbid'. The prosecution was attempting to force the court to legislate and to assume a censorship of the clergy. Stephen urged the court to 'protect us from tyranny, not by the learned, but over the learned'. 'The issue now is whether the church is to strangle free and reverent inquiry, the only test of truth … A cynical and sceptical minority is indignant that a clergyman of the Church of England should dare to use his mind, and should not be punished as a criminal for having done so.'[25]

Phillimore, beginning the prosecution's argument for the admissibility of the articles, said that 'the real issue' was 'is it competent to beneficed clergymen, with cure of souls, who have subscribed the Articles and Formularies of the Church of England … by what they are pleased to call "remorseless criticism", to dispose of all the prophecies of the Old Testament; and by what they are pleased to call a "verifying faculty", to deny all the miracles of the New?' The case was to be decided on the basis of the Articles, formularies and liturgy, which latter included nearly all the Bible as appointed to be read on particular days. Lushington interrupted to ask whether this would require him to judge on points of divinity. Phillimore insisted that the Act of Uniformity 'made the Prayer Book a part of the statute law of the land, and the Prayer Book incorporated in it … very nearly the whole of the Bible'. If the Bible were inadmissible in the only court which could try heresy, then heresy could not be condemned. Lushington repeated his point that there would be no limit to the arguments he would have to consider, but he did not stop Phillimore from presenting his argument. Phillimore insisted that he was not trying to put down reason or criticism, but simply stating that 'if, under the mask of criticism, and under the garb of interpreting the Gospels, you arrive at conclusions and publish conclusions which are wholly inconsistent with the Doctrines and Formularies of your Church, then you ought to leave your office in that church'.[26]

On the specific charges, Phillimore argued that the reference to the preface was proper because Williams could have explained or amended his essay in later editions. This was not an ordinary criminal prosecution but 'a question of the correction of a clerk' for heresy. A clergyman was not free to review any book in any fashion; in quoting heresy without disapprobation he brought scandal upon the Church, and 'a scandal upon the Church may enure even to deprivation of preferment'. Phillimore asserted that canonicity meant inspiration and that Christ and his apostles, in citing prophecies as predictive, gave them that authority. He was not arguing for literal inspiration but only for plenary inspiration, which must mean something different in kind from 'the level of human reason'. His attempt to discuss German divinity was interrupted by Deane's protest and Lushington's fear that he might be forced onto dangerous ground.

Phillimore did not press the matter but pointed out that Williams had imported heretical ideas into England without disapprobation. 'That new mode of teaching I charge to be a departure from the facts of revelation, with a substitution of pure speculation in their place', and that was contrary to the doctrines of the Church. He concluded that 'the Church, while leaving full liberty to her ordained ministers to criticize the text, and examine the history of Holy Writ, has not conceded to them the license [sic] of denying ... all the historical facts of the Bible, with the truth of which all the great doctrines of our salvation ... are inextricably and for ever bound up'.[27]

Coleridge's speech showed his High Church background in its emphasis on authority. He dismissed the defence's appeal for liberty and private judgment as 'declamatory observations' addressed not to the court but to the public. The fact that a reviewer is citing another is no defence: 'if that which is slanderous, if a man who repeats it makes it his own and does mischief with it, it makes him in a court of law responsible'. Williams had in fact adopted Bunsen's positions. He had denied that the Bible was the Word of God, a special revelation of truth. Yet the Church had used the Bible to establish its doctrines, which would only make sense if it held them to be inspired by God to provide the rule of faith. The word 'canonical' in the Sixth Article meant 'inspired'. The Church held that the Bible was inspired in a sense different from that in which others books might be inspired, the direct communication of the mind of God of all that relates to faith. Coleridge allowed all textual questions and even questioning of authorship as long as the inspiration and authority of the book was not denied. On predictive prophecy he asserted that 'it is not open to a beneficed Clergyman to deny that there was running through the Old Testament a constant intended, and distinct reference to the events of the New'. In denying the authenticity of Daniel, Williams had effectively called the book a forgery, which was a denial of its canonicity: 'certain doctrines are laid down by the Church and the Church being the Church of those doctrines has said that they are to be found in those books, and those books are the infallible support of those doctrines'. It was wrong to use an argument, which would be right about an ordinary book, about a book in which there was a divine inspiration. Coleridge also desired that free scope be given to religious inquiry; 'But my Lord, there must be limits somewhere'.[28]

Swabey was allowed to speak as a third prosecutor. His speech was unremarkable except for a blunter statement of reviewer's responsibility – 'Dr. Williams is responsible for the whole except where he has expressed disagreement' – and of the obligation of the court to consider biblical passages as evidence. The latter brought a protesting intervention by Lushington, who also objected to a charge emphasized by both Coleridge and Swabey, on Augustine's idea of the curse of infants, which, Lushington held, was a 'waste of time' to make into a criminal charge.[29]

Deane had the final word, in response. Prophecy was not a doctrine, but merely one of the evidences of religion. 'Canonicity is not inspiration for the

Article does not say so.' Williams had not actually denied the inspiration of any passage relevant to faith. If Williams' words were ambiguous, 'the Court is bound as a Criminal Court to put the least harsh meaning upon the passage' to give the defendant the benefit of the doubt. As for the 'Word of God', 'that Scripture which has reference to Christ as the centre point of the redemption of mankind is in its immediate and divine origin the word of God … and the word of God is in Scripture'.[30] The case concluded with formal but sincere thanks to the court for its patience.

The case of Fendall v. Wilson took only four days, largely because most of the general questions had been traversed and only the specific charges were discussed, but also because only Phillimore and Swabey were briefed for the prosecution. After they had spoken, Lushington pressed them as to whether the Church asserted that every word of Scripture was true, to which Phillimore replied that he knew of no authority for denying the facts of Scripture. The question of authorities other than the formularies troubled Lushington: 'He could understand how he was to construe the Articles and Liturgy, but when he came to other authorities he confessed he got into considerable difficulty'. Swabey argued that criticism must be confined to the examination of manuscripts and editions. But ideology was a system which differed entirely from the legitimate criticism permitted by the Church of England to its members. Phillimore also concentrated his fire on ideology, pointing out that treating miracles ideologically struck at their use as evidences of revelation. Lushington complained that his question had not been answered: 'The Court must therefore draw the line of demarcation for itself'. Deane, in defence, argued that Wilson had never denied the inspiration of Scripture 'in all fundamentals and essentials'. The Thirty-Nine Articles had mostly been directed against the errors of Rome and sixteenth-century sectaries, and only the first six defined doctrine; Wilson had not contradicted any of these.

After this discussion, on March 3, 1862, Lushington announced that he would delay his judgment in both cases until the Privy Council delivered its judgment on the appeal of Burder v. Heath, 'hoping to obtain some guide in the course then laid down'.[31] Williams and Wilson thought this unfair,[32] but they were compelled to wait until the summer.

Stephen, not averse to self-promotion, published his speech as a pamphlet. It made his reputation as a lawyer.[33] Whether it was successful as an argument in court is less certain, but Stephen had made the legal point that this was a criminal proceeding in which the defendant must be given the benefit of the doubt. But the originality of his speech lay in its religious argument that the Christian revelation was contained in the Bible but was not identical with the Bible, rendering meaningless the term 'Word of God'. This was to open a new phase in the religious controversy itself.

Evangelicals, in particular, were attached to the term 'Word of God' and the direct inspiration of the entire Bible which it represented.[34] When Stephen published his argument, the indefatigable McCaul seized the opportunity to make this point central to the debate. McCaul's pamphlet treated 'the distinction between the Word of God and the Bible' as 'the fundamental principle' on which Stephen's argument was based. No such distinction existed, he asserted. '*Canonical* is equivalent to *Inspired*' because the Articles, in making the canonical Scriptures the rule of faith, presupposed their divine authority, inspiration and infallibility.[35] McCaul touched a nerve with the clergy by his emphasis on the Bible as being, not merely containing, the Word of God. The phrase was held dear by the Victorian clergy, simplifying an otherwise abstruse argument for them.

One other inveterate controversialist spoke out in the interval between trial and judgment: Williams, hitherto almost silent in public. His farewell sermon to the students at Lampeter College on May 25, later published as *Persecution for the Word*, was an unrepentant restatement of his positions and attack on his prosecutors. He had sought to bring out 'the living Word, traced immediately and primarily on man's heart, and in the fabric of Nature', rather than postponing it 'to the secondary records of that Word, embodied in books'. The 'exceptional element' in his teaching was 'not a contention for an opinion, but a plea for frankness'. As a scholar he was concerned with facts, with veracity, and he protested against those who would require him to misrepresent facts to correspond with doctrine. The suit against him was 'undertaken in order to procure the falsification of literature, brought forward under untrue pretexts, supported by dislocated quotations, pleaded with rude unfairness, and painfully protracted'. He would submit to the court's decision on doctrinal statements but would insist on the results of his literary researches, especially on prophecy. If need be, he would 'follow where God leads into the wilderness'. He urged his audience to work for tolerance and to suffer rather than 'falsify some simple fact'.[36] Williams had never been content with pleading innocence and seeking toleration; he insisted that he was right on the issues and more orthodox than his opponents.

CHAPTER ELEVEN

Verdict

The decision on the appeal of Burder *v.* Heath was delivered on June 6, 1862. The Judicial Committee of the Privy Council sustained Lushington's verdict and 'the principles of decision' on which it had been based.[1] Lushington was now free to render his decision in the cases of Williams and Wilson. He had not been idle during the interval, having perused the transcript of the hearings and read through *Essays and Reviews*, he was reported to have said, 20 times.[2]

Lushington's judgment, delivered on June 25, was as careful as his preparation. He began by stating his general principles, but he had first to note that the form of a review presented certain difficulties in determining the position of its author. He held that it is not competent to a clergyman, 'when he either states or professes to give the substance of unsound doctrine from the work reviewed, to leave his own opinion in the dark. Were it otherwise ... a Clergyman might with impunity republish even an infidel book'. The court was not trying the theological soundness of Williams' views, but only whether those doctrines were 'at variance with the doctrines of the Church, as declared in the Articles and Formularies'. He could not consider episcopal censures or the views of theologians: 'This is not a Court of Divinity, but a Court of Ecclesiastical Law'. The Privy Council had declared the law that questions not determined by the Articles or formularies were open, so there might be much that 'is deserving of censure, and yet ... the law of the Church may not reach it'. The court would not consider the Bible at all, lest it be drawn into theological questions: 'urged by every motive to preserve peace in the Church, I will not be tempted, in the trial of any accusation against a Clergyman, to resort to Scripture as the standard by which the doctrine shall be measured'. Hence, even in charges which were admitted, the articles must be 'reformed' to eliminate references to the Bible. However, the Articles, using phrases such as 'God's Word written', 'necessarily implied the doctrine that in all matters necessary for salvation the Holy Scriptures emanated from the extra-ordinary and preternatural interposition of the Almighty', and thus a clergyman who maintains that Scripture proceeded from human mental powers maintains 'that the Bible is not God's Word written, but is the work of man', in violation of Articles VI and XX. Scholars can deal freely with the text and authorship but may not question the canonicity or authority of any book.[3]

Lushington then dealt with the individual articles against Williams, admitting the formal ones and (after being reformed) three of the substantive charges, while dismissing all the rest. Williams' statements that the Bible was the 'expression of devout reason' and 'the written voice of the congregation' were 'inconsistent with the doctrine that it was written by the interposition of God', and that article was admitted. Williams' positions on messianic prophecy were 'not consonant with the doctrine of the Church, as usually promulgated by high authority', but they did not contravene a particular Article or formulary, and so that article was rejected. The same held for Williams' statements on Daniel and other prophecies: 'Now all this may be wholly erroneous; but what Article of Religion is contravened?' There was nothing criminal in Williams' construction of the Flood: 'It is a denial of ordinary, or what may be called orthodox, interpretation, but not of the truth of the writing itself'. But Williams' statement on propitiation was 'inconsistent with and contrary to the 31st Article', and this charge was admitted. A charge relating to baptism was not clearly a statement of Williams' own doctrine and must be rejected; but in his remarks on justification 'Dr. Williams employs these words as a form of declaring his own sentiments' and was thus responsible for them, and this article was admitted. The article on the general tendency of the essay was rejected for lack of specificity. Having thus decided, Lushington remarked: 'Looking at the great importance of this case, and that in fact, though not in form, I have pronounced a decision on its merits', he gave both parties leave to appeal the interlocutory judgment to the Privy Council, which leave was also granted in Wilson's case.[4]

Lushington then turned to Fendall v. Wilson, which was 'subject to the same general rules and principles'. On the first charge, he expressed regret that Wilson 'has frequently expressed himself in language so ambiguous as to admit of opposite constructions', but in a criminal case this was a defence, and the article was rejected. On Wilson's remarks about the 'Word of God', Lushington conceded that that Article did 'not contain a declaration of the Bible having been *throughout* supernaturally suggested' and that some parts of it might not have been; but 'God's Word written' implied a 'special interposion' which Wilson had denied, so that article was admitted. Passing on to 'ideology', Lushington repeated '*usque ad nauseam,* that I have no concern with interpretation, save so far as relates to the Articles of Religion or the Formularies'. The liberty of interpretation claimed by Wilson exists in the Church. 'I plainly see to what fearful consequences this doctrine may be carried; but, provided that the doctrines of the Articles of Religion and the Formularies are not contravened, the law lays down no limits of construction, no rule of interpretation for the Scriptures. My authority cannot reach this case.' Wilson's remarks on non-believing subscription might be criminal as to himself; but Wilson was charged only with advising others that it was allowable. This was 'blamable' but did not violate the Canon under which he was charged, so two articles had to be rejected. On some remarks about the heathen to whom Christ had not been preached, it was impossible to put a negative to Wilson's words, so that they did not negate any Article. But his denial of any distinction between covenanted and uncovenanted mercies seemed to Lushington 'to declare that a man may be saved by the law which he professeth', which directly contradicted Article XVIII, so that charge was admitted. A charge about the authorship of 2 Peter did not impugn its canonicity; this charge was in fact withdrawn. But the final passage, on the final salvation of the damned, could not be reconciled with 'the passages cited of the Creeds and Formularies, and I must admit this Article'. Lushington had thus admitted three (reformed) articles against Wilson and rejected the rest.[5]

Lushington concluded by noting that some might think that he had 'taken too limited a view' of his powers. 'I can only say that I have shaped my course according to the authority I am bound to follow, – the authority of the Privy Council.'[6] This was a lawyer-like statement and justification of his acquittal of most of the charges, an acquittal which opened up all questions of text and authorship and most questions of interpretation by a narrow construction of the Articles and Formularies and the allowance of the benefit of the doubt in a criminal case. However, in the articles which he admitted, he did not put the most favourable construction on the author's words and was compelled to make an interpretation as much theological as legal of the doctrinal implications of the Articles. The result was to acquit the Essayists on the points most central to themselves and to condemn them on those least likely to be sustained on appeal. It is not impossible that this was exactly what Lushington intended, but his judgment was consistent with the position of a pre-Broad Church liberal Anglican.[7]

Williams regarded the result as a substantive victory, freeing the clergy from any obligation to falsify biblical criticism. 'Glory be to God ... if we have thus far broken the rod of falsehood, brandished in right reverend hands. Yet, if we gain nothing more, I feel this day that I have not lived in vain; my Master has done by me a work which will abide.'[8] In a postscript to *Persecution for the Word*, published later that summer, he again claimed that 'whatever freedom I have claimed for Biblical investigation, and more ... is judicially conceded as permissible in the Church of England. Whereas the counter-claim of our episcopate to exercise a falsifying influence over hermeneutics, in view of the supposed interest of dogmatic theology, is repudiated as illegal'. However, he complained about the points on which he was convicted, saying that the court had misunderstood his meaning: 'in no one of the reservations unfavourable to the defendant has the manifest meaning of the Essayist been given truly'. He blamed this on a lawyer's incapacity to understand theology or literature. 'The aspect under which Revelation presents itself to the legal mind is not as saving souls, but as material for framing Articles ... With no literary light, there could be no ecclesiastical justice'. But 'if I were technically to withdraw every expression reserved by the Court, in the sense which the Court has technically affixed to it, I should not thereby retract a particle of my meaning, or imply any modification of doctrine. That sentence of the judgment which excluded Scripture from the indictment, decided in my favour every principle maintained by me'. It had restored to the Church the 'right of interpreting Scripture at large'.[9]

Wilson, reviewing the decision in the *Westminster Review*, also hailed the decision as a victory for 'liberty to the clergyman', but he carped at 'the reluctance and ungraciousness' with which Lushington had conceded it. But the question of truth, as distinct from liberty, would be decided by the more open tribunal of the laity, which would bring about a 'second Reformation, when its Protestantism shall be effectually liberated from the bondage of the letter of the Bible'.[10] In a subsequent review, Wilson again criticized Lushington's inclination 'to develop doctrine' in 'his most intricate and inconsistent judgment'.[11] This was in a review of a pamphlet by a clergyman who criticized Lushington's judicial constructions of the Articles as theology by a non-theologian and called his ruling that parts of the Bible were written by the preternatural interposition of God a 'new Article' of religion.[12]

Jowett was 'satisfied and pleased with the Judgment of Dr. L. on the whole. A great step has been gained in freedom for the C[hurch] of England'.[13] To Florence Nightingale he wrote: 'The general result is I think to extend considerably the borders of the Ch[urch] of England. This judgment is to the "Broad Church" (I hate that expression) what the judgment in the Gorham case was to the Evangelicals'.[14]

The High Church journals were unimpressed with the judgment. The *Guardian*, which had all along regarded the prosecution as ill-advised, thought that Lushington's opinion 'will satisfy no one but the lawyers, and perhaps not them'. Most churchmen were 'alarmed to see that out of so many erroneous and heretical propositions so few are held to transgress ecclesiastical law'. Little could be effected by such trials, and the Church had already spoken out decisively in Convocation.[15] Denison's *Church and State Review* expressed 'dissatisfaction' with the limitation of Lushington's judgment, but in any case felt that synodical condemnation was necessary: 'The Church in her corporate capacity has to be relieved by the act of her corporate representation'.[16] There was evidently much dislike of the judgment among evangelicals, but their chief journals put a cheerful face on the matter. The *Record* 'on the whole' thought it 'a gain to the Church'; even Lushington's liberal leanings gave greater weight to his judgment.[17] The *Christian Observer* found it 'all that the Court of Arches either can or ought to do', especially since Lushington determined that 'the Bible is to be received as God's written word'.[18] Lay reactions were generally favourable, though the radical deist Francis Newman, writing in the *Westminster Review*, found the condemnations a sign that the clergy was still in bondage to subscriptions; 'the real question ... is, not what the formularies have said, but what is the Truth?'[19] But *Fraser's Magazine* had 'no doubt that this book will be the beginning of popular biblical criticism in England, and that the Church allows much greater latitude to biblical criticism than is generally supposed'.[20] *Punch* summarized 'Lushingtonianism in Little':

> PARSONS! Believe in a general way:
> And be specially careful of what you say.[21]

One private opinion on Lushington's judgment was promptly put into action. J. W. Colenso, missionary bishop of Natal, had written a study of the Pentateuch which denied its Mosaic authorship and factual accuracy. He felt scruples about publishing because of the words 'believe all the Canonical Scriptures' in the ordination service. His doubts were removed by the judgment, and *The Pentateuch and Book of Joshua Critically Examined* was published in October.[22] In his Preface, Colenso expressly stated his reliance on the judgment, and he urged the Essayists to maintain their positions in the Church 'and to claim for *all* her members, clerical as well as lay, that freedom of thought and utterance, which is the very essence of our Protestant religion'.[23] Thus began the Colenso case, which was intertwined with the case of the Essayists and followed a parallel course – episcopal manifesto, synodical condemnation and Privy Council decision – until 1865.

Meanwhile the legal case proceeded on its slow course. Lushington had given both parties leave to appeal the interlocutory judgment to the Privy Council, and Phillimore wished to do so in order to have some of the rejected articles re-admitted. Hamilton, however, 'on full consideration of the Nature of the Final Court and the Responsibility of bringing before it such momentous questions' of theology, declined to be the appellant.[24] Fendall followed the bishop's lead. The defense did not appeal the interlocutory judgment because it expected to appeal all matters after the final judgment. It sought to re-argue the admitted articles after they had been reformed as to their substance rather than their admissibility; but Lushington plainly stated that such argument 'will have no effect at all'.[25] In fact, by admitting the articles he had declared them worthy of condemnation. But all this procedure delayed the final judgment until December.

Just before the decision, Tait had occasion to deliver his triennial Charge as bishop of London. His subject was freedom of Inquiry: 'after all, we are Protestants. We have been accustomed to speak a good deal of the right and duty of private judgment'. Doubters can only be dealt with by those who enter into their doubts and understand them. 'Nothing is to be gained by haranguing against scepticism to a sympathizing crowd of attentive orthodox believers who never knew a doubt.' Nor should there be alarm 'if we find free inquiry amongst the clergy'. Clergymen 'are not precluded from free inquiry, even at the risk of this inquiry leading them far away from the Church'. He did not look to prosecutions and courts 'for the preservation of orthodoxy in our clergy'. Experience showed that 'determined teachers of error' eventually leave the Church. 'They cannot bear the Liturgy and Articles.'[26]

At last, on December 15, 1862, the Court of Arches was ready to proceed to its final judgment. Phillimore, in praying for judgment, noted that he had not proceeded under the statute of Elizabeth which would have required deprivation, but had rather sought to combine the security of doctrine with 'the reformation of the individual'.[27] He therefore urged that Williams be suspended from his benefice until he retracted his errors. Coleridge added that some security should be required for Williams' future teaching. Deane argued that Williams had not contradicted the Articles, an argument which the court allowed but ignored. Stephen then offered to withdraw the passages on atonement and propitiation, where Williams had merely stated Bunsen's opinions.[28] Phillimore demanded that all three condemned passages be withdrawn, including 'the voice of the congregation', which Williams refused to give up; so Phillimore refused to compromise.[29] Stephen asked the court to consider the charges on which Williams had been acquitted. 'If the expressions held to be illegal were struck out, the substance of the Essay prosecuted was precisely the same. ... The rest was a matter of expression.'[30]

Lushington, in passing judgment, was not convinced by the arguments of defence counsel; he would abide by his former judgment. The sentence would be, not what he considered best, but what was the best that 'the highest tribunal – namely, the Privy Council – would sustain'. The important thing was not punishment but warning the clergy 'that they must not intentionally violate the law of the Church'. Admitting that some might think him too lenient, he refused to suspend Williams until he recanted on the ground that a recantation extorted by pecuniary need might 'not come from the heart'. He therefore suspended Williams for one year and awarded costs to the prosecution. There was no further argument in the case of Wilson, who received the same sentence. The defence immediately announced that it would appeal.[31]

Lushington's decision was indeed lenient. Although loss of a year's income and payment of the considerable costs was a heavy financial burden, it was no more than a financial penalty. It was not the deprivation which had driven the unfortunate Heath out of the Church. As in his interlocutory judgment Lushington refused to condemn Williams and Wilson on the points they considered essential, so in his final judgment (if sustained) he did not force the Essayists out of the Church.

The lenity was generally noticed. The liberal *Daily News* observed that not even Williams' 'warmest friends would say that, supposing the judgment to be right, the sentence is severe'.[32] Wilson, writing anonymously, acknowledged that 'we do not think they can have like reason to complain'.[33] Williams privately said, 'We have gained the principle for which we contended, and are only entrapped by a legal fiction in what we did not contend for.'[34] Only Denison complained of 'the unfitness and inadequacy of the punishment'.[35]

The legal case boosted the sales of *Essays and Reviews*, which had slowed in the latter part of 1861. The smaller and cheaper tenth edition was published in three printings of 1000 copies each in January, March and April of 1862. After the trial, an eleventh edition of 1500 copies appeared in March 1863, with the acquitted and condemned passages indicated. This brought the total sale to 22,250 copies.[36]

CHAPTER TWELVE

Appeals

When the proctor for Williams and Wilson gave notice that he would appeal, the prosecution was presented with a dilemma. The Court of Arches was an ecclesiastical court, the Archbishop of Canterbury's court, applying ecclesiastical law as judged by a civil lawyer. Appeal, however, lay to the Judicial Committee of the Privy Council, an essentially common-law court created in 1833. To be sure, there would be three prelates on the panel, the archbishops of Canterbury (Charles Longley, a stronger figure than J. B. Sumner whom he had succeeded in 1862) and York (the rapidly promoted Thomson) and the bishop of London (Tait), safely orthodox by two to one, but learned rather in theology than in ecclesiastical law. The only civilian on the Privy Council was Lushington, who could not sit on an appeal from himself. This meant that the panel would be dominated by common lawyers, unfamiliar with either theology or ecclesiastical law, and with a professional bias to acquit if there was any doubt. It had previously overturned verdicts in Arches, most notably in the Gorham case. Further, it was an essentially secular court, the agent of the royal supremacy over the Church.[1] Hamilton had doubts as to the fitness of such a court to rule on sensitive questions of doctrine, which had kept him from appealing the interlocutory judgment. Yet he could hardly refuse to 'adhere to the appeal', unless he was prepared to content himself with a moral victory in the ecclesiastical court, declaring the law of the Church, while defaulting in the actual lawsuit.

Phillimore advised Hamilton to adhere to the appeal, to 'say to the Court of Appeal – *to which they take us* – we too are not satisfied with the Judgment', because of 'the inadequacy of the sentence to guard against ... heresy being preached to the parishioners of Broad Chalke' unless Williams was required to recant, and also because of the rejected articles in the interlocutory judgment from which they had not appealed earlier but which, Phillimore thought, might now be challenged.[2] This course was adopted; but it would be several months before the appeal could be heard.

In the interval attention shifted to Jowett at Oxford. He could not be prosecuted in the courts and had so far suffered nothing more than the regular rejection of proposals for the endowment of his chair. Indeed, Oxford itself had been surprisingly devoid of agitation, largely due to the management of the vice-chancellor, Francis Jeune.[3] But Pusey felt increasingly uncomfortable with his position as promoter of Jowett's endowment and opponent of his heresy. As early as February 1862, he felt that Jowett ought to be prosecuted in the court of the University.[4] He was stimulated to take action by Lushington's interlocutory judgment. He sought a legal opinion from Phillimore as to whether a court would find Jowett guilty of heresy and whether he could be prosecuted in the Vice-Chancellor's Court. Phillimore's opinions were delivered in October. He held that statements in Jowett's 1855 essay on the atonement had contradicted several of the Articles; that statements on inspiration in the essay thereon violated the formularies, according to Lushington's judgment; and that a statement on the agreement of the creeds with Scripture contradicted the eighth Article.[5] He further held that the Vice-Chancellor was bound to admit articles charging a resident member of the University with heresy and that he could be compelled by writ of *mandamus* to do so.[6] It remained for Pusey to find someone to institute the prosecution. He was reluctant to do so himself, lest the prosecution should appear to be the work of one party, but he would become a prosecutor along with others.[7] He quickly found Charles Ogilvie, regius professor of pastoral theology, but it was not until the Christmas vacation that he obtained the other, Heurtley, Lady Margaret professor of divinity and (most importantly) an evangelical.

The case opened in the Vice-Chancellor's Court on February 13, 1863. This was a peculiar court, usually employed for the collection of debts from undergraduates; *Punch* satirized it as the 'Small Debts and Heresies Court'.[8] The hearing was postponed for a week after Jowett's proctor gave notice that he would challenge the jurisdiction of the court. The next day the *Times* had a leading article sharply criticizing the prosecutors, 'short-sighted men with a rooted distrust of the power of truth to abide the ordeal of free inquiry ... the *odium theologicum* of a few infatuated dignitaries'.[9]

Pusey defended the prosecution in a letter of February 19, pointing out that this was the only court in which action could be taken against Jowett:

> A claim has been made to affix new meanings to words, and so to subscribe our formularies in senses which they will not take. It is impossible, then, to look upon Professor Jowett's teaching otherwise than as a part of a larger whole – a systematic attempt to revolutionize the Church of England. The publication of the *Essays and Reviews* was a challenge to admit that teaching as one of the recognized phases of faith, in the English Church ... To leave the challenge unnoticed would have been to acquiesce in the claim ... Prosecution is not persecution.[10]

Pusey's letter set off another side-controversy. Matters were not helped when Maurice, pleading for toleration, introduced a red herring with a reference to the 'non-natural' sense of words in Tract 90. This produced an interminable exchange of letters between Pusey and Maurice and the only public intervention in any of these controversies by John Henry Newman.[11]

The case was finally brought to trial on March 20 before the vice-chancellor's 'assessor' or judge, Mountague Bernard, an academic common lawyer who was turning this formerly civilian court into a court of common law.[12] Bernard was one of the founders and editors of the *Guardian*, whose constant deprecation of prosecutions had alienated Pusey. Jowett's proctor, Henry A. Pottinger, entered a protest against the jurisdiction of the court in spiritual matters such as heresy. Bernard would not admit the protest, holding that Jowett was liable if it could be shown that he had violated one of the University Statutes. In a learned discussion of the Statutes, he found them uncertain and in any case not imperative: 'if I have jurisdiction in this matter, which is doubtful, it is a jurisdiction which the Statutes do not imperatively bind me to exercise, and which I ought not to exercise upon this citation'. Bernard's Solomonic decision, which amounted to a dismissal of the case, was as much statesmanlike as legal; he spoke of saving 'the University from the continued agitation and disturbance which these proceedings must occasion'.[13]

Bernard gave the prosecution leave to appeal, and initially Jowett feared that it would: 'You don't know Pusey: he has the tenacity of a bulldog'.[14] But Pusey took further counsel, seeking a joint opinion from Phillimore and Coleridge as to whether a *mandamus* could be obtained from the Court of Queen's Bench. Phillimore, a civil lawyer, had earlier stated that a *mandamus* was issuable, but Coleridge, a common lawyer and the son of a judge, knew that no judge would issue one. They replied that a judge 'would probably be very reluctant to interfere in a matter which was one of academical opinion'.[15] Pusey attributed this to 'an anti-doctrinal bias'.[16] Under the circumstances, the suit against Jowett was withdrawn.

During the proceedings Pattison had been distinctly unhelpful to Jowett, counselling him to submit and to say that he had been misunderstood. Jowett thanked God that he did not submit: 'submission appears to imply that the limits of the Ch[urch] of England in the University are acknowledged to be narrowed'.[17] Stanley, on the other hand, was consistently supportive. When the prosecution failed, he again moved in the University Council to raise the salary of the Greek professorship, but lost by a narrow majority. He shortly thereafter left Oxford on being appointed dean of Westminster.

Other cases were also cutting across that of the Essayists. That spring Colenso was the subject of episcopal discussions resulting in a remonstrance, and proceedings in Convocation would soon follow. That year Ernest Renan published his romantic but unorthodox *Vie de Jésus*. Its English translation produced a small controversy of its own,[18] and references to Renan and to Colenso are frequently found in subsequent denunciations of *Essays and Reviews*.

The delay in hearing the appeal to the Privy Council was due in part to the problem of selecting the panel of legal members for the trial. In High Church circles there were suggestions that the court was packed. One reason for this was that the arrangements were made by the registrar of the Council, Henry Reeve, the editor of the *Edinburgh Review*.[19] Another was Coleridge's disappointment that his father, Sir John Taylor Coleridge, a retired judge who was a privy councillor, was left off.[20] But the elder Coleridge had caused a scandal in Pooley's case, 1857, with a harsh sentence on a blasphemer prosecuted by his son.[21] Although there was no rule against conflict of interest, it was improbable that he would be chosen to hear a case in which his son was of counsel. In fact, the law lords chosen for the case were unimpeachable: the lord chancellor, Lord Westbury, two past chancellors, Lords Chelmsford and Cranworth, and one who had declined the chancellorship, Lord Kingsdown.[22] Two Tories and two Whigs, none was known to be a partisan in religion.[23]

The two cases were heard in five sittings between June 19 and 26, 1863. The appellants argued their own cases, Wilson because he felt the theological issues needed to be explained, and Williams to 'gain for himself the power of explaining what he meant, and disclaiming what he did not mean', though Phillimore suspected that he disagreed with his counsel.[24] In the course of proceedings the article against Williams on propitiation and that against Wilson on uncovenanted mercies were abandoned as untenable. Phillimore tried to limit the appellants to appealing against the sentence only, arguing that they could not argue on the merits of the admitted articles since they had not appealed their admission in the interlocutory judgment; alternatively, if the admitted articles could be appealed, the prosecution could seek to reinstate the rejected articles. The Judicial Committee rejected both parts of this argument, and the appellants were allowed to appeal both verdict and sentence.[25]

Wilson's case was heard first, and the competence of his published speech suggests that he had legal coaching. His argument was that Lushington, in giving a definite interpretation of the Articles and formularies, had developed doctrine on points not defined by the Church. He had misapplied the Gorham Judgment's term 'literal and grammatical sense' by construing 'literal' as opposed to 'figurative', when some of the language of the formularies was in fact figurative. In 'extracting a doctrine from the metaphor "Word of God written"', Lushington had developed a doctrine from an incidental expression, going beyond his office of declaring the law. 'The addition which is here made to the Thirty-nine Articles of the Church of England is most momentous.' 'The Judge has made a law – and made it *ex post facto*', in specifying that inspiration required the 'preternatural interposition' of God. Turning to the question of eternal punishment, Wilson argued that the term 'everlasting' is ambiguous in meaning, 'obviously figurative'. The Article in question was directed against the Roman doctrine of purgatory, and a more specific Article in the 1552 Articles against universal restoration had been deleted when the Thirty-Nine Articles were drawn up. He had not taught as doctrine that all may eventually be restored after the last judgment, but had merely expressed a 'hope' or 'pious opinion'. Phillimore in reply insisted 'that the doctrine of the plenary Inspiration of Scripture was the doctrine of the Church of England', to which Wilson responded that 'plenary' may simply mean 'sufficient'.[26]

Williams' grounds for appeal were that he had not maintained any doctrine contrary to the Articles or formularies, that the passages extracted from his article did not warrant the conclusions drawn from them, and that Lushington had 'ignored the indwelling of the Holy Spirit in the Church of God'. He argued that his phrases 'expression of devout reason' and 'written voice of the congregation' violated no Article, for 'all questions as to the mode, extent, nature, and effect of Inspiration were by law left open'. The other phrases, on propitiation and justification, were statements of Bunsen's views. Any clergyman had the right to deny the 'preternatural interposition' of God in the composition of the Bible, but Williams had not in fact denied it.[27]

After Phillimore and Coleridge replied to Williams, Wilson had his final summing-up. This left only a half hour of the sitting of July 26. To avoid delay, Williams compressed his statement into 40 minutes 'speaking at railway speed', too fast for the shorthand writers, but drawing applause.[28] The court then reserved its judgment.

The usual procedure of the Judicial Committee was to hold a preliminary discussion, after which the presiding member (in this case Westbury) would prepare a draft judgment which would be printed and passed around to the other members for their comments, until agreement was reached. It is not certain that this procedure was followed in this case. It soon became clear that a difference of opinion existed between the lay lords joined by Tait, who wanted to reverse Lushington's judgment, and the two archbishops, who would uphold most of it. Westbury, while regarding *Essays and Reviews* as 'futile and puerile and pointless', nonetheless insisted that 'if the principles referred to in that judgment had been duly applied, the whole of the passages libelled must have been treated as not containing any criminal matter'.[29] But the lay-prelatical division, on a court that usually reached agreement, disturbed the lay lords sufficiently that they requested the prelates individually to write their opinions and have them printed and sent around. Longley was working on his opinion in early October, assisted by Sir John Coleridge.[30] This process delayed the final judgment, which had been expected in the autumn, until February 1864;[31] two meetings in January were needed to settle on the final terms.[32]

A judgment of greater intrinsic weight was rendered in October 1863, when Thirlwall delivered his long-awaited Charge. He acknowledged that the Essayists had rightly denied 'joint responsibility or concert' in their publication. But when the question arose whether some of them taught doctrines inconsistent with that of the Church, their apparent acquiescence involved each of them in 'a responsibility, which he could not shift from himself, for opinions which he did not expressly disavow'. He defended the episcopal manifesto as 'a declaration that, in the opinion of the Bishops, its contents *were* repugnant to the doctrine of the Church'. But a legal proceeding was ill-suited to decide points of theology. He did not regret that a lay judge unlearned in theology should decide 'when civil rights are at stake', but 'the character of the Church as a religious communion can never be compromised by such a decision'; one might acquit judicially that which one condemned theologically.[33]

Thirlwall turned to the individual Essayists, giving 'the foremost place' to 'the Essay which strikes most directly at the root of revealed religion', Baden

Powell's denial of miracles, which 'moves wholly within the circle of a purely materialistic philosophy'. The realms of faith and reason cannot be totally separate, for such things as Christ's own miracles are facts. 'The fact and the doctrine are inseparately blended together. To deny the fact is to reject the doctrine.' Christian doctrine cannot survive 'after its supernatural groundwork has been withdrawn from it'. Turning to Temple's essay, Thirlwall criticized its use of language 'directly suggestive of the most perplexing doubts'. 'It opens the broadest room for an assault on the foundations of historical Christianity, without setting up any defence against it'. Williams' essay was not simply a 'report' but a 'vindication' of the views he described and passed over the question of 'supernatural agency'.[34] Wilson's essay brings 'the Church down to the religious level of those who hold least of Christian doctrine'. 'A Church, without any basis of a common faith, is not only an experiment new in practice and of doubtful success, but an idea new in theory, and not easy to conceive.' Thirlwall dealt briefly and mildly with the other Essayists. Goodwin, a layman, said nothing that a clergyman might not properly have said. Pattison's historical essay could not be charged with the doctrines of the others, nor did Jowett's treatment of inspiration commit him 'to their denial of revelation'. Thirlwall noted that there was no organ of the Church competent to define inspiration; 'I cannot profess to desire that such an organ should be called into action for such a purpose, or that a new article should be framed to bind the opinions of the clergy on this subject'.[35]

As for the volume as a whole, it was the 'product of one school' which was 'mainly negative'. 'That negation does reach to the very essence and foundation of the Christian faith; that after the principles laid down in this work have been carried to their logical result, that which is left will be something to which the name of Christianity cannot be applied without a straining and abuse of language. It will be no longer a religion, and will not yet have become a philosophy.' In such a system, Christ could neither be 'a Teacher of superhuman authority' nor 'an object of personal faith'. 'Their Christology is one which ... *will not bear to be prayed.*' Their ideal was 'a National Church, without a theology, without a confession, without a creed, with no other basis of united worship than a system of universal equivocation'.[36]

Thirlwall turned to the debate over Colenso, in whose episcopal censure he had not concurred. The Church does not 'fence the study of Scripture, either for Clergy or laity, with any restrictions as to the subjects of inquiry ... But if the inquiry is to be free, it is impossible consistently to prescribe its results'. Thirlwall deplored action by Convocation on either case. 'No mistake which Convocation could commit could be more disastrous to its credit and usefulness, or more imperil its very existence, than if it should attempt to circumscribe the freedom of opinion sanctioned by the Church by any new determination of its own.' The bishops had rightly abstained from pronouncing on propositions but had merely marked the character of the book's doctrines 'with reference to the standards of the Church's doctrine. To inquire whether they were tenable or not in themselves was here wholly beside the purpose'. Thirlwall agreed with the proposition that 'the Bible is not itself God's Word', hoped that Convocation would not attempt 'to determine the nature of the inspiration of Holy Scripture' and felt no fear that critical analysis of the Old Testament would endanger the Christian revelation. 'Such questions must be left to every one's private judgment and feeling, which have the fullest right to decide for each, but not to impose their decisions, as the dictate of an infallible authority, on the consciences of others. Any attempt to erect such facts into articles of faith, would be fraught with danger of irreparable evil to the Church, as well as with the immediate hurt to numberless souls.'[37]

Thirlwall's Charge was a magisterial judgment, a rare example of calm and cool reason. Thirlwall favoured free criticism of the Bible and acceptance of its results, and he deplored any attempt to close what had been open questions or to tighten the bonds of doctrine. But fixed doctrine there must be, to maintain the character of the Church as a Church, and that doctrine must be founded on a revelation communicated with supernatural authority, involving miracles. Thirlwall's outlook was similar (even in its legalism) to that of Lushington. Theirs was the judgment of one generation of liberals upon another.

Despite his strictures upon particular essays and upon the Essayists as a group, Thirlwall's pleas for liberty of criticism and against further censures showed that he was moving practically closer to them. This was partly due to his lengthy correspondence with Stanley, ever a mediator on their behalf. Stanley congratulated him on his Charge: 'I cannot doubt that, had the original Episcopal censure been couched in the same terms of discrimination, or had one of the Essayists been freed from the charge of repugnance to the Church of England with the same distinctness as appears in your Charge, the effect on the Church at large and on the fortunes of individuals would have been very different'.[38]

Stanley himself was occupied with another matter, the attempt to modify the terms of subscription to the Thirty-Nine Articles,[39] a side-debate which in part grew out of the debate over *Essays and Reviews*. The original debate had lost most of its life as an issue and was only kept alive by the trials. Only one pamphlet against the book from the standpoint of Anglican orthodoxy was published in 1863.[40] Pattison was able to get off a blow against his orthodox opponents in an article published anonymously in the Unitarian *National Review*,[41] which has been described 'as a fighting reply to the attack on *Essays and Reviews*',[42] but whose main thrust was a denunciation of the High Church party for driving learning out of the Church of England.

Meanwhile the evangelical Bible Society found a sufficient reply to doubt and unbelief, represented by the Essayists and Darwin, in the form of a sixpenny edition of the Bible.[43]

CHAPTER THIRTEEN

Acquittal

Word that the Privy Council would reverse the Lushington judgment began to leak out. Pusey, on a hint 'from some high legal quarter', wrote frantic letters to Tait in hopes of limiting the terms of the judgment,[1] began to prepare for action after it came down and wrote to the *Record* praying that the decision 'might not be against God's truth'.[2] After the last meeting of the Judicial Committee, Longley privately informed several persons.[3] Phillimore also expected an adverse decision.[4]

The judgment was delivered on February 8, 1864, in a crowded Council Chamber, by Lord Westbury, its principal author.[5] He began by noting that only 'a few short extracts' were before the court, and its judgment must be confined to these. If the book as a whole was 'of a mischievous and baneful tendency', it would be liable to that condemnation notwithstanding this judgment. The charges in a criminal case must be specific, but the defence may explain any statement by reference to the context. The standard of judgment was that of the Gorham case. The court must ascertain the true construction of the Articles and formularies and the 'plain grammatical meaning' of the impugned passages. 'On matters on which the Church has prescribed no rule, there is so far freedom of opinion that they may be discussed without penal consequences.' Nor may the court 'ascribe to the Church any rule or teaching which we do not find expressly or distinctly stated' or necessarily implied. 'That only is matter of accusation which is *advisedly* taught or maintained.' Writers cannot be held responsible for 'more than the conclusions which are directly involved' in their statements.[6]

After these general observations, Westbury turned to Williams' case. Williams had 'nowhere in terms asserted that Holy Scripture is not the Word of God'. His phrases 'devout reason' and 'voice of the congregation' were shown in context not to bear the sense ascribed to them. Even if Williams were thought to approve of them, they were hardly 'a full statement of his own belief or teaching'. On the question of the 'fiction' of the transfer of the merits of Christ, the Articles were silent, and 'we cannot say therefore that it is penal in a Clergyman … however unseemly' to use those words. On the question of 'justification', the court concluded that the charge against Williams wrongly interpreted his meaning. Williams had not asserted that justification meant *only* peace of mind or sense of divine approval.[7]

With regard to Wilson, against whom only two charges remained, Westbury noted that the proposition that 'every part of the Scriptures was written under the inspiration of the Holy Spirit is not to be found either in the Articles or in any of the Formularies'. Terms such as 'Word of God' 'cannot be affirmed to be clearly predicated of every statement and representation contained in every part of the Old and New Testament'. 'The framers of the Articles have not used the word "inspiration" as applied to the Holy Scriptures; nor have they laid down anything as to the nature, extent, or limits of that operation of the Holy Spirit. The caution of the framers of our Articles forbids our treating their language as implying more than is expressed.' None of the passages extracted from Wilson's essay 'are contradicted by or plainly inconsistent with the Articles or Formularies to which the Charge refers, and which alone we are at liberty to consider'. That left only the question of eternal punishment. The passage extracted did not warrant the charge that Wilson had 'advisedly' maintained a denial of the last judgment. He had only expressed 'the hope that the punishment of the wicked may not endure to all eternity'. The formularies do not make 'any such distinct declaration of our Church upon the subject as to require us to condemn as penal the expression of hope by a clergyman'.[8]

Westbury repeated that 'the meagre and disjointed extracts which have been allowed to remain in the reformed Articles, are alone the subject of our Judgment'. The court could not and did not pronounce on 'the design and general tendency' of the book or 'the effect or aim' of any essay. 'On the short extracts before us, our Judgment is that the Charges are not proved.' The Judicial Committee would recommend to the Queen that the sentences be reversed. Costs of the appeal were awarded to the appellants; each party would bear its own expenses in the Court of Arches. Westbury noted that the two archbishops did not concur in those parts of the judgment against Williams on 'the expression of devout reason' and against Wilson on inspiration.[9]

The judgment was substantively a victory for the Essayists. Coupled with Lushington's judgment, which had already stricken out most of the charges, it opened a large area of biblical criticism and theological inquiry to free discussion among the clergy, and it rendered a large part of the conventional teaching of the Church unenforceable at law. Not only was it a victory for liberty of thought, it was a gain for literature in general, establishing in Williams' case that a reviewer is not responsible for the statements he cites. But Westbury's language made it appear that the victory was awarded grudgingly. His references to 'meagre and disjointed extracts' which were capable of constructions not entirely contradictory to Articles and formularies seemed to reduce the acquittals to technical escapes from imprecise laws by imprecise language. His refusal to comment on the general character of the essays or their theological soundness implied a disapproval of them. His careful limitation of the judgment to rejections of specific charges against specific phrases was correctly intended to demonstrate that this secular court was not legislating for the Church. But the court did in fact legislate, and it legislated against orthodoxy. A mock epitaph on Westbury concludes:

> He dismissed Hell with costs,
> And took away from orthodox members of the Church of England

Their last hope of everlasting damnation.[10]

The victorious Essayists were only moderately enthusiastic. Williams privately found the judgment 'timid and uninstructive, and about three parts satisfies me with a redress, for which I ought to be thankful; but falls short of a justice with which I should be contented … the step in the direction of freedom for the Church is very decided'.[11] Wilson, in the *Westminster Review*, was self-congratulatory and triumphant: the decisions 'declare the existence of an amount of liberty in the Church of England which the public generally little dreamed of'.[12] Privately he was as disappointed with Westbury as he had been with Lushington: 'there was a tone of Apology hardly consistent with the dignity of the Judgment Seat'.[13] Their supporters were more enthusiastic on their behalf. Stanley told Tait that 'it is impossible to overstate the importance, both in what it gives and what it prevents. It is worth all the painful struggles and anxieties of the last three years'.[14]

Hamilton was disheartened by the judgment. He had evoked a definition of the law of the Church the very opposite of what he had intended, and he now sought to show 'that I have not done a great wrong to the C[hurch] of E[ngland] through imprudence and disregard of the warnings of others'.[15] Phillimore, who thought the decision 'disgraceful'[16] to the court, Pusey and others wished Hamilton to issue a pastoral letter to his clergy, but he did not feel up to it. He wrote a letter to his archdeacons but reserved his main statement until his visitation, scheduled for that summer.[17] In his Charge to a sympathetic audience, Hamilton acknowledged that he had 'been an instrument of placing the majesty of the law on the side of error' but insisted 'that my present responsibility is nothing to what it would have been had I allowed myself … to be deterred from the discharge of an act of duty'.[18] This had all along been his simple position.

Hamilton's more pressing problem was to pay his legal costs. He had to pay Williams' costs on appeal – not a great sum, as Williams had not employed counsel[19] – and his own costs in both trials, a total of some £2308. The costs were more than covered by a subscription, mostly from the clergy of his diocese, but with contributions from his fellow bishops and others.[20] Fendall's costs were to be covered by another subscription and the Essayists' by the Williams and Wilson Appeal Fund organized by Stanley.

The judgment was fully reported in the press. *The Times*, in the leader it devoted to the subject, reverted to its previous unfriendly line towards the Essayists. They had escaped penal consequences 'by the skin of their teeth'. The court had taken special care not to differ 'from the very general censure which has been passed on the book'. Yet 'the broad fact remains that a book which has roused the greatest public dissatisfaction, and which was almost judicially condemned by the Bench of Bishops, has been found practically unassailable in point of law'. The 'orthodox clergy' should rely on 'the inherent goodness of their cause', and these 'rash and unfounded opinions' would 'disappear into absolute oblivion'.[21]

The religious newspapers took different positions. The *Guardian*, which had deprecated prosecutions all along, was tempted to say 'we always told you so'. 'The gains to be secured by success bore no proportion' to the risk of failure and its consequences. 'They have secured for those opinions a recognized place within the limits of the Church of England.' But the decision was not as bad as appeared. The court had guarded itself against any misconception that the judgment 'lends any kind of sanction to *Essays and Reviews*'. The only way to suppress new heresies was by new dogmatic decisions, but that process might 'lead to far worse evils than the occasional endurance of an unsound ecclesiastic in a country parish'.[22] The moderation of the *Guardian*'s position so offended Keble that he cancelled his subscription, and Pusey, who had already given up hope for his party's paper, decided to write in the evangelical *Record*.[23] That journal had duly denounced the judgment as 'adverse to the Christian faith' and 'involving grave mischief'. But evangelicals, who had won the Gorham case, could hardly criticize the court for applying its principles here, and the actual decision was minimized as no more than 'a Scotch verdict of "Not Proven"'. The *Record*'s harshest condemnation was reserved for Tait's concurrence in the result.[24]

Counsel in the case were able to speak anonymously through the press. Swabey, assisted by Phillimore, criticized the judgment in the conservative *Quarterly Review*. 'By restraining the Church from putting her own discipline in force against the false teacher, the Court does by necessary consequence interfere with doctrine.' The problem was traced back to Lushington, who 'had first removed from the pleadings the articles which would have justified the condemnation which, after removing what would have justified it, he arbitrarily pronounced'. But the decision was limited: 'the Court, whilst it has acquitted the teacher, has left the teaching unsanctioned'. The Church was not committed to actual heresy. The true remedy was to alter the court of final appeal.[25] On the other side, Stephen wrote in two magazines at once. In *Macmillan's Magazine*, he hailed the judgment as 'the Magna Charta of honest inquiry in the Church'. It established that 'the clergy are fully at liberty to criticise every part of the Bible, and to inquire not merely into the truth of, but the morality of every part'.[26] In *Fraser's Magazine*, Stephen argued on erastian lines that 'the judgment of the Committee of Council was not merely legally right, but was the only one which would have been consistent with the existence of the Church of England as a national Church or, indeed, as anything wider than a sect based on mere popular prejudice'. The Anglican Church 'is an institution adapted, not for the teaching of any particular form of doctrine, but for the common worship of God by many people of very various theological views'. He exulted in the gain of liberty of thought by the clergy.[27]

Anglican periodicals, while critical of the decision, minimized it in favour of other themes. The evangelical *Christian Observer* attached little importance to the result. 'It is not an acquittal on the broad question at issue ... nor is it punishment the Church wants, but protection.' It was disturbed by Westbury's remarks on inspiration, eternal punishment and justification but hoped they were only *obiter dicta*. 'But this is a state of things which cannot, and ought not to last. A house divided against itself cannot stand.' A new tribunal was needed.[28] The High Church *Christian Remembrancer* cautioned against despondency, even though the law had been strained to a denial of justice. 'It certainly seems to open the door to unbounded licence as regards the criticism of Holy Scripture: though here the dissent of the two Primates is certainly a very important fact when the committal of the Church is being considered.' But 'we will not yet despair'.[29] Denison, in his *Church and State Review*, returned to his old theme that not a legal but a synodical condemnation was needed. 'The Church, though she be established by Law, does not speak by the Law courts, but by her Synods.' He proposed action by Convocation, 'the ONLY means whereby the church can speak in her corporate capacity'.[30]

Nonconformists pointed to the decision as the consequence of legal establishment. The Congregationalist *British Quarterly Review* urged evangelical clergy to rebel against the law. 'To remain in the system is to be implicated, more or less, in all the evils which belong to it ... On this remnant, and on the Free Churches of the land, it will devolve to become the guardians of the Inspired Records, and of the truth deposited in them.'[31] The *Liberator*, organ of the disestablishment movement, called for 'a new crusade' to disestablish a Church degraded by submission to the law. 'If the Establishment is weakened, truth is strengthened.'[32]

Roman Catholics also saw an advantage in a decision which revealed the dependency of Anglicanism upon the State. The *Dublin Review* held that in England 'religion is a function of the state, a department of the administration', and has 'nothing to do with faith'.[33] H. E. Manning, himself a convert, urged in two clever pamphlets that the decision proved that the Anglican Church was not part of the universal Church. 'A Church that can hold its peace in the presence of heresy is not the Church of God.' Its Catholic members should 'come forth' to the true Church.[34] Even protests such as the declaration being circulated were not adequate, because they did not change the system. 'The real culprit is the Anglican system, which generates the heresies which the tribunals only legalise.'[35] Manning and others hoped that the decision, like that in the Gorham case, would generate a wave of converts to the Roman communion. That no defections, either to Rome or to orthodox dissent, took place may have been due to the orthodox reaction within Anglicanism.

The judgment was followed by another wave of pamphlets.[36] The most notable was Keble's *A Litany of our Lord's Warnings*, a catena of Christ's statements on the subject of eternal punishment. 'From wresting Thy Holy Scriptures; from mistrusting Thy Holy Church; from bigotry and indifference; from respect of persons; from making God's Word of none effect ... Good Lord, deliver us.'[37]

The strongest reaction to the judgment was that of Pusey, who had anticipated the legal result: 'The radical evil of Law judges is their bias to acquit the accused'.[38] He was utterly dismayed by that part of the decision denying the binding doctrine of eternal punishment. This was 'demoralizing', opening 'a floodgate of immorality, for nothing will keep men from any sin, except the love of God or the fear of Hell, and most commonly the fear of Hell drives people to God'.[39] In this sense the judgment was literally 'soul-destroying'. Pusey's concern here was pastoral, for the common people who needed the dread of eternal punishment to keep them from sinning.[40] This aspect of the decision galvanized Pusey into prompt action on several fronts.

Pusey issued his personal protest in the form of a letter to a newspaper. Since he had given up the *Guardian*, he chose to publish in the organ of the opposite party, the *Record*, a call for common action against the 'common enemy, unbelief … The recent miserable, soul-destroying judgment surely requires united action on the part of every clergyman and every lay member to repudiate it'.[41] This marked the beginning of a *rapprochement* of the two great parties in the cause of their common orthodoxy. The *Record* hailed Pusey's 'admirable and faithful letter'.[42] The lay leader of the evangelicals, Lord Shaftesbury (Pusey's cousin), wrote to him to urge 'combined action in the cause of our Common Master … We have to struggle not for Apostolical Succession or Baptismal Regeneration, but for the very Atonement itself'.[43] Pusey accepted the proposal: 'This soul-destroying Judgment may … be overruled in God's mercy to good, if it binds as one man all who love our blessed Lord, in contending for the Faith assailed'.[44]

Even before the decision came down, Pusey had planned another action, an agitation to reform the court of final appeal in matters ecclesiastical, to get rid of the domination of the common lawyers.[45] He began work on this immediately, but it was the last of his projects to mature.[46] He also took a major part in the efforts to draft and get signatures for a declaration of the clergy of the doctrine impugned by the judgment. Both these efforts brought him into collaboration with Wilberforce, bringing about a *rapprochement* between two men hitherto estranged. Yet another project was an attempt to minimize the legal force of the judgment itself. To this end, he sought and obtained a legal opinion from the two leaders of the bar, Sir Roundell Palmer, the Liberal Attorney-General and a High Churchman, and Sir Hugh Cairns, his Tory and evangelical counterpart. Their opinion stated that the judgment did not 'furnish the means of determining, in the abstract, any of the legal questions raised by the present case'. The court had merely determined that two specific propositions were not rigorously binding upon clergymen. Pusey published this terse opinion with a less terse preface in which he stated that the legal force of the judgment was 'very narrow indeed'. He went on to criticize Westbury's language as a 'profanation of justice' and to maintain that 'the unjust decision of the Supreme Court does not, in itself, alter the doctrine of the Church of England'.[47]

In the midst of his frantic activity immediately after the judgment, Pusey received an invitation from Stanley, newly installed as dean of Westminster, to join in a series of distinguished guest preachers from all parties at the Abbey. Pusey was troubled by an invitation at this time which would require him to join with Stanley and his party. 'It gives an appearance of unreality if people, who are at that moment in active antagonism on what they believe to be of vital moment, unite as if there were nothing at issue between them ... I believe the present to be a struggle for the life or death of the Church of England, and what you believe to be for life I believe to be for death.'[48] He asked for the names of other preachers, and when Jowett was named said 'I do not know what single truth we hold in common'.[49] Finally Pusey sought the advice of Hamilton, who recommended declining. 'The essence of your scheme seems to be to exhibit as one those whose differences I believe to be vital; and so ... I cannot with a safe conscience accept it.'[50] Pusey's fierceness at this time was matched by Liddon, who also was invited and declined.[51]

Pusey's most effective action in the immediate aftermath of the judgment was to obtain from the archbishops an explanation of their concurrence in the acquittal of Wilson's remarks on eternal punishment. Pusey wrote to Longley; at Pusey's suggestion Keble wrote; and at Keble's suggestion Bishop Philpotts of Exeter also wrote.[52] The problem for the archbishops was that the rules of the Privy Council allowed only the decision of the Judicial Committee, without individual opinions, to be made public, and individual Privy Councillors were not allowed to publicize their advice to the Queen. Longley hoped to be able to indicate his grounds in response to an inquiry from a clergyman and was concerned only with selecting the right occasion.[53] So intense was the pressure from Pusey that Longley anticipated his chosen occasion and gave a private statement on March 4 which was published in the *Guardian* on March 16:

> I wish it to be generally understood that, in assenting to the reversal of the Judgment of Dr. Lushington on the subject of eternal punishment, in the case of Mr. Wilson, I did so solely on technical grounds, inasmuch as the charge against him was so worded that I did not think it could be borne out by the facts. The eternity of punishment rests, according to my mind, exactly on the same ground as the eternity of blessedness; they must both set and or fall together; and the Church of England, as I maintain, holds both doctrines clearly and decidedly.[54]

This statement satisfied the orthodox on the point on which they were most troubled by the archbishop's concurrence. But the alarm among orthodox clergymen about the judgment as a whole was so great that Longley felt that a more extended public statement was necessary. This he gave later in March in the form of a pastoral letter, a typically Roman Catholic format which this Low Churchman helped to naturalize in the Church of England. Longley justified his judgments both as to conviction and acquittal. 'I was in nowise called upon to attempt any justification of inspiration, seeing that the Church had not thought fit to prescribe one.' On the other hand, 'the Church authoritatively declares Holy Scripture to be identical with all those Canonical Books ... that it is "The Word of God", and "God's Word written" ... by the term "Canonical Books" is meant, Books which lay down a rule of faith authoritatively'. Williams' words were inconsistent with the formularies, as were Wilson's in denying God's Word to be co-extensive with Scripture. The Articles, in identifying Scripture with 'God's Word written,' 'make the one co-extensive with the other'. The issue was 'whether a clergyman should be permitted to proclaim to his people that the term "Word of God" is not to be identified with "Holy Scripture"'; whether, in fact, the Bible is still to be our guide in matters of faith'. The Bible would 'cease to be an infallible Rule of Faith' if some portions were merely human, for we have 'no certain criterion' to distinguish between the human and divine elements. His acquittal of Wilson did not arise from any doubt as to the doctrine of the Church, 'nor do I conceive that the Church has any more sure warrant for belief in the eternal happiness of the saved than it has for belief in the eternal suffering of the lost'. However, 'there was so much obscurity in the forms of expression used by Mr. Wilson' that the passages extracted did not warrant the charge. While textual criticism was allowable, 'criticism in the case of a Minister of our church must have its limits'. Longley warned the clergy against interpreting the word 'everlasting' other than as 'eternal' in the sense of 'never-ending': 'our certainty of never-ending bliss for penitent believers is gone, if the word bears not the same signification' for punishment.[55] The *Record*, praising the pastoral, said that 'the Archbishop has spoken out with a force and a precision which will prevent it being said that the Church acquiesced in those sentiments in which the Lay Lords and the Bishop of LONDON had seemed to abandon the ancient orthodoxy of the Church'.[56]

The next month Thomson issued a pastoral letter to his province of York, 'to remove misapprehensions, and to reassure'. The novel element in his letter was a distinction between 'the so-called Judgment', the opinion read by Westbury, and the real judgment, which was the formal report to the Queen, merely reversing the verdict; only the latter was binding on the clergy.[57] Thomson concluded that 'there is no reason for immoderate fear' as a result of a legal decision. 'The Church of England knows little of courts and prosecutions; and her stability and soundness in the faith rest upon a different and far surer guarantee.'[58]

The dissentient among the prelates on the Council, Tait, found an occasion to state his case in a preface to a volume of his sermons, *The Word of God and the Ground of Faith*. Tait deplored the 'public clamour ... excited by some well-intentioned men, who seem to have thought that the calm decision of the highest court of judicature could be overborne by the protest of individuals'. He deprecated the orthodoxy which maintained itself 'rather by loud declarations than by sound argument'. Affirming his own belief in eternal punishment, Tait noted that 'it is one thing to allow that an opinion is not punishable by law, and quite another to maintain that it is true'. He found it satisfactory that clergymen were not required to maintain 'the unwarranted position ... that the Bible is an infallible guide in questions of physical science'. On the question of inspiration, 'the most important theological question of the day', Tait commended the caution of the framers of the Articles who had not defined it so as to come 'into a dangerous antagonism with God's other gifts of reason and conscience'.[59] But Tait could not prevail against the two archbishops, whose statements gave the sanction of the authorities of the Church to the orthodox counter-offensive initiated by Pusey.

CHAPTER FOURTEEN

Condemnation

The orthodox counter-offensive took two forms: a declaration by the clergy reaffirming the chief points of doctrine impugned by Westbury's judgment, and a synodical condemnation by Convocation of *Essays and Reviews* as a book. The latter was a revival of an effort almost carried to success in 1861. The former, however, raised issues that had not been central in the original debate, which had centred upon the 'verifying faculty' and the evidential apologetic. The Privy Council judgment involved two new doctrinal issues: the Bible as the 'Word of God' and the eternity of punishment. The first was a simplified statement of the inspiration of Scripture, the underlying issue of the entire controversy; but in its specific focus on the phrase 'Word of God', it had not surfaced until Stephen's defence of Williams was attacked by McCaul in 1862. The matter of eternal punishment was but one out of numerous charges against Wilson; it owed its prominence to the accident of surviving Lushington's winnowing of the charges and to Pusey's particular pastoral concern with the issue. The issues of the controversy had been changed by the controversy itself.

The idea of a clerical declaration or protest was initiated by an Oxfordshire rector, W. R. Fremantle, in a letter to his bishop, Wilberforce.[1] Wilberforce sent the letter to Pusey who, after some consultation, drafted a declaration.[2] Advantage was taken of a University Convocation scheduled for February 25 on the new examination statute, which would be widely attended by the clergy. A hasty notice was given of a meeting to be held in the Music Hall immediately following Convocation.[3] After some confusion, the meeting adopted a motion proposed by Denison and seconded by a Low Churchman to elect a committee to draw up a declaration for general signature by the clergy. The committee was a representative mixture of Low and High Church figures, including Pusey and Denison, with Fremantle as secretary.[4] It met immediately afterward and agreed upon a declaration, a modified version of Pusey's draft which remarkably harmonized Low and High Church themes:

> We, the undersigned presbyters and deacons in holy orders of the Church of England and Ireland, hold it to be our bounden duty to the Church and to the souls of men, to declare our firm belief that the Church of England and Ireland, in common with the whole Catholic Church, maintains without reserve or qualification the inspiration and Divine authority of the whole canonical Scriptures, as not only containing, but being, the Word of God, and further teaches, in the words of our blessed Lord, that the 'punishment' of the 'cursed' equally with the 'life' of the 'righteous' is 'everlasting.'[5]

Fremantle had the declaration printed and sent to every clergyman with a list of the committee and 157 other sponsors and a prefatory letter, dated February 29, earnestly entreating each recipient, 'for the love of God', to return his signature.[6] The declaration was further publicized by letters and notices in the religious newspapers and an advertisement in *The Times*.[7] The procedure differed from the 1861 clergy petition in that it included the Irish Church (still part of the same Establishment) and that signatures were sought from all clergy, curates as well as incumbents.

The declaration achieved considerable success, gathering 10,000 signatures by March 23.[8] Fremantle extended the period for signatures to Whitsunday (May 15) to 'sweep up all the stray and unmoved minds as far as possible'.[9] But support for the declaration was far from unanimous, even among those who substantially agreed with it. Complaints from Low Churchmen about cooperation with Puseyites were quickly smothered by Hugh M'Neile, fiercest of evangelical partisans, and the *Record*.[10] In the *Guardian*, a young layman, D. C. Lathbury, expressed fears for the integrity of the High Church party in Pusey's cooperation with the evangelicals, leading to an exchange of letters with Liddon as Pusey's surrogate.[11] Some High Churchmen had difficulties about the word 'presbyter' rather than 'priest' (Pusey had introduced the word). Other objections were that the declaration was ambiguous, that it went beyond the formularies and added a new test, that it was drawn up by a small group without authority, or that it challenged the royal supremacy by contradicting a judgment of the Queen in Council. There were also objections to the moral pressure, especially on curates, to sign.

The declaration produced side-controversies of its own. The dean of Ripon, William Goode, who agreed with its doctrines and would have supported a voluntary declaration of belief, was disturbed by language which stated that these were articles of faith maintained by the Church of England and so contradicted the judgment which held that they were not, impugning the royal supremacy to which the clergy were bound.[12] He obtained a formal opinion from two barristers, A. J. Stephens and J. C. Traill, that 'the Declarants impeach the Judgment of the Judicial Committee by affirming the converse of the propositions established by the Judgment', and this evinces 'an intention on the part of the Declarants not to submit to the Judgment pronounced by the Queen'.[13] Pusey quickly obtained an opinion from Palmer and Cairns, that 'it is not in any way unlawful for clergymen, either singly or together, in their preaching or otherwise, to affirm the words of the Declaration'.[14] This storm, which temporarily disturbed the progress of the declaration, blew over; like much else, it enriched none but the lawyers.

The other notable side-controversy was carried on in a series of letters to *The Times*. Maurice opened it on March 5 with a letter criticizing the declaration for being so ambiguous on 'Word of God' and 'everlasting' that Williams and Wilson might as easily sign it as Pusey.[15] Pusey replied on March 8 that there was no ambiguity, the meaning of words being determined by the context; the words were chosen because they were found in the formularies.[16] Maurice expanded his argument the next day.[17] Pusey's response on March 11 cited a letter by Wilson to the *Daily News* quoting a Rotterdam pastor who denounced eternal punishment as inconsistent with God's attributes. 'We do not believe in the same God. God Whom we adore in His awful and inscrutable justice and holiness, these writers affirm to be cruel.'[18] Maurice's reply on March 12 explained why he would never sign the declaration. 'An irresponsible self-elected committee has no right to frame a new test for the Church of England.' It was not honest, meaning more than it said: 'a special notion about inspiration which I, for one, believe to be dishonourable to the Word of God' and 'the notion that God condemns men to everlasting sin which I, for one, hold to be an accursed notion'. The adjuration to sign 'for the love of God' was in fact a threat to junior clergy that they would suffer if they do not sign. 'I accept Dr. Pusey's statement, tremendous as it is. I say that the God whom we are adjured to love, under these penalties, is not the God of whom I have read in "the Canonical Scriptures".'[19] Pusey closed the debate on March 15 with a refutation of Maurice's charges of dishonesty, blasphemy and oppression, a denial that the declaration was a new test, and an assertion that it 'will have a great moral effect on the country ... What else could they do who feared lest people should be encouraged to disbelieve the Bible and Hell, and that they were in risk of losing their faith and their souls?'[20]

The declaration eventually obtained the impressive number of 11,200 signatures. This is often cited as a majority of the clergy,[21] but that statement is based on the number of clergy in England only, whereas the declaration included Ireland and was numerously signed there. The total number of clergy in the United Church was 24,800, so the signers amounted to 45 per cent of the clergy.[22] But when it is considered that numerous signatures were withheld because of technical objections by men who agreed with the doctrine,[23] it is fair to say that the sentiment expressed by the declaration was that of a majority of the clergy.

The declaration was formally presented on May 12, by Archdeacon Clerke of Oxford, on behalf of the committee, to Archbishop Longley, who was joined by five other bishops. Longley had originally intended to utilize this occasion to deliver his response to the judgment,[24] but this had been anticipated. In accepting the declaration on behalf of the episcopate, he stated his 'conviction that the clergy of our Church will never be disposed to propagate opinions which tend to subvert the fundamental doctrines of Christianity. We, on our part, should ever feel it to be our duty to maintain the authoritative teaching of the Church'.[25]

Two other declarations were prepared during this period. One was an address of thanks to the archbishops by laymen, a sort of lay counterpart to the clergy declaration. In five weeks 137,000 signatures were collected, an impressive figure even in that age of monster petitions, demonstrating the existence of a substantial orthodox laity.[26] The other was a declaration of scientists that there was no conflict between science and Scripture. 'We, the undersigned Students of the Natural Sciences, desire to express our sincere regret, that researches into scientific truth are perverted by some in our own times into occasion for casting doubt upon the Truth and Authenticity of the Holy Scriptures.' This was announced in May 1864 but not presented until the following year, while efforts were made to collect signatures from fellows of scientific societies. Meanwhile a controversy arose in which the declaration was denounced by scientists of the stature of Sir John Herschel and Augustus de Morgan. Altogether the declaration received 716 signatures from a variety of 'scientists'.[27]

The judgment and the declaration produced a resurgence of the pamphlet and sermon controversy over *Essays and Reviews*.[28] Charges delivered about this time also alluded to the subject.[29]

The revival of the controversy over *Essays and Reviews* also put an end to the most promising attempt to endow Jowett's Greek professorship. Late in 1863, Stanley and Pusey had agreed on a statute to have the University raise the salary to £400 with a clause, suggested by Keble, 'that the University shall be held to have pronounced no judgment upon his writings, in so far as they touch the Catholic faith'. This compromise easily passed Congregation (the assembly of resident members) in early February, just before the judgment. But that decision so hardened opinions that when, on March 8, the measure came before Convocation, the country clergy came in great numbers and, led by Denison, defeated it by 467 to 395.[30] A similar effort in October did not pass the Hebdomadal Council. In April Lord Westbury introduced a bill in the House of Lords to endow the Greek chair with a canonry in the Chancellor's gift. Westbury's bill was thrown out by 55 votes to 25. In this case the motive was not *odium theologicum* but an objection to this use of a canonry.[31]

The next, and virtually the last, stage of the controversy was the effort to obtain a synodical condemnation of *Essays and Reviews* by Convocation. When it met on April 19, a number of *gravamina* were introduced in the Lower House, as well as a petition from Williams requesting to be heard before being condemned. None of these was acted upon, but Denison's *gravamen,* with 40 signatures, requesting that the Upper House act upon the condemnation passed by the Lower House in 1861, was brought as a petition to the Upper House by the prolocutor the next day.[32]

The Upper House had met on April 19 with closed doors for an hour and a half 'that we might rub off if possible any points of contact'.[33] In its open session Wilberforce presented petitions for a judgment and gave notice of his motion 'that this house will take into its consideration the Message of the Lower House, sent on the 21st of June, 1861, for the purpose of considering whether the house shall accede to the prayer of the petition' for synodical censure.[34] Wilberforce's leadership of the Upper House stemmed from his coming ready with a proposal; the mover of a motion sets the terms of the debate.

On April 20, the Prolocutor presented Denison's *gravamen*, 'That, the suit now having been brought to a close, the injury done to the Church by the delay of Synodical judgment may in part be repaired by proceeding to such judgment'. Wilberforce immediately arose to reopen a matter which had 'slumbered' since 1861. 'This Synod must take that course by which alone the Church can officially and as a body record her protest' against the teaching of the Essayists. He then moved 'that this house resume the consideration of the subject, and that a committee of this house be appointed' to consider the messages of the Lower House and the contents of the book and to report on them.[35]

Thirlwall, who might have supported condemnation in 1861, now opposed it as unnecessary, inexpedient and useless. His speech was directed against Denison and the clerical declaration, scoffing at the signatures: 'the framers of this Declaration believe that the youngest literate[36] or illiterate – they often mean the same thing – who has been last admitted into Deacon's orders is competent to express an opinion upon the subject'. He considered the number of signatures 'in the light of a row of figures preceded by a decimal point, so that however far the series may be prolonged, it never can rise to the value of a single unit'. He denounced the 'moral torture' by which signatures had been coerced. Queried by Hamilton as to the relevance of discussing the declaration, Thirlwall replied that the real ground of the *gravamen* was the dissatisfaction in the Church at the Privy Council judgment, and the declaration was a true exponent of this. The fact was that the Judicial Committee had ruled that the two doctrines of the declaration were not the doctrines of the Church of England. Controversy existed in the Church on these questions, and Convocation possessed no authority to settle them. He counted it 'the greatest of all possible blessings' that no such authority existed which could make 'a new article of faith'. He was 'averse to any new restriction either of the terms of communion or the conditions of entering the ministry of the Church'.[37]

After Alfred Ollivant of Llandaff spoke briefly in favour of the motion, Tait arose to urge that each bishop calm the excited feelings of his own clergy by following the example of Thirlwall's Charge. 'This is the proper mode of dealing with this matter.' *Essays and Reviews* was 'falling into oblivion', but condemnation would create a new demand for it. He disparaged the *gravamen* as a mere petition of individual members of the Lower House, disregarding 'the totally changed aspect of things' in that it 'disinters from the dead an unfortunate paper' of 1861. 'To define what is contrary to the doctrine of the Church would, I presume, be to make a new Article.'[38]

John Jackson of Lincoln and John Lonsdale of Lichfield spoke against the motion and Hamilton spoke in favour of it. Harold Browne, now bishop of Ely, opposed it, feeling that the result of the controversy would ultimately be not the shaking of faith but its confirmation. 'I wish to see as much as possible of fair, calm, open discussion, and not any check or control, except in a case of absolute necessity, by authority.' Ellicott, now bishop of Gloucester, favoured appointing a committee which might have a 'tranquillising effect'. Wilberforce pointed out that there was no conflict between synodical condemnation and the Privy Council judgment, which had stated that it did not consider the 'tone and character of the book'. Synodical action was a 'protest against the presence of false doctrine' in the clergy. 'Why does agitation prevail? Because authority is silent. What stops agitation? Authority speaks.'[39]

The bishops then voted, dividing five on either side. Archbishop Longley, who had not voted,[40] then gave his vote in favour of the motion on the ground that it was only a motion to refer the matter to a committee. The bishops then appointed themselves collectively the committee.[41] The work of preparing the report took two months.

On June 21, Wilberforce presented the report of the committee to a thin Upper House; Thirlwall and Browne were among the absentees. The committee, 'being of opinion that the Synod cannot avoid pronouncing upon the doctrinal character of such a work', reported 'that the book contains false and dangerous statements, and reasonings at variance with the teaching of the Church of England, and deserving the condemnation of the Synod'. This was followed by several broad specifications supported by extracts from particular essays. The committee considered 'that a tendency to unsettle belief in the revelation of the Gospel pervades the book'. 'Besides the general teaching, which the committee consider as striking at the root of all Revelation, they have found frequent contradictions of the particular truths of the Christian faith, or insinuations of their falsehood.' They observed throughout 'a mode of treating the Holy Scripture which subverts the authority it has always possessed in the Church as the inspired Word of God'. Singled out for particular censure were Williams' 'verifying faculty', Wilson's 'private opinion' on eternal punishment and his 'proposition, that men may, as the condition of being invested with the office of teachers in the Church, subscribe to Articles of Religion without believing them to be true'. On all these grounds the committee reported 'that this book does, in their judgment, merit the condemnation of this Synod'.[42] Wilberforce moved that the report be received and adopted 'to clear themselves from any complicity in what they believed to be the false and dangerous statements contained in that book ... It would be treason to our common faith to suffer the members of our ministry to put forth to the world such doctrines without a repudiation of those doctrines by the Church'.[43]

Tait, who had not attended the meetings of the committee, opposed the report on the ground that it was their duty rather 'to calm the public mind than to excite it'. This had already been done by the episcopal manifesto of 1861 and by Thirlwall's Charge. Tait objected to citing extracts because 'you are generally obliged to condemn the particular statement in question by some general statement' which may lead to dangerous consequences. The committee should not have raised any questions besides the two in the clergy declaration, which he disparaged, pointing out that it was signed by less than half the clergy and a

distinct minority of deans, heads of colleges and professors. He questioned
Thomson's assertion that Westbury's opinion was not the judgment. By stating
that Williams and Wilson were at variance with the doctrine of the church on
points on which they had been acquitted by the Privy Council, Convocation
'will exhibit a rather unseemly antagonism between the two great bodies'. He
held 'that the appointment of this committee was a mistake, and that its report
will do harm to the Church'.[44]

Ollivant of Llandaff defended the committee's practice of 'extracting passages
from the book which are utterly at variance with the idea of the Bible being a
book of inspired authority'. It was 'necessary for the Church as a Church to
purge itself from any complicity with this book'. Jackson of Lincoln differed
from Tait on the relevance of the declaration but doubted that condemnation by
Convocation would 'allay the irritation which now prevails' and would vote
against it. Wilberforce deprecated the desire for 'quietness': 'excitement, when
the truth is threatened, is the very evidence of a living Church'. Convocation
would not come into conflict with the Privy Council as long as it accepted only
the 'legal consequences' of the judgment. 'We are free, without blaming the
Court, to declare what are matters of faith.' He asked that the bishops state
synodically 'that as a Church, by the Church's voice, we repudiate this false
teaching'.[45]

Longley, who had been silent previously, now stood forth, stating that Convocation had the power to condemn erroneous books and that it was 'its
province and function' to do so. He read a legal opinion which the committee
had obtained from Sir Hugh Cairns and John Rolt 'that the Convocation of the
Province of Canterbury is not estopped by the 25th Henry VIII, c. 19, or by any
other statute, from expressing by resolution or otherwise their condemnation or
disapprobation of a book, although no special Royal licence is given for that
purpose'.[46] Longley felt strongly that 'If ever there was a book which deserved
such condemnation, it is the book entitled *Essays and Reviews*'. He believed 'that
there are many minds most seriously disturbed which will receive great comfort,
and have their fears and apprehensions allayed, when they find the Church in its
corporate capacity expressing its opinion'. Condemnation would prevent
secessions from the Church.[47] Longley desired 'a moderate censure, a moderate
condemnation of the book'.[48]

Wilberforce then made the operative motion:

> That the Upper House of Convocation having received and adopted the
> report of the committee of the whole house appointed by them to examine
> the volume entitled *Essays and Reviews* invite the Lower House to concur
> with them in the following judgment: – 'That this Synod, having ap-
> pointed committees of the Upper and Lower Houses to examine and
> report upon the volume entitled *Essays and Reviews*, and the said commit-
> tees having severally reported thereon, doth hereby Synodically condemn
> the said volume, as containing teaching contrary to the doctrine received

by the United Church of England and Ireland, in common with the whole Catholic Church of Christ.

Wilberforce stated that this language 'had been studiously made as little offensive as it was possible to make it'. Without further debate, the motion was passed by six votes to two, Tait and Jackson being the negatives. The resolution was immediately given to the prolocutor of the Lower House.[49]

There seems to have been a strategy here to reassert the leadership of the bishops. The Lower House had initiated the procedure for censure, but in the definitive action the bishops took the initiative and invited the Lower House to concur, thereby forcing one final debate. The debate was curious in that the greater part of the moving and talking was done by the proponents of the Essayists. This was partly due to changes in membership: McCaul had died, and Stanley had his first opportunity to participate as dean of Westminster. But a political factor was also involved. The session of Parliament, with which Convocation was concurrent, might be ended at any moment by prorogation, and Denison, leading the majority in favour of condemnation, wanted to get the business over as speedily as possible. This may also explain the plethora of motions and speeches by the minority.

Denison immediately moved 'that this house do thankfully accept and concur in the condemnation of the book by the Upper House'. Debate proceeded by way of successive dilatory amendments, each defeated by decisive majorities. It was first moved to await a report from a committee which had been assigned to examine precedents, then simply to request more time to deliberate. Stanley, who seconded both motions, deplored 'precipitation' and held that 'what the doctrine of the Church of England was, and what it was not, had lately been settled by the highest court of appeal in the land. (Loud cries of "No, no.")'.[50] Debate on the second amendment was carried into the next day, June 22.

The next amendment called for a delay in order to hear Williams, who had requested to be heard. Harvey Goodwin, now dean of Ely, urged that they 'hold out the hand of Christian fellowship to him'. Stanley, on the basis of his 'more intimate knowledge' of the Essayists, denied that there had been any concert among them. The amendment was defeated, although Williams' petition was entered on the minutes. A substitute motion to decline to concur in the censure because it was 'unwise to revive the judicial functions of Convocation' was then moved. This brought Fendall into the debate, appealing from the decision of the Judicial Committee to Convocation 'as a higher court than the Committee of Council, to reverse again by their decision the decision of that court, not as practically affecting the men, but as affecting the sentence as regards the Church of England'. The lengthy debate brought cries of 'Divide', and the motion was defeated. After an adjournment was voted down, the main question was debated. Stanley challenged Convocation, if it condemned *Essays and Reviews*, to condemn his own biography of Thomas Arnold, which 'contains passages identical in principle and almost in words with the extracts taken from the *Essays and*

Reviews'. He noted the case of Denison, who had narrowly escaped the courts: 'if ever there was a case that called for Synodical judgment, it is his case'. He acknowledged that his speech was 'useless as far as votes are concerned', but continued until the debate had to be adjourned.[51]

On June 24, Stanley resumed his great speech, giving 'four great objections' to the condemnation: 'first, it is ambiguous; secondly, it is undiscriminating; thirdly, it is unfair; and fourthly, it is nugatory'. It was not only futile but 'a superfetation of futility'. He concluded by thanking those members who had come forward 'at the peril of their professional reputation and worldly interests, and exposed themselves to the poisoned shafts of the most envenomed controversy for the sake of upholding what they believe to be the cause of common sense, Christian justice, and Christian charity. (Cheers.)' Christopher Wordsworth, no liberal, again asked that Williams be heard. The prolocutor ruled against further amendments. After several other speeches, Denison brought 'an exhausted debate to a close'. The greatest cruelty was that of the Essayists, who 'have spent all their intellect and energy in the unsettling of God's truth, but have not given us, for they could not, one thing in its place'. It was essential to this synod, as guardian of the faith, 'that it have and that it exercise the judicial function as against heresy. It is not essential to it that it exercise the judicial function as against heretics'. The house divided, and the condemnation was passed by 39 votes to 19. Wordsworth moved a rider to provide for subsequently hearing Williams. 'I have discharged a duty ... *liberavi animam meam*.' This was defeated, and Convocation was then prorogued.[52]

Essays and Reviews was synodically condemned. The condemnation, coupled with the indication of majority feeling in the declaration of the clergy, gave a clear judgment against the book by the clergy. The judgment of the Privy Council had been countered by the judgment of Convocation. It has been characterized as one of those 'non-binding authoritative pronouncements that reinforce the claim of one side or the other to carry the authentic tradition of the church, but do nothing to dissuade or unchurch the opposite side'.[53] It was, in fact, an outburst of clericalism.

Clerical reactions were favourable. The *Guardian* rejoiced in the 'purgation of the Church' which was no longer answerable for false doctrine: 'as a spiritual society, and as an ecclesiastical corporation, she has, through the only regular organ she possesses, and in the only way open to her, expressly disowned and repudiated their errors'.[54] Denison in the *Church and State Review* could say 'the book is now, therefore, Synodically condemned' and turn his attention to the reform of the court of final appeal in ecclesiastical cases.[55] But the lay response to clericalism was unsympathetic. *The Times*, which regarded *Essays and Reviews* as an 'obnoxious volume', found in the 'folly and mischievousness' of the proceedings 'an assumption of authority which almost passes belief'. Such proceedings were 'in direct violation of the principles of our Establishment' and escaped the state's interference only by their 'complete insignificance'.[56] Robert Browning noted the hold which the debate had taken on the lay mind:

> The candid incline to surmise of late
>   That the Christian faith proves false, I find;
> For our Essays-and-Reviews' debate
>   Begins to tell on the public mind,
> And Colenso's words have weight.[57]

The most thorough critique of the agitation which culminated in the condemnation came from Stanley, in the *Edinburgh Review*. Stanley called the condemnation 'a measure of doubtful legality', expressing an 'uncompromising determination ... to secure victims at any cost'. But the declaration and the synodical judgment would pass away, while 'the permanent blessings' of the Privy Council judgment would remain. Stanley justified the Crown's supremacy over the Church, exercised through the law, as the security of its members. It was 'a triumph, not of a party but of the whole Church'. 'We shall have lost the expensive luxury of prosecutions, but we shall have gained the blessings of truth and peace.'[58]

One anticlerical reaction was evinced in a debate in Parliament. Lord Houghton (Monckton Milnes) had received a letter from Williams, complaining of being condemned unheard. Houghton gave notice of a question to the chancellor, on behalf of the government: 'Whether they have taken or are willing to take the Opinion of the Law Officers of the Crown as to the Powers of the Convocation of the Province of Canterbury to pass a Synodical Judgment on Books written either by Clergymen or Laymen; as to the immunity of Members of that body from Proceedings at Common Law consequent on such Judgments; and as to the Forms according to which such Judicial Power must be exercised if it belongs to that Body?' Presenting his question in the Lords on July 15, Houghton said that his sole interest 'is for the freedom of opinion and the liberties of literature'. He feared that the condemnation was 'a very perilous precedent' for a general censorship of literature. Citing precedents, he argued that Convocation lacked the privilege to pass judgments.[59]

Westbury, seeking to put down by ridicule the clerical criticism of his judgment, responded that the action of Convocation was clearly illegal. He pointed out, however, that the penalties for *praemunire* were extremely severe: the bishops would have to appear at the bar of the House as penitents in sackcloth and ashes and be fined £30,000, and the members of the Lower House would also be mulcted. He shrunk from such action, and asked instead whether indeed there was a synodical judgment. There was none: 'what is called a synodical judgment is a well-lubricated set of words – a sentence so oily and saponaceous that no one can grasp it. Like an eel, it slips through your fingers. It is simply nothing ... it is literally no sentence at all'. The phrase 'oily and saponaceous' was a gratuitous slap at Wilberforce, who was nicknamed 'Soapy Sam'. Westbury compounded this by stating that 'as no one is hurt by this oily form of words ...

having regard to the impotency of the thing, Her Majesty's Government intend to take no action in the matter'. He concluded with a lecture on the supremacy of the Crown and Convocation's lack of jurisdiction.[60]

Longley, replying for the bishops, regretted that malice had been imputed to Convocation, whose 'object was simply and solely to vindicate the Church of England from complicity with opinions which we considered most mistaken and dangerous'. He had sought an opinion from the Attorney- and Solicitor-General but had been refused, so he had taken that of Cairns and Rolt. He defended the condemnation as necessary: 'I ask your Lordships whether since the Reformation there has been any crisis in the English church of so grave a character as that through which it is now passing, and whether there is ever likely to occur in the next 200 or 300 years so serious a case or one calling so urgently upon Convocation, the Synod of the Church, to pronounce its opinion' on a book 'that strikes at the root of Christian belief'. Tait supported the Archbishop on the question of legality, nothing that the Law Officers had refused to rule: 'they must know what the law is before they obey it, and you do not tell them'. Tait could not resist a gentle criticism of Longley's sense of urgency: 'Men always exaggerate the importance of the questions of their own time'. He thought it likely that 'the Church, having had its attention called to the subject, will think it desirable to treat these matters in another way'.[61]

Wilberforce took advantage of Westbury's personal attack on him:

> If a man has no respect for himself, he ought, at all events, to respect the tribunal before which he speaks; and when the highest representative of the law of England in your Lordships' House, upon a matter involving the liberties of the subject and the religion of the realm, and all those high truths concerning which this discussion is, can think it fitting to descend to a ribaldry, in which he knows that he can safely indulge, because those to whom he addresses it will have too much respect for their character to answer him in like sort – I say this House has ground to complain of having its high character unnecessarily injured in the sight of the people of the land, by one occupying so high a position within it.

After being cheered for putting down Westbury, Wilberforce went on to justify the action of Convocation. 'Our action was for the maintenance of truth, and to hold to engagements, and it was not to put down opinion.' It was 'one thing to condemn a man, and another to censure a book'. They were 'set in trust in this land for this – that we may be the true depository of the truth which God has revealed'. The synodical judgment was the 'best means of preserving peace in the Church', which should be allowed 'in her authorized manner to pronounce for her followers, as she has done in this instance, that she disclaims for her living ministry this erroneous teaching'.[62]

Westbury's use of personalities had weakened his case so that Wilberforce's dignified rebuke seemed to give him, and his Church, the advantage in this debate,[63] which ended without action. The *Guardian* showed its scorn for

Westbury: 'a man may be made a Peer, and yet fail sometimes to show the breeding of a gentleman'.[64] His 'gratuitously insolent and offensive' speech, with its 'unseemly and scurrilous personalities', had evoked 'the dignified but crushing reply of the Bishop of Oxford, which carried the house completely with it'; and the Archbishop had clearly shown that 'the object of that proceeding was, not to condemn the men, but to repudiate the book', which has given 'deep satisfaction' to the clergy.'[65]

Houghton's question, and even Westbury's remarks, had another effect: to remind churchmen that the clericalism manifested in the synodical condemnation was liable to evoke a laic counter-reaction. Tait's speech showed that he had taken the point. Gladstone, the High Church spokesman in the Commons, was troubled enough to have a discussion with Houghton the next day.[66] But the most striking reaction was that of the *Record*, which had not joined in rejoicing over Convocation's action and always distrusted the High-Churchmanship of Wilberforce. It felt that 'a Convocation, in which there is no lay element, ought to be watched with suspicion' and had 'no confidence in Convocation as at present constituted'. Westbury had been right to turn on Wilberforce. 'We cannot trust the schemes of those who hold the Ultramontane views of the Bishop of OXFORD, nor can we regret that he should have met with so decisive a check.'[67] The temporary alliance of High and Low Church, having accomplished its purpose, was beginning to fall apart, and the most aggressive organ of the evangelicals realized that they had been drawn into a union organized by High Churchmen for the High Church purpose of upholding the corporate and authoritative character of the Church of England.

The debate in the House of Lords was the last formal proceeding in the *Essays and Reviews* controversy. The Essayists had been acquitted in the courts, and *Essays and Reviews* had been condemned by the clergy. This should not be regarded as a draw. Orthodoxy had mobilized the clergy; it was not in the nature of the Broad Church to mobilize anybody. The hint at the end that there was a substantial opposition between the clerical and lay mentalities remained only a hint. In the short run, orthodoxy won the battle. Controversies do not have a long run.

CHAPTER FIFTEEN

Aftermath

The orthodox (and largely High Church) counter-offensive continued after the synodical condemnation. The next objective in Pusey's agenda was the reform of the court of final appeal in ecclesiastical cases so that bishops, not lay lawyers, would determine the doctrine of the Church. This was already under discussion among Pusey, Keble and Liddon in the immediate aftermath of the judgment. Action was postponed until the more urgent matter of the declaration was attended to, but there was much consultation. W. E. Gladstone, as a cabinet member, was applied to but saw no ready legislative solution.[1] There were difficulties about the precise reform to be sought. Pusey at various times talked about making the bishops equal in number to the lay lords or separating out the bishops as the sole judges on questions of doctrine; but Wilberforce wanted to remove the bishops altogether from the Judicial Committee 'so that it should be a merely civil court, without having any plea of having an Ecclesiastical sanction'.[2] This was also the opinion of Palmer, and it was to be adopted uncontroversially when Palmer (then Lord Chancellor Selborne) reformed the entire judicial system in 1873.[3]

Denison had presented a *gravamen* for reform of the court of final appeal at the same time as he moved for synodical condemnation. This was referred to a committee of which, as the proposer of the motion, he was chairman. He wrote the report, presented in the final days of Convocation, asserting that the Judicial Committee was 'absolutely a lay court without any admixture of the spirituality' and therefore unsuited to be the supreme ecclesiastical court. Denison's report, postponed by the debate over condemnation and then by prorogation, was lengthily discussed in the Convocation of 1865. But nothing came of it: the Upper House tabled the matter, and the Lower House passed only a tame statement that the court was 'open to grave objection'.[4]

The efforts of Pusey and Keble to reform the final court of appeal resumed in the summer of 1864 in the form of a project of an organization to agitate for this purpose. This was the object of the lengthy preface appended to the brief opinion of Palmer and Cairns as to the legal force of the judgment, which Pusey published in September. After a diatribe against Westbury's opinion, Pusey urged the clergy to call for 'tribunals of their own'. 'Let men league together to support no candidate for Parliament, who will not pledge himself to do what in him lies to reform a Court, which has in principle declared God's Word not to be His Word, and Eternity not to be Eternity.'[5] Criticism of the preface brought letters by Pusey and Keble to *The Times*.[6] Meanwhile Pusey and Keble had prepared a circular, sent to clergy in October, proposing an Association for

Amending the Law of Final Appeal in matters affecting Doctrine, whose 'Provisional Committee' would meet on November 9.[7] Meetings continued well into 1865,[8] but neither a general petition for redress nor an organized political campaign ever developed. It is possible, however, that Gladstone's unreadiness to act on this issue cost him High Church support in his 1865 defeat for re-election as member for Oxford University, which was the culmination of the reaction against liberalism in the university.[9]

One reason for the failure of this effort was the refusal of Low Churchmen to join in what they regarded as a High Church measure:[10] a purely clerical tribunal might as easily reverse the Gorham judgment as that on the Essayists. On this issue the temporary alliance of High and Low Church broke down. But the decisive blow to the movement came from Thirlwall in his Charge of 1866. Surveying the events of the last three years, Thirlwall disparaged both the declaration and the synodical condemnation as inefficacious against the judgment: 'as long as the law under which we live remains unchanged, no number of voices, either of individuals or of clerical assemblies, can contract' the lawful latitude of opinion of the clergy. Importance was attached to those acts 'with a view to some ulterior object', a change in the constitution of the court of appeal to exclude the laity from decisions affecting doctrine. 'I consider it as a ground for the deepest thankfulness, as one of the most precious privileges of the Church of England, that principles which I believe to be grounded in justice, equity, and common sense, are still the rule of judgment in ecclesiastical causes.' A decision of the present court 'can only affect the position of individuals in the Church, but leaves the doctrine of the Church just where it was'. But the object of the reform of the court was 'to enable an ecclesiastical council to pronounce a Declaration of faith' which would be 'a new, more or less authoritative, definition of doctrine; in other words, a new article of faith'. Thirlwall pointed to the Colenso case to show how release from the royal supremacy meant 'a no less complete emancipation from the rules and principles of English law and justice. The result showed how dangerous it would be to entrust a purely ecclesiastical tribunal with the administration of justice in ecclesiastical causes: how surely the divine would get the better of the judge'.[11] The ex-lawyer Thirlwall had given the clearest rationale for the subjection of the Church to the law of the state as a protection for liberty within the Church.[12]

Not only did the Church have to live with the Judicial Committee of the Privy Council, it had to make use of it. This was immediately shown in the case of Colenso. Robert Gray, the High Church bishop of Capetown, exercised his metropolitan authority over the province of South Africa by summoning Colenso for trial for heresy by his synod. Colenso, who did not attend, was deposed from his bishopric. He appealed to the Privy Council, not as the final court of appeal in ecclesiastical cases (Gray would not adhere to an appeal to a secular court on a point of doctrine) but in its civil capacity as the court of appeal in common law for the colonies. Gray was supported by Pusey, Keble and Wilberforce; the

Colenso defence fund received contributions from Jowett and from scientists such as Darwin and Lyell.[13] In 1865 the Judicial Committee ruled for Colenso on the surprising ground that Gray had no authority over Colenso since the Queen's patent, which purported to convey it, was null and void after the grant of legislative autonomy to the Cape colony. Colenso kept his stipend, endowment and cathedral. Gray excommunicated him in 1866. At the Convocation of that year Wilberforce proposed a declaration that the Church of England was in communion with Gray and not with Colenso; Tait and Thirlwall watered this down into a statement that they were in communion with Gray. The problem of independent colonial bishops, revealed by the Colenso case, led to the calling of the first pan-Anglican Lambeth conference in 1867. Tait ensured that the conference was not directed against Colenso, but he was condemned in a private document circulated among the bishops. Gray consecrated a rival bishop of Natal, producing a schism in which Colenso kept only a minority of the churches. The later volumes of his *Pentateuch* included much solid scholarship, but the controversy which his first volumes aroused may have set back biblical scholarship in England even more than that over *Essays and Reviews*.[14]

One further heresy case came before the Privy Council. Charles Voysey was encouraged by the judgment to preach a sermon on July 10, 1864, later published as *Is Every Statement in the Bible about our Heavenly Father Strictly True?* Going beyond the Essayists, he directly challenged the inspiration of the Bible and, in this and later writings, other doctrines explicit in the Articles and formularies. Voysey was tried in the Chancery Court of York in December 1869, and was convicted on several charges. The committee to defray the cost of his appeal included Jowett and Stanley, who disagreed with Voysey but hoped to keep him within the Church. But his case, like that of Heath, was hopeless, and the Judicial Committee was unanimous in upholding the conviction.[15]

The Heath and Voysey cases showed that the courts of the 1860s were still able to convict for heresy, though they did not do so in the cases of the Essayists. But the real importance of the Voysey case is that it was the last such case. 'With it, the series of doctrine cases comes to an end. Never again was a clergyman of the Church of England required to answer for his doctrines in an English court.'[16] Subsequent legal proceedings were for ritualistic practices, directed against the High Church by the evangelicals, which may explain why the High Church lost its taste for prosecutions.

If heresy could not be prosecuted, it might at least be refuted, and this was another side of the orthodox counter-attack. Pusey was already engaged on a multi-volume commentary on *The Minor Prophets* (1860–77), not controversial but displaying his considerable learning with a total absence of criticism. As Regius Professor of Hebrew he felt it his duty to defend the Old Testament, and Williams' denial of predictive prophecy in the book of Daniel provided Pusey with a target. His commentary on Daniel was published in 1864, in the midst of all his other activities. Pusey replied to Williams' assertions with his own counter-assertions, convincing only those who wanted to be convinced. But there were many who wished to think that the Essayists had been refuted when they had merely been contradicted; Lord Shaftesbury thought that Pusey's *Daniel* and Payne Smith's *Isaiah* had stopped the critics.[17]

The other pillar of the orthodox apologetic, miracles, received a more original defence. J. B. Mozley, perhaps the finest theological mind among the tractarians, delivered the Bampton Lectures of 1865 on the subject of miracles. Like Mansel, he borrowed his argument from the sceptics, Hume's theory of causation. The so-called laws of nature are not really laws; the order of nature is merely our perception of sequence and expectation of its continuance. Thus miracles are not violations of law, because there is no inherent law to prevent them. Mozley's argument was so triumphant that it was never followed up, and he stands as 'the last great exponent of the evidential idea of miracles'.[18]

The definitive statement and ablest defence of the orthodox position was made by Liddon in his Bampton Lectures of 1866 on *The Divinity of our Lord.* Seeking to refute the negative criticism of Renan, Baur and Strauss, Liddon rested the case for the truth of the Old Testament on the infallibility of Christ, who cited Moses as the author of the *Pentateuch,* David as the author of a psalm, and so on. To disbelieve the Old Testament was to disbelieve Christ. This was presented so ably and appealingly that it became 'the most famous course of Bampton Lectures ever given ... These lectures hurled the old faith at the heads of dons and undergraduates and at the world; with learning, force, devastation of the follies of opponents, and no power to persuade waverers'.[19] The lectures, published in 1867, became a bestseller.[20]

And then, nothing. Orthodoxy had reasserted its position. Since it was not again attacked directly, there was nothing more for it to do. It was a position not capable of further development, so it did not develop further. An exhausted orthodoxy died of its own victory. The evidential apologetic, having survived the onslaught of the Essayists, was never again invoked and disappeared from view. The next generation knew it not.

Some concessions were quietly made. The 1864 reform of the Oxford examination statutes dropped Butler from the required curriculum; this had been engineered by Pattison. The Bampton Lectures for 1864, by T. D. Bernard, cautiously allowed a progressive revelation, in the sense of a growing apprehension by man of God's truth.[21] Subscription to the Thirty-Nine Articles, travestied by Wilson and criticized by Stanley, was reformed for different reasons with surprising ease. The requirement to declare one's 'unfeigned assent and consent to all and everything contained in' the Book of Common Prayer and the Articles was deterring to ordinands and embarrassing to officiants, and some evangelicals, led by Lord Ebury, had been seeking milder terms since 1857. Though a motion was defeated in the Lords in 1863, a royal commission was appointed in 1864 and recommended more general terms. Convocation agreed, and the Clerical Subscription Act was passed in 1865, requiring only a simple 'assent' to the

Articles and the Book and a belief that their doctrines were 'agreeable to the Word of God'.[22]

There was even a victory for one of the Essayists. The increase in Jowett's stipend as Regius Professor of Greek, seemingly impossible to enact at Oxford, was won for him by history. The historian E. A. Freeman published, in October 1864, a pamphlet (originally a letter in the *Daily News*) on *The Oxford Regius Professorship of Greek*, pointing out that this was the only one of the ten regius professorships founded by Henry VIII which still received its original stipend of £40. The others had been increased in proportion to the increase of value of the lands which had funded them, and Christ Church, to whom these lands had been granted, had actually proposed in 1854 to do the same for the Greek chair, before Jowett obtained it. Dean Liddell of Christ Church sought to take advantage of a gap in Freeman's argument by stating in November that, if it could be shown that the chapter held lands specifically granted for the purpose, he would propose an augmentation of the stipend. The challenge was taken up by a young lawyer, Charles Elton, who discovered that the lands which supported the Divinity, Hebrew and Greek chairs had first been granted for the purpose to Westminster Abbey and, when it declined, re-granted to Christ Church. He published this in *The Times* on January 16, 1865. Even then the chapter did not yield, but obtained an opinion from Palmer and Cairns that there was no legal obligation to pay more than £40. This enabled the chapter to surrender gracefully, announcing in February that it would raise the salary to £500.[23] Jowett was relieved of financial cares but deprived of a grievance.[24]

Jowett had been silent throughout the controversies. When they were over, he remained silent as a critic and theologian. It seemed as if the reaction to his commentary and essay had driven him out of the field,[25] flying for refuge to the calm of Platonic translation. In fact his theological interests remained active, though only intimates knew this. Throughout his life he preached and published sermons, and he always intended to return to a theological work. He explained his position to Florence Nightingale:

> I know that it is very doubtful whether I could in any degree succeed in working them out and I certainly could not succeed without entire health and a good deal of reading and thought. But then at present I have the translation and Edition of Plato in hand, and besides this my pupils: in the last is a perfectly unlimited field and when I see men passing through College or in the University to whose career I might have given a twist in the right way if I had only time or energy I feel very strongly the responsibility of this.[26]

By the time he was finished with Plato, Jowett had become master of Balliol, and academic life had come to absorb him fully. Teaching was for him a religious activity. 'The truth probably is that he had come to realise that he could much more effectively propagate his beliefs through the institutional structure of the college and the university than by publishing his theological writings.'[27] But he had also expressed doubts about whether he could succeed in working his ideas out. Jowett was the theologian *manqué* of the Broad Church; but had he published his theology, it is not certain that he would have resolved his own difficulties or lived up to his promise.[28]

Of all those connected with the Essayists, only Stanley, not an Essayist but their most constant defender, actually carried forward the work for which *Essays and Reviews* was a prospectus and prolegomenon. His *Lectures on the History of the Jewish Church*, published in 1863 and 1865, made no original contribution to scholarship but offered the public an acceptable presentation of a critical and historical approach to the Bible. Stanley's reverence and cautious use of criticism produced 'a work that undoubtedly commended the critical method to fair-minded people'.[29] In his frequent essays in several periodicals he maintained a witness for liberal Anglicanism. An 1865 address on 'The Theology of the Nineteenth Century', later published in *Fraser's Magazine*, presented *Essays and Reviews* as part of a large historical tendency which brought men closer to the Scriptures and might be called a 'new Reformation'.[30] But Stanley's real achievement was in another sphere: he could not make the National Church liberal, but he made Westminster Abbey the national church.

The Essayists themselves never developed their ideas further. A twelfth edition of *Essays and Reviews* was published in 1865, with suitable notations indicating the passages acquitted in 1862 and in 1864.[31] Wilson, at least, wanted to go further. He continued his reviewing of religion and philosophy in the *Westminster Review* throughout 1870.[32] In that year he proposed a second volume of *Essays and Reviews*. But a stroke in 1871 put him and his project out of action.

Williams pugnaciously reasserted his old positions, especially on prophecy as moral witness rather than prediction. He did this through a translation of the Hebrew prophets, published in 1866 and 1871. An 1868 article in the *Fortnightly Review* on 'The Theory of Clerical Obligation' strongly asserted the obligation of believing subscription to the Thirty-Nine Articles but held that this did not require 'the concealment of truth'.[33] But he did not develop his position further before his death in 1870; and his widow's 1874 biography may have expressed his views more clearly than his own writings.

The remaining Essayists were silent as to criticism or theology. Powell was dead. Goodwin had made his only contribution to religious thought in *Essays and Reviews*; his main contributions were in Egyptology, and he wrote on music and literature before going off to the Orient as a judge. Temple had never written any original scholarship, and his duties as headmaster of Rugby left him no time. He was to reappear in the public eye in 1869; but it was only in 1884 that he advanced the liberal cause by giving Bampton Lectures which, without controversy, announced the Christian acceptance of Darwin.[34] The only active original scholar was Pattison, but after 1860 his was a purely historical scholarship not on religious subjects, while personal embitterment served to attenuate his religious convictions.[35]

The Broad Church movement did not move forward after the publication of *Essays and Reviews*. It effectively came to an end amid the controversies surrounding the book; but those controversies did not put an end to it. Rather, the Essayists (except for Jowett) simply had nothing more to say. As Anglican orthodoxy had exhausted itself during the controversy, the Broad Church had exhausted itself in precipitating it. The first concerted effort of the Broad Church was also its last.

CHAPTER SIXTEEN

Epilogue

The bench of bishops was transformed at the end of the 1860s. For a decade until 1865, Lord Palmerston had steadily promoted Low Churchmen. That did not much change under his immediate successors. When Archbishop Longley died in 1868, Disraeli, in his first ministry, was prepared to nominate the Low Churchman Ellicott to the primacy. But he did not press his choice against Queen Victoria, who was determined to name Tait, and so a moderate Broad Churchman, unpopular among the clergy, became archbishop of Canterbury.[1] A short time later Gladstone became prime minister. He promoted his friend Wilberforce to Winchester on C. R. Sumner's retirement in 1869. That year saw several deaths and retirements, enabling Gladstone to realize his program of distributing bishoprics more evenly among all parties within the Church, with a preference for those politically Liberal.

In October 1869, on the death of the High Church Bishop Phillpotts, Gladstone appointed Temple to the vacant see of Exeter. Gladstone's motive may have been political, for Temple supported Gladstone, but the choice conformed to his policy of balancing appointments, and the Queen did not disapprove. Temple's main qualification was being headmaster of Rugby, but, in the Church of England, flogging schoolboys is considered good preparation for governing clergymen. But what mattered to the orthodox was that Temple was an Essayist, an author of a book synodically condemned, and he had refused to separate himself from his colleagues.

The shock to clerical opinion was magnified when the publisher of *Essays and Reviews* seized the occasion to reprint the last edition of the book with only one change: the Table of Contents now described Temple as 'Bishop elect of Exeter'.[2] Temple had allowed the reprinting, wanting 'neither to break up the book nor stop it suddenly' but to print sufficient copies to exhaust the demand 'and then let it die out as it was dying before'.[3]

The explosion of outrage in 1869 was, as in 1864, led by Pusey. He immediately wrote to Gladstone to announce that they were politically separated. 'As a public man, he is a lost friend; as an individual, I love him still.'[4] If Gladstone could inflict such an injury on the Church, any other prime minister would do worse. 'I must henceforth long, pray, and work, as I can, for the severance of Church and State.'[5] Pusey wrote to the *Guardian*, protesting against the 'horrible scandal of the editor of the Essays and Reviews to be a Christian bishop'. As in 1864, he joined forces with his evangelical counterpart, and a committee issued the announcement: 'The Earl of Shaftesbury and the Rev. Dr. Pusey having consented to act in unison in using every effort to prevent the scandal to the Church caused by the Premier's nomination of Dr. Temple, clergymen and laymen willing to support their brethren in the Diocese of Exeter are requested to communicate without delay to the secretaries'.[6]

Notwithstanding Shaftesbury's cooperation, the protests against Temple's bishopric had a decidedly High Church flavour. In nominating Temple, Gladstone had disregarded the synodical condemnation of *Essays and Reviews*, one of the rare exercises of independent authority by the Church. Denison took the lead in protesting, reprinting his 1861 *Analysis of 'Essays and Reviews'* with a fiery preface: 'If a writer in a book, condemned *without reservation* by a Synodical Judgment, may, without retractation, or explanation, or disavowal, or remission or qualification of Sentence, be raised to the Episcopate, then The Church of England, *as by law established*, is a profane absurdity'.[7] Denison later published a letter to the prolocutor of Convocation asserting that this was 'contrary to the Canon Law of the Church Catholic' and giving notion of a *gravamen* of protest which he intended to introduce in the Lower House.[8] He had already read his personal protest at his church of East Brent. Another vociferous protest came from Burgon in two pamphlets.[9] Seven other clergymen issued protests or pamphlets against Temple's bishopric.[10] There were also pamphlets by a Roman Catholic convert and a leader of the Plymouth Brethren.[11]

Not everybody joined in the outcry. The *Guardian* deplored the campaign against Temple. R. W. Church thought it 'unjust' and 'discreditable'.[12] Even the *Church Times*, the new organ of the extreme High Church, would not take part.[13] But outright support for Temple was uncommon. Lord Russell, the former prime minister, wrote privately to Temple, congratulating him.[14] A few friends spoke out, notably E. W. Benson, headmaster of Wellington, who wrote to *The Times* on October 22 in defence of Temple.[15]

Efforts were made to make Temple's appointment acceptable by persuading him to withdraw his essay from the book or explain his differences from the other authors. Dean Wellesley of Windsor, the Queen's ecclesiastical advisor, was acutely aware of Temple's problem: 'it is difficult for a man to make explanations with a bishopric hanging over his head'.[16] Harold Browne, Christopher Wordsworth, now bishop of Lincoln, and Wilberforce all wrote to Temple urging him to withdraw or explain. To all these entreaties he returned the same refusal. The book had been useful 'to break through the mischievous reticence which was crusting over the clergy';[17] a wide latitude of opinion was necessary for the English Church; he was upholding religious liberty. Above all, it was imperative to make no other declaration than those required by law, lest he set a precedent by which unauthorized declarations might be required as a condition of obtaining a bishopric. 'The one safe rule for me to follow is the law of the Church of England.'[18]

Those opposed to Temple's bishopric sought to interfere with his progress through the process by which a nominee actually becomes a bishop. The first step was his election by the cathedral chapter of Exeter. This was more symbolic than practical, for the Queen could appoint by letters patent if the chapter refused to elect, and the dean and chapter were liable to the penalties of *praemunire* if they refused to elect the person named in the royal *congé d'élire*. Nonetheless the effort was made. About 200 of the 1000 clergy of the diocese of Exeter signed a memorial urging refusal to elect. The dean wrote that 'from all parts of the country I have letters about the sword of the Lord and of Gideon, exhorting us to go to Prison, and promising us visits there'.[19] On November 11, 1869, the dean and 12 prebendaries voted to elect Temple, while the sub-dean (W. J. Trower, retired bishop of Gibraltar) and five others voted in opposition.[20]

The next step was the confirmation of the election, normally a formality. But a question was raised about Temple's legitimacy (he was born in the Ionian islands, where there were no parish registers), and his eldest sister had to be called at short notice to testify that he was legitimate; and other testimony was required to his personal character. Bishop Trower and a beneficed clergyman of the diocese protested against the confirmation. But Sir Travers Twiss, the archbishop's vicar-general who conducted the confirmation, ruled that he had no option but to act upon the royal mandate and could not judge the merits of the case.[21]

The final step was the consecration. There was some difficulty in making a quorum of bishops to perform the act. Many, perhaps most, of the bishops shuddered at the thought of consecrating an author of a book synodically condemned, who had, moreover, stubbornly refused to recant or explain. Wilberforce was named in the royal commission but declined 'because he did not as I continually hoped he would, clear himself from compli[cit]y with E & R'.[22] Harold Browne agreed to consecrate but not to present Temple for consecration, and felt it necessary to write a letter to his archdeacons explaining 11 reasons for participating, principally that Temple was personally free from heresy, 'a man of singular probity, and sincere Christian and believer in all the Articles of the Christian faith'.[23] Tait was willing to consecrate but was prevented by ill health. Finally, there were assembled Browne, the liberal Thirlwall, the mild Philpott of Worcester, and Jackson, now bishop of London, who presided in Tait's absence.

The final scene was at the consecration at Westminster Abbey on December 21, 1869. Jackson announced that he had received protests from four bishops led by Wordsworth of Lincoln,[24] claiming that the archbishop could not consecrate in face of a protest from his suffragans. He had taken legal opinion that the consecration must proceed, but he asked the assistant bishops for their opinions. Each spoke against receiving the protests, Browne with a learned reference to the primitive church, and Thirlwall with a blunt 'My judgment is that they cannot be received.' Temple was consecrated.[25]

Even the fact that Temple was now bishop of Exeter did not end the controversy. Denison had given notice of a *gravamen* of protest in Convocation, which met on February 9, 1870. The Lower House defeated the motion. A few minutes later, Philip Freeman, archdeacon of Exeter, mistakenly thinking that he had Temple's authority to do so, announced that Temple's essay would not appear in any future edition of *Essays and Reviews*.[26] Denison was elated: 'We have got rid of the stigma laid upon the Church by the book; we shall see no more of the book'.[27] He announced that he would withdraw from the opposition he had planned to offer to Temple's election as a vice-president of the Society for the Propagation of the Gospel on February 18.[28]

Temple was embarrassed by this announcement. Conservatives interpreted it as a recantation and liberals felt it as a betrayal. It became necessary for him to speak out. He justified both the essay and its withdrawal in a speech to the Upper House on February 11.

> Now, so long as there was any legal right at stake, it seemed to me the strongest of all possible duties that I should not sacrifice any such right ... I felt certainly that the publication of one essay amongst others was a thing which might be allowed to Frederick Temple, but which was not, therefore, to be allowed to the Bishop of Exeter ... his position would give it a kind of authority that it would not have of itself ... my reason for agreeing to join was that I could not help being very much struck with the extraordinary reticence which then prevailed among the younger University men ... Men were unwilling to express doubts and perplexities which it was certainly far better that they should express ... I think there is a more reasonable and better tone in discussing great questions in consequence of the publication of that book ... I thought that the work had really been done, and that to persist in the publication of that book now was not to persist in advocating certain principles, but to persist in maintaining a particular discussion ... in all these cases a mischief ... is almost a necessary accompaniment of the progress of investigation; but as God made us, it is simply impossible to stop that progress ... I am quite sure that the belief in the most fundamental points, if once it were supposed to be absolutely free from all investigation and all question, would begin to lose its real vitality, and a belief without vitality seems to me to be not merely a negation, but a most positive and real mischief ... I think that such a discussion ought to be allowed the greatest freedom that can possibly be given it, consistent with the acknowledgment of the Bible as the supreme revelation, and with a reverent – a really reverent – spirit in the treatment of all subjects connected with it ... I am quite sure that no one has a more real reverence for God's Word, or a more entire desire to make it the guide of his life, than I have myself; and that there is no one who feels more confident that the result of the freest inquiry in a reverent spirit will be to uphold the dignity and honour of that Word.[29]

Though it received criticism from both sides, Temple's speech effectively ended the controversy over his bishopric. It clearly manifested his integrity and consistency: 'granite on fire', as he was later described.[30]

Almost unnoticed in the uproar over Temple, Williams died suddenly early in 1870. His funeral sermon was preached on January 30 by a former pupil, John Owen, under the title of *The Ideal of the Christian Minister*. Speculating that Williams might have become a bishop had he been less rigid in devotion to conscience and truth, Owen denied that he was a 'neologian' inventing new beliefs. His purpose had been to preserve freedom of thought in the Church of England 'from the narrowing influences of a slavish liberalism on the one hand, or a blind ecclesiasticism on the other', by subordinating text and dogma 'to the paramount authority of Reason and of Conscience'.[31]

The banner that Williams dropped was picked up by Wilson. Already in mid-1869 he had proposed to Jowett, who eagerly agreed, a second volume of *Essays and Reviews*, reviving the original notion of a series of volumes.[32] Wilson undertook two essays on the principles of the Reformation, and Jowett was to write two essays on the Reign of Law and another topic which eventually became the Religions of the World. His Balliol colleague and future biographer Lewis Campbell agreed to write on mistranslations in the English New Testament, but Sir Alexander Grant, who had withdrawn from the first *Essays and Reviews*, declined to join the second lest it endanger his educational work in Edinburgh.[33] Further planning was suspended during the crisis over Temple's bishopric, but as soon as he was consecrated Wilson and Jowett resumed work. Wilson wrote to Pattison to seek a sequel to his essay, but Pattison, now soured, thought that the English public could not understand theology.[34] Jowett wrote to the philosopher Edward Caird about a volume which 'should be adequate to the subjects of which it treats, and should be written in a religious spirit'.[35] Williams would have been asked to write had he lived. Others who were considered were a reluctant Max Müller, Stanley, the lawyer Charles Bowen, Dean Elliott of Bristol, W. H. Fremantle (later dean of Ripon) and Samuel Davidson, who had been dismissed from the Lancashire Independent College in 1857 for his biblical criticism.[36] But Wilson suffered a stroke which effectively put an end to the project of a book.

Some of the writers did, nonetheless, continue with their essays. Campbell thought that his own essay, which appeared in the *Contemporary Review* in 1876, was the only essay to be published, but Davidson's tract *On a Fresh Revision of the English Old Testament* (1873) was a larger version of the essay he had been asked to contribute.[37] Jowett was hard at work on 'The Religions of the World' and wrote 30 pages in the summer of 1871, but the project was laid aside in the next vacation.[38] He continued to show interest in writing on theology, but he published no more.

The last battle fought over the Broad Church came in 1872, when Stanley's election as a select preacher at Oxford was contested but carried.[39] Absolutely the last shot fired in the controversy was the funeral sermon for Wilson in 1888, preached by his pupil Kennard, who went over all the old ground in justifying his master.[40] The dead were left to bury their dead.

CHAPTER SEVENTEEN

The Night Battle

The most important fact about the controversy over *Essays and Reviews* is a negative and unrecorded fact. There is no evidence that any person had his mind changed by the arguments in the debate.

The failure of argument, the essential absence of discourse, in this greatest of Victorian controversies suggests some reflections about the nature and function of Victorian controversy. The parties never really engaged each other, but simply asserted their positions which remained unchanged in the debate.[1] The characteristic absence of interaction was pointed out by the greatest of Victorian controversialists, John Henry Newman:

> Half the controversies in the world, could they be brought to a plain issue, would be brought to a prompt termination. Parties engaged in them would then perceive, either that in substance they agreed together, or that their difference was of first principles ... Controversy, at least in this age, does not lie between the hosts of heaven, Michael and his Angels on the one side, and the powers of evil on the other; but it is a sort of night battle, where each fights for himself, and friend and foe stand together. When men understand what each other means, they see for the most part that controversy is either superfluous or hopeless.[2]

Despite the futility of controversy, and its inherently ephemeral character, Victorians controverted with great zeal and utmost seriousness. The intensity of religious controversy is largely explained by the fact that most of the participants were clergymen. To be sure, in a Protestant church laymen could take part, and in a church 'by law established' lawyers played an important role; but clergymen were best suited to deal with the issues, and they willingly did so. The evangelical and tractarian revivals had transformed the clergy into a distinctive profession, single-mindedly devoted to their religious duties, serious beyond all others, taught to magnify religious issues. The clergy were in the business of making religious affirmations which they were expected to state with absolute certitude. Yet the repeated shocks which the Church had faced since 1828 had produced in them a nervousness, almost an institutional hypochondria, about 'the Church in danger' or 'the faith in danger'.

The potential for controversy was always there. The struggles between the High and Low Church parties would erupt periodically into controversy. Attacks, or perceived attacks, on the Church by dissenters or secular liberals kept up the sense of 'the Church in danger'. From the mid-century there was recognized a danger from 'rationalism' without and within the Church, fuelled by 'doubt' and leading to 'infidelity'. The dangers were not unreal, though clerical minds incapable of doubting were equally incapable of understanding doubt. In such an atmosphere, a controversy could be triggered by writings such as *Essays and Reviews* or Colenso's *Pentateuch* or by actions such as the Privy Council judgment or Temple's appointment.

Media were readily available in which such controversies could be conducted. The periodical press – newspapers, magazines and reviews – were at the height of their influence. The 1860s were the optimal period for widely read periodical controversies: the repeal of the 'taxes on knowledge' in the 1850s had cheapened periodicals, especially newspapers, but the 'yellow press' had not yet developed to turn them from their original seriousness. Letters to the editor allowed individuals a voice of their own. Tracts and pamphlets could readily be published; larger works such as *Essays and Reviews* or *Replies* were profitable speculations for publishers. There was the oral medium of the ubiquitous sermon, or the occasional Charge, which could then be published as a pamphlet. The old-fashioned device of the signed petition allowed large numbers to indicate their position.

It was difficult for a controversy not to arise when a suitable trigger such as *Essays and Reviews* appeared. It was bound to be reviewed, at least in the religious press. Orthodox reviewers were duly appalled. It required only that this opinion be vented in the general press, and Harrison's provocative article in the *Westminster Review*, followed by Wilberforce's call to action in the *Quarterly*, supplied the necessary prods. After that, the controversy took on a life of its own, with clerical declarations and episcopal censures on the one hand and pamphlets and books on the other. There was no stopping it. Once started, the controversy fed on itself.

The controversy took an unpredictable course. It was unusual in that it was largely a one-sided controversy, the Essayists spoiling the fun by their refusal to defend themselves (except for the defences in court and some guerrilla actions by Wilson and Williams) and being defended by few other than Stanley. This gave undue prominence to what were essentially tactical differences among the champions of orthodoxy. Had Hamilton's prosecution not aborted the action of Convocation in 1861, the book would have been synodically condemned at that time, and the controversy would have died out with the publication of *Replies* and *Aids to Faith* at the beginning of 1862. But the arguments and judgments in Arches and the Privy Council changed the very issues of the controversy. The two points of the clergy declaration of 1864 – the Word of God and eternal punishment – had not been central issues in 1861, when miracles and the verifying faculty were of most concern; and the acquittal by the Privy Council turned the synodical condemnation into a confrontation between the clergy and the civil power. Temple's bishopric in 1869 brought on a brief reprise of a controversy which otherwise died in 1864.

The *Essays and Reviews* controversy was also notable for the way in which it spun off side-controversies and agglomerated to itself other controversies. These might be trivial, for numerous persons had their own hobby-horses to ride. They might be forced: the *Record* (which regularly generated controversies) started a side-controversy over the report of Bunsen's death which almost split the Evangelical Alliance. But they might also be significant or interesting, as the debate over Wilberforce's sermons on revelation and probation. Ongoing controversies could also be worked into this debate, whether the reform of the liturgy or dissenters' attacks on the established Church. Major contemporary controversies interacted with this one. Darwinian evolution was frequently mentioned in the debate, usually as a stick wherewith to beat the Essayists; but it was not as central to the clerical mind as the myth of 'the warfare of science and religion' would make it appear. But the Colenso controversy was thoroughly intertwined with that over *Essays and Reviews*.

One question remains. To whom did the controversialists address themselves? The Essayists had a sense of the 'public' they were addressing: the educated elite, lay as well as clerical, largely graduates of their own universities, especially the younger generation. But *Essays and Reviews* was their last as well as first concerted effort. Their orthodox opponents also had an audience in mind: what was known as 'the religious world', the mass of believers and practisers of the faith. It was supposed that these people were disturbed by the novel doctrines and doubts of the Essayists, and the early declarations and much of the pamphlet literature were largely intended to reassure them that the faith was secure and that the clergy as a whole were faithful to the doctrines that their people expected them to teach. 'Such works do not stand as landmarks ... they do not greatly affect the progress of science or the interests of religion, but they lull the distress felt by conscientious people and produce a calming effect when controversy is running high.'[3] But it is difficult for works of controversy to produce a calming effect. What reassured the religious public was the very volume and vociferousness of the condemnations.

It was not the religious public that the orthodox clergy had to reassure: it was themselves. Already nervous about 'rationalism', 'neology', 'doubt' and 'infidelity', the clergy of 1860 was in the throes of a conservative reaction of which the orthodox apologetic was the core. Suddenly the Essayists appeared with a direct challenge to the fundamentals of that apologetic. All the orthodox could do was to reassert their belief loudly and often, for the orthodox apologetic was so self-sufficient as to be capable only of assertion. Something more seemed to be needed to convince themselves that the faith had survived the attack and that the Church was pure despite the heretics in it. The Church had to purge itself from their taint by condemning their doctrines and by protesting its own faith, whether by the authority of the bishops and Convocation, by declarations of the clergy as a body, or by individual protests in sermons and tracts. The pamphlet literature is one howl of protest, and throughout it runs the note of *liberavi animam meam*. It was more important to vent one's soul, to express one's faith, than to convince any audience. More than anything else, controversy met a psychological need. The ultimate function of controversy was catharsis.

Notes

Chapter 1

1. Ieuan Ellis, *Seven Against Christ: A Study of 'Essays and Reviews'* (Leiden, 1980), p. ix. *The Origin of Species* was published on November 28, 1859; *Essays and Reviews* on March 21, 1860. The debates overlapped and sometimes interacted.
2. Basil Willey, *More Nineteenth Century Studies: A Group of Honest Doubters* (London, 1956), and A. O. J. Cockshut, *Anglican Attitudes: A Study of Victorian Religious Controversies* (London, 1959).
3. Ellis, *Seven Against Christ.*
4. For example, M. A. Crowther, *Church Embattled: Religious Controversy in Mid-Victorian England* (Newton Abbot, 1970), on Rowland Williams and H. B. Wilson; several biographies of Benjamin Jowett and numerous Victorian lives of other figures; and Pietro Corsi, *Science and Religion: Baden Powell and the Anglican Debate* (Cambridge, 1988).
5. See Josef L. Altholz, 'The Mind of Victorian Orthodoxy: Anglican Responses to *Essays and Reviews*, 1860–1864', *Church History,* 51 (June 1982) 186–197, reprinted in Gerald Parsons, ed., *Religion in Victorian Britain,* vol. 4: *Interpretations* (Manchester, 1988), pp. 28–40.
6. Ellis, *Seven Against Christ,* p. x.
7. I had Ellis in mind when I wrote this; but another exemplar of religious studies came to my attention afterwards: Nigel M. de S. Cameron, *Biblical Higher Criticism and the Defense of Infallibilism in 19th Century Britain* (Lewiston, NY, 1987). Cameron considers the Essayists categorically with their successors in the critical school ('the Critics') and against the opponents of any or all of them ('the Conservatives'), always with an eye to the revival of infallibilism in the present day. Cameron's final chapter ('An Anatomy of Controversy') was not the source of my title.

Chapter 2

1. Clement C. J. Webb, *A Study of Religious Thought in England from 1850* (Oxford, 1933), p. 9.
2. Hamish F. G. Swanston, *Ideas of Order: Anglicans and the Renewal of Theological Method in the Middle Years of the Nineteenth Century* (Assen, 1973), pp. 5–10, points out that Paley was most popular between 1794 and 1830 and Butler between 1830 and 1860. Paley remained in the Cambridge curriculum into the twentieth century, Butler at Oxford between 1832 and 1864.
3. The argument here stated baldly is developed in Josef L. Altholz, 'The Mind of Victorian Orthodoxy: Anglican Responses to *Essays and Reviews*, 1860–1864', *Church History,* 51 (June 1982) 186–197, reprinted in Gerald Parsons, ed., *Religion in Victorian Britain,* Vol. 4: *Interpretations* (Manchester, 1988), pp. 28–40. A different line is taken by Nigel M. de S. Cameron, *Biblical Higher Criticism and the Defense of Infallibilism in 19th Century Britain* (Lewiston, NY, 1987), who holds that 'the Conservative school developed in reaction to the Critical' (p. 115) and does not acknowledge that the 'lines of defence' were fully prepared before 1860.

4. H. D. McDonald, *Ideas of Revelation: An Historical Study A.D. 1700 to A.D. 1860* (London, 1959), p. 130.
5. Henry L. Mansel, *The Limits of Religious Thought* (Boston, 1859), pp. 168 (Lecture VI), 213 (Lecture VIII).
6. See R. V. Sampson, 'The Limits of Religious Thought: The Theological Controversy', in *1859: Entering an Age of Crisis*, P. Appleman, W. A. Madden, and M. Wolff, eds (Bloomington, IN, 1959), pp. 63–80.
7. John William Burgon, *Lives of Twelve Good Men*, new ed (London, 1891), p. 339.
8. Cf. Duncan Forbes, *The Liberal Anglican Idea of History* (Cambridge, 1952).
9. [W. J. Conybeare], 'Church Parties', *Edinburgh Review*, 98 (October 1853) 273–342.
10. [A. P. Stanley], 'The Gorham Controversy', *Edinburgh Review*, 92 (July 1850) 263–292.
11. Samuel Taylor Coleridge, *Aids to Reflection* (London, 1890), p. 273.
12. Coleridge, *Confessions of an Inquiring Spirit*, H. StJ. Hart, ed. (Stanford, CA, 1957), pp. 41, 42.
13. Cited in Bernard M. G. Reardon, *From Coleridge to Gore: A Century of Religious Thought in Britain* (London, 1971), p. 57.
14. Ieuan Ellis, *Seven Against Christ: A Study of 'Essays and Reviews'* (Leiden, 1980), p. 11.
15. Balliol College, Jowett Mss., 'Brown Tin Box', Notebook O, 16. The argument that Stanley was not the leader is made by Peter Hinchliff, *Benjamin Jowett and the Christian Religion* (Oxford, 1987), p. 70.
16. Owen Chadwick, *The Victorian Church*, 2 vols (London, 1966–70), 1: 552.
17. Benjamin Jowett, *The Epistles of St. Paul to the Thessalonians, Galatians, Romans: With Critical Notes and Dissertations*, 2 vols (London, 1855), 2: 459, 469.
18. Jowett, *The Epistles of St. Paul to the Thessalonians, Galatians and Romans*, Lewis Campbell, ed., 2 vols, 3rd edn (London, 1894), 2: 317–18; based on the 2nd edn (1859).
19. *The Times*, October 15, 1859, cited in Evelyn Abbott and Lewis Campbell, *The Life and Letters of Benjamin Jowett, M.A., Master of Balliol College, Oxford* (New York, 1897), p. 255.

Chapter 3

1. Cited in Vernon F. Storr, *The Development of English Theology in the Nineteenth Century* (London, 1913), p. 430.
2. Wilson was criticized by the Low Church newspaper, the *Record*, and in a pamphlet, *Rationalism in the Pulpit of the University of Oxford* (1854); see Crowther, *Church Embattled*, p. 115. Even the biblical scholar F. J. A. Hort thought the lectures 'perfectly horrible': Arthur F. Hort, *Life and Letters of Fenton John Anthony Hort* (London, 1896), p. 210.
3. See Dennis R. Dean, 'John W. Parker', *Dictionary of Literary Biography*, vol. 106: *British Literary Publishing Houses, 1820–1880* (Detroit, 1991), pp. 233–236.
4. Hort to Gerald Blunt, March 11–12, 1855, in Hort, *Life of Hort*, p. 310.
5. Temple to Canon Cook, 1869, in E. G. Sandford, *Frederick Temple: An Appreciation* (London, 1907), p. 204.
6. See Mark Francis, 'The Origins of "Essays and Reviews": An Interpretation of Mark Pattison in the 1850's', *Historical Journal*, 17 (December 1974), 797–811;

and Josef L. Altholz, 'Periodical Implications and Origins of *Essays and Reviews*', *Victorian Periodicals Newsletter*, **10** (September 1977) 140–154.

7. Mark Pattison, *Memoirs* (London, 1885), p. 208. See also John Sparrow, *Mark Pattison and the Idea of a University* (Cambridge, 1967).

8. Francis, 'Origins', 802, citing Chapman to Pattison, January 3, 1854, Bodleian Mss. Pattison 50, ff. 301–2, paying Pattison for reviews of books. It is not clear what this represents. Pattison's own list of 'Papers in Various Periodicals' (Bodleian Mss. Pattison 112) lists nothing in the *Westminster* prior to April 1857, so this is not an article. *The Wellesley Index to Victorian Periodicals 1824–1900*, Walter E. Houghton, ed. (Toronto, 1979), 3: 620, gives attributions for all sections of the new 'Contemporary Literature', but some are only 'probable'.

9. Francis, 'Origins', pp. 802–3, citing Chapman to Pattison, October 30, 1854, Bodleian Mss. Pattison 50, ff. 402–3. Francis errs in assuming that Pattison became theology and philosophy editor of the *Review* as a whole; he merely edited (and largely wrote) this section of 'Contemporary Literature'.

10. *Wellesley Index*, 3: 623. *Wellesley's* thorough research is to be preferred to Francis, 'Origins', 814, who says that Wilson took theology while Pattison retained philosophy. Pattison did contribute one philosophical notice in July 1855 and substituted for Wilson in January 1857. On Wilson's writing for the *Westminster*, see Ieuan Ellis, *Seven Against Christ: A Study of 'Essays and Reviews'* (Leiden, 1980), pp. 20–21, 43.

11. 'They are even destitute of that instrument, which every fractional subdivision of the smallest sects possesses, an organ in the periodical press.' [W. J. Conybeare], 'Church Parties', *Edinburgh Review*, 98 (October 1853): 334. See Josef L. Altholz, *The Religious Press in Britain, 1760–1900* (New York, 1989), pp. 33–35.

12. Francis, 'Origins', 805, citing Pattison to Chapman, October 9, 1857, Bodleian Mss. Pattison 51, ff. 386–90.

13. Wilson to Pattison, January 27, 1858, Bodleian Mss. Pattison 52, ff. 95–96. Wilson and Pattison had already corresponded on January 5 and 8.

14. Wilson to Pattison, March 19, 1858, Bodleian Mss. Pattison 52, ff. 93–94. Francis, 'Origins', 806, reads the date as January 19, but this is unlikely. 'Mr. Sanders' is probably Thomas Collett Sandars, a barrister who contributed to *Fraser's Magazine* and the *Westminster Review*.

15. J. J. Stewart Perowne, ed., *Remains Literary and Theological of Connop Thirlwall*, 2 vols (London, 1877), 1: 308, 292, 294.

16. Ellen Williams, *The Life and Letters of Rowland Williams, D.D.*, 2 vols (London, 1874), 2: 3.

17. Terence Thomas, 'The Impact of Other Religions', in Gerald Parsons, ed., *Religion in Victorian Britain*, vol. 2: *Controversies* (Manchester, 1988), pp. 219–293. The volume won for Williams the friendship of Bunsen: Ralph A. D. Owen, *Christian Bunsen and Liberal English Theology* (Madison, WI, 1924), p. 69.

18. Connop Thirlwall, *A Letter to the Rev. Rowland Williams ... in Answer to His 'Earnestly Respectful' Letter to the Lord Bishop of St. David's* (London, 1860), p. 19.

19. Warren R. Dawson, *Charles Wycliffe Goodwin 1817–1878: A Pioneer in Egyptology* (London, 1934), p. 25.

20. Dawson, *Who Was Who in Egyptology* (London, 1951), p. 63. Goodwin also translated the travel story of Sinuhe.

21. E. G. Sandford, ed., *Memoirs of Archbishop Temple*, 2 vols (London, 1906), 1: 223.

22. Quoted in Sandford, *Temple: An Appreciation*, p. 204.

23. Quoted in Desmond Bowen, *The Idea of the Victorian Church* (Montreal, 1968), p. 179.

24. Jowett to Stanley, August 15 (1858), Balliol College, Jowett Mss.

25. Stanley to Jowett, August 16 (1858), Balliol College, Jowett Mss.

26. Jowett to Stanley, August 15 (1858), *loc. cit.*

27. Ellis, *Seven Against Christ*, pp. 51–52.

28. Hort to Williams, October 21, 1858, in Hort, *Life of Hort*, pp. 399–401.

29. Pietro Corsi, *Science and Religion: Baden Powell and the Anglican Debate, 1800–1860* (Cambridge, 1988), a superb intellectual biography. See also Michael Ruse, 'The Relationship Between Science and Religion in Britain, 1830–1870', *Church History*, 44 (December 1975): 505–522. The sons of Powell's last marriage hyphenated both his names; one was the founder of the Boy Scouts.

30. Peter Hinchliff, *Benjamin Jowett and the Christian Religion* (Oxford, 1987), p. 72. Ellis, *Seven Against Christ*, p. 51, comments more acidly on 'the haste and lack of thought in the preparation of the volume as a whole'.

31. Jowett to Stanley, March 10, 1859, Balliol College Jowett Mss.

32. 'I am glad to think that you are now really at work on the Essay ... I must still continue gently to apply the whip.' Wilson to Pattison, November 21, 1869, Bodleian Mss. Pattison 52, f. 551. Previous delays are mentioned in Wilson's letters of July 4, September 27 and October 7.

33. Pattison sent 60 pages to Parker on January 13, 'felt an enjoyable sense of deliverance' after finishing the essay on the 14th, and delivered the rest to Parker in London on the 17th. Bodleian Mss. Pattison 130, diary entries.

34. Corsi, *Science and Religion*, p. 217. Powell had time to insert references to Darwin and to Archbishop Whately's review of his *Order of Nature*.

Chapter 4

1. The 1855 *Oxford Essays* said: 'This volume ... is not intended to advocate any particular set of opinions, theological, social, or political. Each writer is responsible for his own opinions, and for none but his own; and no attempt has been made to give a general unity of thought to the publication ... in accord with the independent character of the separate contributions, the names of the writers have been affixed in the Table of Contents to the several Essays.' The 1856 *Oxford Essays* remarked: 'It may not, perhaps, be superfluous to repeat that these essays are not intended to advocate any one set of opinions, and that the writers are quite independent of one another, and wish, by affixing their names to their respective contributions, to incur each the sole responsibility of what he writes'. For the 'ambiguity and brevity' of the preface, see Ieuan Ellis, *Seven Against Christ: A Study of 'Essays and Reviews'* (Leiden, 1980), pp. 50–51.

2. Goodwin had no title; Pattison did not give his title until he became Rector of Lincoln College.

3. Wilson's correspondence with Pattison (Bodleian Library Mss. Pattison 52–53) indicates that the articles were set up in type as they were received.

4. Ernest G. Sandford, ed., *Memoirs of Archbishop Temple, by Seven Friends*, 2 vols (London, 1906), 1: 280. But Provost Hawkins of Oriel claimed to have detected heresy: Hamish F. G. Swanston, *Ideas of Order* (Assen, 1973), p. 187, n. 73.

5. Geoffrey Faber, *Jowett: A Portrait with Background* (London, 1957), p. 234.

6. Otto Pfleiderer, *The Development of Theology in Germany since Kant, and its Progress in Great Britain since 1845* (London, 1890), p. 388.

7. Arnold taught 'God's religious education of the human race, from its earliest infancy down to the fulness of times'. A. P. Stanley, *Life and Correspondence of Thomas Arnold, D.D.*, 2 vols, 3rd American edn (Boston, 1860), 1: 199 (printed from the plates of 'the last London edition'). Arnold often spoke of the 'boyhood' of mankind. The derivation from Arnold is so obvious that it has eluded all previous writers. Ellis, *Seven Against Christ*, cites F. W. Robertson's 1858 translation of Lessing.

8. Frederick Temple, 'The Education of the World', *Essays and Reviews* (London, 1860), pp. 5, 41, 43, 44, 45, 47.

9. J. J. Stewart Perowne, ed., *Remains Literary and Theological of Connop Thirlwall*, 2 vols (London, 1877), 2: 29.

10. C. C. J. Webb, *A Study of Religious Thought in England since 1850* (Oxford, 1933), p. 95.

11. David L. Edwards, *Leaders of the Church of England 1828–1944* (London, 1971), p. 292, attributes this to Temple's 'own experience of being liberated at Oxford from the over-simplicity of his mother's religion'.

12. Williams to his sister-in-law, January 8, 1870, in Ellen Williams, *The Life and Letters of Rowland Williams, D.D.* (London, 1874), 2: 366.

13. See J. W. Burrow, 'The Uses of Philology in Victorian England', in Robert Robson, ed., *Ideas and Institutions of Victorian Britain* (London, 1967), pp. 180–204.

14. The exception is John Rogerson, *Old Testament Criticism in the Nineteenth Century: England and Germany* (London, 1984), pp. 121–129.

15. Dated 1855, quoted in Williams, *Williams*, 1: 347. Also Williams to James Stephenson, December 13, 1858, *ibid.*, 407: 'although such writers as *Bunsen* have been of great aid to me, I am by no means their blind follower; and in some cases I could prove myself to have *preached* some of Bunsen's critical notions before he had published them to the world'.

16. Rowland Williams, 'Hints to my Counsel in the Court of Arches', 1862, cited in *ibid.*, 2: 54.

17. Williams, 'Bunsen's Biblical Researches', *Essays and Reviews*, p. 53.

18. *Ibid.*, p. 50. The next sentence anticipates form-criticism: 'Nor should the distinction between poetry and prose, and the possibility of imagination's allying itself with affection, be overlooked.' The anticipation is pointed out by Basil Willey, *More Nineteenth Century Studies* (London, 1956). The literary significance of this sentence, and the failure to develop its theme, is noted by James E. Reidy, *Higher Criticism in England and the Periodical Debate of the 1860s* (unpublished PhD dissertation, University of Minnesota, 1971), p. 121.

19. Williams, 'Bunsen's Biblical Researches', pp. 51, 52, 53.

20. 'He could not have vindicated the unity of mankind if he had not asked for a vast extension of time, whether his petition of twenty thousand years be granted or not. The mention of such a term may appear monstrous to those who regard six thousand years as a part of Revelation.' *Ibid.*, p. 54.

21. *Ibid.*, p. 56. This passage was acquitted by the Court of Arches in 1862.

22. *Ibid.*, pp. 60–61. This passage was condemned in 1862 and acquitted by the Privy Council in 1864. (Further references will be simply 'acquitted 1862' or 'condemned 1862'.)

23. *Ibid.*, p. 61. Condemned 1862. G. M. Young, *Victorian England: Portrait of an Age*, 2nd edn (New York, 1954), p. 181, n. 3, cites the first sentence 'to show what passed for heresy in 1861'. There were in fact two theological errors; and 'a supposed external authority' was offensive to the orthodox.

24. Williams, 'Bunsen's Biblical Researches', p. 62.
25. Williams cited Coleridge: 'Of prophecies in the sense of *prognostication* I utterly deny that there is any instance.' *Ibid.*, p. 66, n. 1. This footnote, consisting entirely of Coleridge quotations, was condemned 1862.
26. *Ibid.*, pp. 66–67. Acquitted 1862. Ewald was Bunsen's principal guide.
27. *Ibid.*, pp. 76–77. Acquitted 1862.
28. *Ibid.*, pp. 77–78. Condemned 1862. 'The written voice of the congregation' seemed to deny divine inspiration.
29. *Ibid.*, pp. 80–81. Condemned 1862. The passages on justification and propitiation gave the greatest offence. Williams regarded them as 'Bunsenian sentences', not basic to his own position. Williams, *Williams*, 2: 81.
30. Williams, 'Bunsen's Biblical Researches', p. 83. The 'verifying faculty' became central to the ensuing debate.
31. Ibid., pp. 92–93. Condemned 1862. Williams concluded with a poem of his own. A note at the end of the volume (p. 434) updated the essay with a comment on two later volumes of the *Bible for the People*. In later editions, the note was revised to notice Bunsen's death.
32. Williams, *Williams*, 2: 24.
33. See Josef L. Altholz, 'Periodical Origins and Implications of *Essays and Reviews*', *Victorian Periodicals Newsletter*, **10** (September 1977): 140–154.
34. Baden Powell, 'On the Study of the Evidences of Christianity', *Essays and Reviews*, p. 100. Powell protested against passing moral judgments on any who are not convinced by the evidences, denying that 'honest doubts evince a moral obliquity': p. 96.
35. *Ibid.*, pp. 107, 109, 115.
36. *Ibid.*, p. 120, quoting Coleridge's words about 'evidences of Christianity.'
37. *Ibid.*, pp. 127, 128.
38. *Ibid.*, p. 139. Powell saw Darwin's law of natural selection as further evidence of 'the grand principle of the self-evolving powers of nature'. He was the only Essayist to mention Darwin. This was inserted when Powell revised his proofs in January, 1860: Pietro Corsi, *Science and Religion: Baden Powell and the Anglican Debate, 1800–1860* (Cambridge, 1988), p. 217.
39. Powell, 'Evidences of Christianity', pp. 142, 143.
40. 2 Cor. 1: 24; 1 Cor. 2: 5. Powell (p. 144) modified the first passage.
41. Corsi, *Science and Religion*, p. 209.
42. It was 'the Essay which strikes most directly at the root of revealed religion'; 'by the absolute rejection of all supernatural interpositions, [it] subverts the historical basis of Christianity'. Thirlwall, *Remains*, 2: 26, 48. S. C. Carpenter, *Church and People 1789–1889* (London, 1933), p. 506, agrees; but Bernard Reardon, *From Coleridge to Gore* (London, 1971), p. 327, argues that 'the distinction … between science and religion was one which the future was to render increasingly common as the only way of securing an anchorage for faith without inhibiting the progress of knowledge'.
43. H. B. Wilson, 'Séances Historiques de Genève – The National Church', *Essays and Reviews*, p. 150.
44. *Ibid.*, p. 153. Condemned 1862.
45. *Ibid.*, pp. 157, 165, 173, 174.
46. 'Holy Scripture containeth all things necessary to salvation: so that whatever is not read therein, nor may be proved thereby, is not to be required of any man, that it should be believed as an Article of the Faith, or be thought requisite or necessary to salvation. In the name of the holy Scripture we do understand those

Canonical Books of the Old and New Testament, of whose authority was never any doubt in the Church.'

47. Wilson, 'The National Church', p. 175. Condemned 1862.
48. *Ibid.*, p. 176; included in a passage condemned 1862.
49. *Ibid.*, pp. 176–177. Acquitted 1862.
50. *Ibid.*, p. 180.
51. *Ibid.*, p. 181. Acquitted 1862. The phrase 'the strictly legal obligation is the measure of the moral one' became the focus of a controversy over the 'ethics of belief'. See James C. Livingston, *The Ethics of Belief: An Essay on the Victorian Religious Conscience* (Missoula, 1974), pp. 7ff.; Gerald Parsons, 'On Speaking Plainly: "Honest Doubt" and the Ethics of Belief', *Religion in Victorian Britain*, vol. 2: *Controversies* (Manchester, 1988), pp. 191–219; and Frank M. Turner and Jeffrey Von Arx, 'Victorian Ethics of Belief: A Reconsideration', *ibid.*, 4: *Interpretations*, pp. 198–217.
52. Wilson, 'The National Church', p. 186. Acquitted 1862.
53. *Ibid.*, pp. 188, 187.
54. *Ibid.*, p. 195. Acquitted 1862.
55. *Ibid.*, pp. 204–205. Acquitted 1862.
56. *Ibid.*, p. 206. Condemned 1862.
57. Wilson referred to Coleridge (p. 191) in connection with the 'Nationalty', the endowment of the Church.
58. Quoted in R. E. Prothero and G. G. Bradley, *The Life and Correspondence of Arthur Penrhyn Stanley, D.D., Late Dean of Westminster,* 2 vols (London, 1893), 2: 4.
59. This paragraph was Wilson's most evident heresy, but it touched an issue regarded as difficult by many. For this debate, see Geoffrey Rowell, *Hell and the Victorians: A Study of 19th-Century Theological Controversies Concerning Eternal Punishment and the Future Life* (Oxford, 1974), followed by Michael Wheeler, *Death and the Future Life in Victorian Literature and Theology* (Cambridge, 1990).
60. Wilson, 'The National Church', p. 151.
61. M. A. Crowther, *Church Embattled: Religious Controversy in Mid-Victorian England* (Newton Abbot, 1970), p. 110.
62. Ellis, *Seven Against Christ*, p. 28.
63. Charles C. Gillispie, *Genesis and Geology* (Cambridge, MA, 1951), holds that the problem was not the opposition of religion to science but the intrusion of religion into science, even by scientists.
64. C. W. Goodwin, 'Mosaic Cosmogony', *Essays and Reviews*, p. 238.
65. *Ibid.*, pp. 209, 211.
66. Specifically chapter 1 and the first three verses of chapter 2. Goodwin noted the variant second account in the rest of chapter 2.
67. Goodwin, 'Mosaic Cosmogony', p. 223.
68. The Bridgewater Treatises were eight Paleyan works by scientists in the 1830s. William Buckland wrote on geology and mineralogy. Goodwin also cited the similar argument of Archdeacon Pratt.
69. Goodwin, 'Mosaic Cosmogony', pp. 227, 252, 250, 253.
70. Willey, *More Nineteenth Century Studies*, p. 149.
71. Goodwin had not yet read *The Origin of Species*, as appears from: 'unless time can effect transmutation of species, an hypothesis not generally accepted by naturalists'. 'Mosaic Cosmogony', pp. 214–215.
72. Faber, *Jowett*, p. 244.

73. Vernon F. Storr, *The Development of English Theology in the Nineteenth Century* (London, 1913), p. 445.

74. 'It had always struck me as a surprising fact that Deism, which had been the prevailing form of thought among the educated classes in England during the first half of the eighteenth century, should have abruptly disappeared somewhere about 1760 ... the usual solution offered by the orthodox, viz. that Deism had been triumphantly refuted in argument, did not explain the fact. I attempted an original inquiry ... into the philosophic causes of the sudden rise and as sudden extinction of Deism.' Mark Pattison, *Memoirs* (London, 1885), p. 313.

75. Leslie Stephen, *History of English Thought in the Eighteenth Century*, 2 vols (London, 1876). Stephen acknowledged in his preface that Pattison's essay had suggested the 'plan' of his work, 'a more detailed and systematic account of the movement so admirably characterised in that essay'.

76. Pattison, 'Tendencies of Religious Thought in England, 1688–1750', *Essays and Reviews*, p. 255. Yngve Brilioth notes: 'It was Mark Pattison who ... first attempted to do justice to eighteenth-century theology.' *The Anglican Revival* (London, 1925), p. 21.

77. Pattison, 'Tendencies', pp. 255, 257, 262, 264. Pattison paid tribute to Coleridge for reviving theology in England (pp. 263–264).

78. *Ibid.*, pp. 297, 329.

79. Owen Chadwick, *The Victorian Church*, 2 vols (London, 1966–70), 2: 76.

80. Reardon, *From Coleridge to Gore*, pp. 247, 329. I possess Norman Sykes' copy of *Essays and Reviews*. Pattison's essay is marked up extensively, evidently for use in Sykes' work on the eighteenth-century Church.

81. Willey, *More Nineteenth-Century Studies*, p. 151.

82. Pattison 'knew exactly how to barb his shaft without danger to himself'. Faber, *Jowett*, p. 244. The suggestion that Pattison drew his fellow-authors into danger while saving himself was advanced by Mark Francis, 'The Origins of "Essays and Reviews": An Interpretation of Mark Pattison in the 1850s,' *Historical Journal*, 17 (December 1974): 797–811, but refuted by Altholz, 'Periodical Origins', and Martha S. Vogeler, 'More Light on *Essays and Reviews*: The Role of Frederic Harrison', *Victorian Periodicals Review*, 12 (Fall 1979): 105–116.

83. Tennyson is said to have 'moderated' the essay. L. E. Elliott-Binns, *Religion in the Victorian Era*, 2nd edn (London, 1964), p. 146, n. 6, citing Hallam Tennyson, *Alfred, Lord Tennyson: A Memoir*, 2 vols (London, 1897), 1: 472.

84. The phrase was used by Jowett, 'On the Interpretation of Scripture', *Essays and Reviews*, p. 387.

85. *Ibid.*, p. 338. Jowett's canon has a precedent in Bishop Lowth: 'He who would perceive the particular and interior elegancies of the Hebrew poetry, must imagine himself exactly situated as the persons for whom it was written, or even as the writers themselves; he is to feel as a Hebrew. ... we must see all things with their eyes, estimate all things by their opinions: we must endeavour as much as possible to read Hebrew as the Hebrews would have read it'. Robert Lowth, *Lectures on the Sacred Poetry of the Hebrews*, trans. G. Gregory (London, 1787; originally published 1753), 1: 114, 113. (I owe this reference to Stephen Prickett.) Curiously, Lowth was almost never cited in this debate.

86. Jowett, 'Interpretation of Scripture', pp. 340, 343, 348, 361.

87. Owen Chadwick comments: 'Sometimes ... Jowett left the reader with a helpless sense that he could not get the truth out of Scripture by any method whatever.' *Victorian Church*, 2: 77.

88. Jowett, 'Interpretation of Scripture', pp. 372, 373, 374, 375.

89. *Ibid.*, p. 377. This and the previous quotation are echoes of Coleridge.
90. Jowett, 'Interpretation of Scripture', pp. 384, 404.
91. *Ibid.*, pp. 409, 431–432, 433.
92. Faber, *Jowett*, p. 244. 'It has not dated.' Swanston, *Ideas of Order*, p. 149.
93. Willey, *More Nineteenth-Century Studies*, p. 158, speaks of Jowett's 'sanctified shrewdness' in proceeding *suaviter in modo* but *fortiter in re*.
94. James Barr, 'Jowett and the "Original Meaning" of Scripture', *Religious Studies*, **18** (1982): 434. A more favourable view of Jowett's 'process of simplication' is Peter Hinchliff, *Benjamin Jowett and the Christian Religion* (Oxford, 1987), p. 73.
95. Chadwick, *Victorian Church*, 2: 77. Others have noted that Jowett 'seems never to have resolved the conflict between his critical instincts and his religious feeling'. L. E. Elliott-Binns, *English Thought, 1860–1900: The Theological Aspect* (London, 1956), p. 126.
96. Evelyn Abbott and Lewis Campbell, *The Life and Letters of Benjamin Jowett, M.A., Master of Balliol College, Oxford*, 2 vols (London, 1897), 1: 297.
97. At this time, periodical articles were unsigned.
98. The extent of English awareness of German criticism is discussed in chapter 12 of Rogerson, *Old Testament Criticism*.
99. There are 52 references to 32 Germans, more than half by Williams (27, not counting Bunsen, *passim*). Ewald is the most frequently cited (five times by Williams). Baur is cited once by Wilson (p. 184) without praise. Strauss is cited by Wilson (p. 200) as 'an example of the critical ideology carried to excess'.
100. Wilson and Pattison were well acquainted with German thought. Powell refers to several Germans, but probably did not read them in the original.
101. Ellis, *Seven Against Christ*, pp. 285, 308.
102. '*Essays and Reviews* does not mark any advance in the critical method. Its importance lies rather in the way in which it indicated a growing tide of opinion against traditional orthodox opinions: a readiness of liberals to come out into the open.' Rogerson, *Old Testament Criticism*, p. 209.
103. An excellent alternative presentation of these themes is Chadwick, *Victorian Church*, 2: 76–77.
104. But see H. G. Wood, *Belief and Unbelief Since 1850* (Cambridge, 1955), pp. 63, 64: 'the essayists were asking for trouble … *Essays and Reviews* was an attempt to let in fresh air by breaking a window'.
105. 'The significance of *Essays and Reviews* lay in its timing.' Nigel M. de S. Cameron, *Biblical Higher Criticism and the Defense of Infallibilism in Nineteenth Century Britain* (Lewiston, NY, 1987), p. 58.
106. He edited the *Evidences* in 1859. He was a special target of Powell, responding with *Danger from Within* in 1861.

Chapter 5

1. Treated in Josef L. Altholz, 'Early Periodical Responses to *Essays and Reviews*', *Victorian Periodicals Review*, 19 (Summer 1986): 50–56.
2. *Spectator*, April 7, 1860, pp. 331–333. The reviewer was not the editor at that time, who later described *Essays and Reviews* as 'a series of very fanciful and very feeble pamphlets'. *Ibid.*, April 20, 1861, p. 417.
3. Cited in Ieuan Ellis, *Seven Against Christ: A Study of 'Essays and Reviews'* (Leiden, 1980), p. 104. The volume in the British Library was missing.

4.   *The Press*, April 21, 1860, p. 385.
5.   'The Credibility of Miracles', *Evangelical Magazine*, n.s. 3 (May 1861): 296.
6.   'Table-Talk', *Guardian*, April 4, 1860, p. 1.
7.   Letter of April 15, 1860, in Ellen Williams, *The Life and Letters of Rowland Williams, D.D.*, 2 vols (London, 1874), 2: 18.
8.   'Broad Church Theology', *Christian Observer*, 60 (May 1860): 398.
9.   'The New Essayists: Dr. Temple', *Ecclesiastic*, 22 (May 1860): 229. The article singled out Pattison for his criticism of the evidential theologians.
10. 'The New Essayists: Dr. Williams and Others', *ibid.*, 22 (June 1860): 245–260. This 'spirited article' was praised in the *Literary Churchman*, 6 (June 16, 1860): 234.
11. *Record*, May 4, 1860, Supplement.
12. 'A Member of the Presbytery of London', *ibid.*, May 21, 1860, p. 3.
13. *Ibid.*, May 21, 1860, p. 2.
14. *Guardian*, May 23, 1860, pp. 473–474. It noted (p. 474) that some Essayists embraced 'Mr. Darwin's theory of species, though it is well known that that theory, so far from being as yet substantiated by proper scientific evidence, is held to be unsound by the greatest living authority on such a point – Professor Owen'.
15. *Ibid.*, p. 475. Tait's biographers, noting that *Essays and Reviews* 'awakened at first no very absorbing interest', make an exception for this 'severe but discriminating review': Randall Davidson and William Benham, *Life of Archibald Campbell Tait, Archbishop of Canterbury*, 2 vols (London, 1891), 1: 277.
16. *Record*, June 1, 1860, p. 4.
17. *Ibid.*, June 8, 1860, p. 2. Leaders in the *Record* were probably written by the editor, Edward Garbett, who directed against the Essayists his new monthly, the *Christian Advocate*, through 1861, and his Boyle lectures, *The Bible and Its Critics* (London, 1861).
18. *Record*, June 18, 1860, p. 4. Cockin's remarks were criticized by 'Mr. Dawson (the well-known public lecturer)'. The *Record* supported Cockin.
19. It was advertised in the *Guardian* on May 30, a week after its review.
20. Joseph Barker's section of *National Reformer*, June 30, 1860, p. 4. The occasion was the death of Powell, liked for his denial of miracles. See Ellis, *Seven Against Christ*, pp. 145–146. Still more damaging was a letter, *National Reformer*, November 24, 1860, p. 7, and reviews on December 1, pp. 1–2, and December 22, pp. 1–2, implying that the Essayists endorsed free thought and repudiated the Bible.
21. 'P.S.', *Christian Remembrancer*, 40 (July 1860): 236.
22. 'Theodore Parker and the Oxford Essayists', *Christian Observer*, 60 (July 1860): 486–487. The Essayists were asked to leave the Church.
23. *Record*, July 11, 1860, p. 4. *Church of England Magazine*, 49 (July 31, 1860): 72: 'There is an able article on "Essays and Reviews", a neologian production.'
24. 'The Oxford Essayists', *London Review*, 14 (July 1860): 512, 519, 525, 527. (This was temporarily the title of the *London Quarterly Review*.) The article was reviewed, as 'Bunsen and His English Admirers', by the *Journal of Sacred Literature*, 12 (October 1860): 233–236.
25. 'The Oxford School, II', *Eclectic Review*, n.s. 4 (August 1860): 118. The first part of the article was (July 1860): 1–12. N. A. D. Scotland, '*Essays and Reviews* (1860) and the Reaction of Victorian Churches and Churchmen', *Downside Review*, 108 (April 1990): 150, notes hostile reviews in the Baptist *Freeman*, June 27, 1860, and the *Primitive Baptist Magazine* (July 1860).

26. *Inquirer,* July 7, 1860, p. 565, cited in Dennis G. Wigmore-Beddoes, *Yesterday's Radicals: A Study of the Affinity Between Unitarianism and Broad Church Anglicanism in the Nineteenth Century* (Cambridge, 1971), p. 48. Similarly, Charles Beard later noted that Jowett's essay 'embodies an undesigned justification of Unitarianism', 'Essays and Reviews – the Broad Church', *Christian Reformer,* 16 (October 1860): 598, cited, *ibid.*

27. W. D. W[atson], 'Essays and Reviews', *Fraser's Magazine,* 62 (August 1860): 228–242. (Attributions from the *Wellesley Index to Victorian Periodicals.*)

28. 'Recent Rationalism in the Church of England', *North British Review,* 33 (August 1860): 227, 252.

29. 'R. B. S.', 'Religion Without a Creed', *Christian Observer,* 60 (August 1860): 556–560.

30. *Record,* August 27, 1860, p. 2.

31. 'Dr. Temple's Place amongst the Oxford Essayists', *Christian Observer,* 60 (September 1860): 632, 636–637. The evangelical journals stressed the Oxford character of the Essayists (though two were Cambridge men).

32. *Record,* September 3, 1860, p. 2.

33. [H. B. Wilson], 'Contemporary Literature: Theology and Philosophy', *Westminster Review,* n.s. 18 (July 1860): 225–228; see next chapter.

34. *Record,* September 12, 1860, p. 4; September 14, 1860, p. 4. These drew a pained letter from T. D. H. Battersby, *ibid.,* October 5, 1860, p. 4. The editor refused to apologize. The *Record* later began a side-controversy on Bunsen's allegedly edifying death on November 28, which eventually forced the Evangelical Alliance to rescind its condolences to Bunsen's family.

35. *Record,* September 21, 1860, p. 4.

36. *Ibid.,* September 28, 1860, p. 4.

37. *Ibid.,* October 3, 1860, p. 4; October 10, 1860, p. 4. Also, 'The Oxford Essayists and the Thirty-Nine Articles', November 9, 1860, p. 4; a leader, November 26, 1860, p. 2; another, December 10, 1860, p. 2; the end-of-year leader, December 31, 1860, p. 2, and the first article by Alexander McCaul, *ibid.,* p. 3.

38. 'Essays and Reviews', *Christian Remembrancer,* 40 (October 1860): 351, 353.

Chapter 6

1. Perhaps the most celebrated and misleading account of the subject is the chapter 'Septem contra Christum' in Basil Willey, *More Nineteenth Century Studies: A Group of Honest Doubters* (London, 1956).

2. [H. B. Wilson], 'Contemporary Literature: Theology and Philosophy', *Westminster Review,* n.s. 18 (July 1860): 225–228.

3. Frederic Harrison, *The Creed of a Layman* (London, 1907), p. 28. Newman is identified by Martha S. Vogeler, 'More Light on *Essays and Reviews*: The Role of Frederic Harrison', *Victorian Periodicals Review,* 12 (Fall 1979): 105–116. See also Vogeler, *Frederic Harrison: The Vocations of a Positivist* (Oxford, 1984).

4. Harrison, *Creed of a Layman,* pp. 27, 30n.

5. [Harrison], 'Neo-Christianity', *Westminster Review,* n.s. 18 (October 1860): 293.

6. *Ibid.,* pp. 294, 295, 299.

7. *Ibid.,* pp. 300, 303, 304–305.

8. *Ibid.,* pp. 316, 322, 323.

9. 'What becomes of the Christian scheme when the origin of man is handed over to Mr. Darwin ...?' *Ibid.,* p. 326.

10. *Ibid.*, pp. 328, 329, 330.
11. *Ibid.*, pp. 331, 332. For a different reading of this article, see Christopher A. Kent, 'Higher Journalism and the Promotion of Comtism', *Victorian Periodicals Review,* 25 (Summer 1992): 52.
12. A. P. Stanley, *Essays chiefly on questions of Church and State from 1850 to 1870,* new edn (London, 1884; orig. 1870), p. 37n.
13. See Vogeler, 'More Light', pp. 110–113, and Evelyn Abbott and Lewis Campbell, eds, *Letters of Benjamin Jowett, M.A., Master of Balliol College, Oxford* (London, 1899), pp. 14–16.
14. Pusey had called Wilberforce's attention to the article on October 31, 1860: H. P. Liddon, *Life of Edward Bouverie Pusey,* 4 vols (London, 1898), 4: 16.
15. Conclusion of Wilberforce's Charge, *Guardian*, November 21, 1860, p. 1020.
16. [Samuel Wilberforce], 'Essays and Reviews', *Quarterly Review,* 109 (January 1861): 249–250.
17. *Ibid.*, pp. 250, 251. Wilberforce hoped that Temple would separate himself from the others.
18. *Ibid.*, pp. 255, 256, 258, 260, 269.
19. *Ibid.*, pp. 270, 272, 273.
20. *Ibid.*, pp. 274, 275, 277, 281–282.
21. *Ibid.*, p. 284, citing *National Reformer,* November 24, 1860.
22. Wilberforce, 'Essays and Reviews', pp. 286, 287, 290.
23. *Ibid.*, pp. 293, 294, 299.
24. *Ibid.*, pp. 302, 303, 304, 305.
25. A. R. Ashwell and Reginald G. Wilberforce, *Life of the Right Reverend Samuel Wilberforce, D.D.* (New York, 1883), p. 313. Wilberforce was paid 100 guineas: p. 321.
26. [Arthur Penrhyn Stanley], 'Essays and Reviews', *Edinburgh Review,* 113 (April 1861): 461.
27. *Ibid.*, p. 464. Harrison complained to Stanley about these personal remarks, and Stanley deleted them when he republished the article.
28. *Ibid.*, pp. 465, 466, 469. The episcopal letter and Convocation had supervened between the two articles; see the next chapter.
29. *Ibid.*, pp. 471, 472, 473, 474.
30. *Ibid.*, pp. 475, 476.
31. *Ibid.*, pp. 477, 478, 479.
32. *Ibid.*, pp. 479, 480, 482, 483, 485, 486.
33. *Ibid.*, pp. 489, 490, 491, 492, 494.
34. *Ibid.*, pp. 496, 497, 498, 499. Stanley ended with a quotation from Jowett's essay.
35. Stanley to Henry Reeve, editor of the *Edinburgh*, cited in Rowland E. Prothero and G. G. Bradley, *The Life and Correspondence of Arthur Penrhyn Stanley, Late Dean of Westminster,* 2 vols (New York, 1894; orig. London, 1893), 2: 33–34.
36. See the Tait–Stanley correspondence in Randall Davidson and William Benham, *Life of Archibald Campbell Tait, Archbishop of Canterbury,* 2 vols (London, 1891), 1: 284–287, 308–312.
37. 'Stanley has written an article in the *Edinburgh* trying to bring off his friends Dr. Temple and Jowett, and to drop Wilson and myself in the mud, particularly poor me.' Williams, April 27, 1861, quoted by Ellen Williams, *The Life and Letters of Rowland Williams, D.D.,* 2 vols (London, 1874), 2: 39.
38. *Guardian*, May 15, 1861, p. 475; inexactly cited by Ieuan Ellis, *Seven Against Christ: A Study of 'Essays and Reviews'* (Leiden, 1980), p. 112n. Yet Ellis' treatment of the essay (pp. 111–114) is worthy of note.

39. Merle M. Bevington, *The Saturday Review 1855–1868* (New York, 1941), pp. 28–30.
40. Prothero and Bradley, *Stanley*, 2: 41.
41. Willey, *More Nineteenth-Century Studies*, p. 171. A. O. J. Cockshut describes it better as 'a partial and apologetic defence': *Anglican Attitudes: A Study of Victorian Religious Controversy* (London, 1959), p. 72.
42. 'Dizzy to the Rescue', *Punch*, December 29, 1860, p. 253.
43. 'Abuse for Argument', *Punch*, March 9, 1861, p. 105. The allusion was to Sidgwick's letter to *The Times*.

Chapter 7

1. Liddon to Keble, March 31 and 'Easter Tuesday', 1860, in John O. Johnston, *Life and Letters of Henry Parry Liddon* (London, 1904), pp. 63, 64.
2. In 1859 Hamilton told Williams that he had taken legal advice as to whether he could safely refuse Williams' institution to the vicarage of Broad Chalke; evidently he had been advised against it. Ellen Williams, *The Life and Letters of Rowland Williams, D.D.*, 2 vols (London, 1874), 1: 387.
3. *Remains Literary and Theological of Connop Thirlwall*, ed. J. J. Stewart Perowne, 2 vols (London, 1877), 1: 349.
4. Pusey to Wilberforce, October 31, 1860, quoted in H. P. Liddon, *Life of Edward Bouverie Pusey*, 4 vols (London, 1898), 4: 16.
5. Letter of 'B. A. Cantab.', 'The Bishop of Winchester on Essays and Reviews', *Guardian*, January 2, 1861, p. 7.
6. See Josef L. Altholz, 'Publishing History of *Essays and Reviews*', *Notes and Queries*, n.s. 29 (August 1982): 312–313. Pattison's records show that he received £304 10s. 3d. for his share of the authors' profits from Longmans in 1861, considerably more than he would have been paid for a similar article in a periodical. He received a further £74 11s. in 1862–64. This gives over £2673 for the authors' total profits and over £1326 for Longmans. The individual returns from Parker's three editions appear to have been about £36. Figures for the final edition are not available, and some payment may have been made by Tauchnitz for a European edition; but we may estimate the total return to each author at about £430.
7. Müller was liberal but not heterodox, as Pusey had discovered by interviewing him. Pusey endorsed him, but could not control his followers, including Liddon. Pusey to Keble, September 17, [1860], Pusey House.
8. M. A. Crowther, *Church Embattled: Religious Controversy in Mid-Victorian England* (Newton Abbot, 1970), p. 65.
9. *To the Most Reverend Father in God, John Bird, Archbishop of Canterbury, Primate of All England and Metropolitan* (undated copy in British Library). The words in quotation marks are from the service of consecration of bishops.
10. *Record*, January 30, 1861, p. 4. There were 326 signatures.
11. *Guardian*, January 30, 1861, p. 102; see also *Record*, January 28, 1861, p. 2.
12. Letter of H. B. Williams, rural dean, *Guardian*, February 20, 1860, p. 166.
13. Thirlwall to Stanley, July 11, 1870, in Connop Thirlwall, *Letters Literary and Theological*, ed. J. J. S. Perowne and L. Stokes (London, 1881), p. 237.
14. Randall Davidson and William Benham, *Life of Archibald Campbell Tait, Archbishop of Canterbury*, 2 vols (London, 1891), 1: 283n. The meetings were confidential, and Wilberforce had made this notation on his memoranda.

15. A. R. Ashwell and Reginald G. Wilberforce, *Life of the Right Reverend Samuel Wilberforce, D.D.*, 3 vols, 2nd edn (London, 1883), 3: 2–4.

16. See the letters to Tait, February 4, 1861, in Lambeth Palace Library, Tait Mss., vol. 80.

17. Ieuan Ellis, *Seven Against Christ: A Study of 'Essays and Reviews'* (Leiden, 1980), p. 165. Philpotts thought the letter was not strong enough.

18. He later stated that he would have signed. *Guardian*, May 15, 1861, p. 458.

19. Quoted in Ellis, *Seven Against Christ*, p. 166.

20. *The Times*, February 16, 1861, p. 10. Fremantle's letter is dated February 13; the episcopal letter is dated February 12.

21. Tait corrected this in a letter to the *Times*, February 19, 1861, p. 3.

22. See Hamish F. G. Swanston, *Ideas of Order* (Assen, 1973), pp. 186–187.

23. G. M. Young, *Victorian England: Portrait of an Age*, 2nd edn (New York, 1954), p. 181. Young spoke of 'that marmoreal intellect'; *ibid.*, p. 114.

24. John Connop Thirlwall, Jr., *Connop Thirlwall, Historian and Theologian* (London, 1936), p. 228.

25. Thirlwall to Thomas Keightley, February 27, 1861, in Thirlwall, *Letters Literary and Theological*, pp. 235–236.

26. Davidson, *Life of Tait*, 1: 281, quoting Tait's journal, January 20, 1861.

27. Jowett to Stanley, n.d., Balliol College Jowett Mss.

28. Temple to Tait, February 25, 1861, in Davidson, *Life of Tait*, 1: 290–293. The entire correspondence is *ibid.*, 1: 288–301.

29. Tait to Temple, February 27, 1861, *ibid.*, 1: 296. See also *The Times*, March 4, 1861, p. 10, for Temple's correspondence with Bishop Philpotts of Exeter.

30. Temple to Wilberforce, February 6, 1861, Bodleian Library Mss. Wilberforce c. 13; Temple to Scott, February 12, 1861, in E.G. Sandford, *Frederick Temple. An Appreciation* (London, 1907), pp. 214–215.

31. Temple to Scott, n.d., *ibid.*, p. 210. The danger ended in early May: Earl of Denbigh to Tait, May 3, 1861, Lambeth Palace Library, Tait Mss., vol. 80.

32. David L. Edwards, *Leaders of the Church of England 1828–1944* (London, 1971), p. 292. For similar difficulties involving E. W. Benson, master of Wellington College, see Alec R. Vidler, *The Church in an Age of Revolution* (London, 1961), p. 123.

33. E. G. Sandford, ed., *Memoirs of Archbishop Temple, by Seven Friends*, 2 vols (London, 1906), 1: 220 and n. 3, 223–225.

34. Stanley to Tait, February 19, 1861, in Davidson, *Life of Tait*, 1: 286.

35. The entire correspondence is in *ibid.*, 1: 284–310.

36. Prothero and Bradley, *Life of Stanley*, 2: 37.

37. 'Anglicanus', 'The Episcopal Manifesto', *The Times*, February 18, 1861, p. 12.

38. 'A Cambridge Graduate', *The Times*, February 20, 1861, p. 12. This was a protest from Cambridge, where the theological environment was less heated than in Oxford. Sidgwick specifically quoted Westcott: 'they love their early faith, but they love truth more'.

39. Leading article, *Record*, February 18, 1861, p. 2. See also *Guardian*, February 20, 1861, p. 161.

40. *Record*, March 1, 1861, p. 2.

41. Jelf had taken a leading part in Maurice's dismissal from King's College. He had presided over a meeting of clergy in January which unanimously voted against 'any joint or concerted action ... being persuaded that the answer to them will be better left to individual Scholars and Divines'. Jelf to Tait, January 30, 1861, Lambeth Palace Library, Tait Mss., vol. 80. But by February 8 Jowett knew that Jelf would make his motion: Ellis, *Seven Against Christ*, p. 165.

42. R. W. Jelf, *Specific Evidences of Unsoundness in the Volume Entitled 'Essays and Reviews'* (Oxford, 1861), p. 2, a republication of his speech and its appendix.

43. The debate is in *Guardian*, February 27, 1861, pp. 188–195, probably the best record, and also in the clerical *Hansard, Chronicle of Convocation*, 1861, pp. 364–413.

44. George Anthony Denison, *Notes of My Life, 1805–1878* (Oxford, 1878), p. 290. Denison held that 'Spiritual censure, the authority exercising, the manner of its exercise, are among the first principles of the Faith of Christ': *ibid.*, p. 288. His fondness for censure may seem surprising in view of his own earlier condemnation for preaching the Real Presence, from which he escaped on a legal technicality.

45. *Guardian*, March 6, 1861, pp. 230–232.

46. Davidson, *Life of Tait*, 1: 204; Geoffrey Faber, *Jowett: A Portrait with Background* (London, 1957), p. 262.

47. A. C. [Tait], *The Dangers and Safeguards of Modern Theology* (London, 1861), pp. 3, 5, 19, 21, 22.

48. Tait's diary, March 7, 1861, in Davidson, *Life of Tait*, 1: 307.

49. *Guardian*, March 13, 1861, quoted in Ellis, *Seven Against Christ*, p. 173. Sumner also spoke out in April by republishing his *Evidence of Christianity* with a preface and appendices directed against *Essays and Reviews*.

50. Bodleian Library Mss. Wilberforce, c. 13. Although these notes are marked 'Destroy', a summary of the discussion was printed in Ashwell and Wilberforce, *Life of Wilberforce*, 1: 316.

51. *Guardian*, March 20, 1861, p. 283.

52. *Ibid.*, pp. 281–283.

53. *Ibid.*, p. 287.

54. 'The man who moves for the Committee is the proper Chairman of it': Denison, *Notes of My Life*, p. 292.

55. 'The thing to be done with a view to avoiding desultory and confused proceedings in Committee is that the Chairman should be ready with a draft Report ... It was too strong and decided for a good many members': *ibid.*, pp. 292–293. Denison published it as *Analysis of 'Essays and Reviews'* (London, 1861), which was praised by 'my dear, kind friend Dr. McCaul'. The two struck up a personal friendship which transcended their party differences.

56. *Record*, March 25, 1861, p. 2. The direct statement of the evidential apologetic is noteworthy.

57. *Record*, May 3, 1861, Supplement.

58. Leading article, *Record*, May 8, 1861, p. 2.

59. Thirlwall, *Thirlwall*, pp. 229–231.

60. *'Essays and Reviews' Anticipated* (London, 1861). Editorial comment in Thirlwall, *Letters Literary*, p. 234. Eliot's biographer, Gordon Haight, does not mention the pamphlet. It was published by Mainwaring, who had succeeded to Chapman's publishing business.

61. *Spectator*, April 20, 1861, quoted in Thirlwall, *Thirlwall*, p. 229.

62. Crowther, *Church Embattled*, p. 121; Ellis, *Seven Against Christ*, p. 178.

63. H. B. Wilson, *Three Sermons composed for the opening of a new organ at St. Chrysostom's Church, Everton* (London, 1861).

64. *Guardian*, May 29, 1861, p. 502. The *Guardian* (p. 497) expressed its regret at this action, and cited the *Standard* as also regretting it.

65. *Guardian*, June 19, 1861, pp. 581–582, cited in Ellis, *Seven Against Christ*, p. 175.

66.   *Guardian*, June 19, 1861, pp. 570–571.

67.   *Guardian*, June 26, 1861, pp. 604–611.

68.   Faber, *Jowett*, p. 249. For the All Souls case, see the article on the college in the *Victoria County History* of Oxford, vol. 5.

69.   This was no mere excuse. Bishop Phillpotts had warned that action might disqualify the bishops in a legal case, allowing the defendants to escape judgment. Phillpotts to Wilberforce, March 14, [1861], Bodleian Library Mss. Wilberforce c. 5.

70.   *Guardian*, July 10, 1861, p. 647.

71.   Faber, *Jowett*, p. 249, is wrong on this point.

72.   Wilberforce to Alfred Ollivant, July 3, 1861, in R. K. Pugh, ed., *The Letter-Books of Samuel Wilberforce* (Oxfordshire Record Society XLVII, 1970), p. 655.

73.   Denison, *Notes of My Life*, pp. 295–297.

74.   *Spectator*, November 16, 1861, p. 1250; *Guardian*, November 20, 1861, p. 1065. *Punch*, November 23, 1861, p. 203, satirized the speech as 'St. Disraeli to the Rescue'.

Chapter 8

1.   The printed date of most pamphlets is 1861, but it is possible to date most of them to the approximate month. Occasionally there is internal evidence. Copies in the British Library have the date of receipt stamped on the last printed page; this is generally a month or two after publication. *Termini a quo* are supplied by reviews in journals which regularly followed the literature, such as the *Literary Churchman*. The term 'pamphlets' is used to cover the entire range of publications including tracts, published sermons or lectures, and books.

2.   Steuart Adolphus Pears, *The Weapons of our Warfare* (London, 1860).

3.   William Gresley, *Idealism Considered, chiefly with reference to a volume of 'Essays and Reviews' lately published* (London, 1860), pp. 40, 28. The date of acquisition by the British Library is October 10.

4.   George Moberly, *Sermons on the Beatitudes ... to which is added a Preface relating to the recent volume of 'Essays and Reviews'* (Oxford, 1860). Moberly published his preface as a separate pamphlet: *Remarks on 'Essays and Reviews': Being the Revised Preface to the 2nd Edition of 'Sermons on the Beatitudes'* (Oxford, 1861).

5.   John H. Pratt, *Scripture and Science not at Variance*, 4th edn (London, 1861), 'with additional illustrations from Bunsen, Homer, Darwin and Goodwin'.

6.   John Bird Sumner, *Evidence of Christianity, derived from its nature and reception*, new edn (London, 1861).

7.   A. M'Caul [sic], *Rationalism and Deistic Infidelity: Three Letters to the editor of 'The Record' newspaper* (London, 1861).

8.   A. M'Caul, *Some Notes on the First Chapter of Genesis, with reference to statements in 'Essays and Reviews'* (London, 1861).

9.   Charles Girdlestone, *Negative Theology an Argument for Liturgical Revision* (London, 1861), followed by the anonymous *The Further Revision of the Liturgy, with a reference to the Clergy, 'Essays and Reviews', etc., etc.* (London, 1861).

10.   Charles Hebert, *Neology Not True, and Truth Not New: three short treatises concerning the Rev. F. D. Maurice's Vere St. Sermons, the Rev. Prof. Jowett's doctrine on 'The Righteousness of God', the Rev. J. L. Davies' reply to 'Atonement by Propitiation', with that treatise also, and a summary of the atonement controversy*, 3rd edn, *with a post script, and a concise account of the 'Essays and Reviews'* (London, 1861).

11.   John Cumming and R. P. Blakeney, *Modern Infidelity and Rationalism exposed and refuted, in answer to the Essays and Reviews* (London, 1861), pp. iii–iv. For the Protestant Reformation Society, see John Wolffe, *The Protestant Crusade in Great Britain, 1829–1860* (Oxford, 1991).

12.   Because they were separately published, the titles must be given (all London, 1861): *The Atonement, in its twofold aspect, toward English 'Essays and Reviews' and Romish 'Decrees and Canons'; The Bible: as treated by the Essayists and Reviewers; Precious Truths persecuted by the Essayists and Reviewers; Mosaic Cosmogony. A Vindication of the Scripture Narrative, in answer to Mr. Goodwin in his essay on the above subject* (in two parts); *Scripture Miracles Vindicated, in answer to Mr. Powell in his essay on the above subject* (in two parts); *Scripture Prophecies Vindicated, in answer to Mr. Williams in his review on the above subject* (in two parts); *Scripture and Chronology, Egyptology, Glottology, and Ethnology, etc. In answer to Mr. Williams in his review on the above subjects; Scripture Interpretation and Inspiration Considered, in answer to Mr. Jowett in his essay on the above subject* (in two parts); *The Theology of the Church of England vindicated, in answer to Mr. Wilson in his essay on the above subject; The Education of the World, Dr. Temple's Essay on, considered. With some notice of Mr. Pattison; The Right Way, and a way which seemeth right; or, a warning to Essayists and Reviewers; The Ground of Glorying: or, The Gospel not negative religion* (not expressly controversial).

13.   In order of delivery, [R. J. Eden], *The Charge of the Right Hon. the Bishop of Bath and Wells* (London, 1861); Richard Whately, *Danger from Within* (London, 1861); Walter Kerr [Hamilton], *A Charge ...* (Salisbury, 1861); Samuel Waldegrave (of Carlisle), *The Charge ...* (London, 1861); Robert [Bickersteth, of Ripon], *A Charge ...* (London, 1861); John Jackson (of Lincoln), *A Charge ...* (London, 1861). This last caused a stir by blaming rationalism on a reaction against High Church excesses, 'substituting credulity for reason' (p. 42). Baring of Durham and Longley of York also charged against the Essays but apparently did not publish.

14.   Edward Bickersteth, *A Charge ...* (London, 1861).

15.   R. W. Jelf, *Specific Evidence of Unsoundness in the Volume entitled 'Essays and Reviews'* (Oxford, 1861), and George Anthony Denison, *Analysis of 'Essays and Reviews'* (London, 1861).

16.   G. W. Dalton, *Notes on Neology. An Appeal to Antiquity on behalf of the authenticity of Holy Scripture, as against the Oxford 'Essays and Reviews'* (Dublin, 1861).

17.   Cyprian T. Rust, *'Essays and Reviews'. A Lecture delivered before the Norwich Church of England Young Men's Society, March 18, 1861* (London, 1861), and Charles Bullock, *'Essays and Reviews'. The False Position of the Authors: An appeal to the Bible and the Prayer Book. A lecture* (London, 1861). As the latter meeting was organized by the speaker, the 'request' may not have been spontaneous.

18.   B. M. Cowie, *An Address on the Chief Points of Controversy between Orthodoxy and Rationalism* (London, 1861), pp. 17, 21, 29. Tait was present in the audience and suggested amendments before publication. *Record*, March 27, 1861, p. 3.

19.   Edward Garbett, *The Bible and its Critics: An enquiry into the objective reality of revealed truths. Being the Boyle Lectures for MDCCCLXI* (London, 1861), pp. 361, 390.

20.   T. Loughnan, *'Essays and Reviews'. An Answer to certain Statements in the essay entitled 'On the Study of the Evidences of Christianity'* (London, 1861); Julius Lloyd, *Abraham's Faith. A Sermon on present controversies* (Wolverhampton, 1861).

21.   Daniel Wilson, *The Inspired Scriptures, not man's 'verifying faculty', the final ground of appeal in matters of faith* (London, 1861); James Booth, *The Bible and*

its Interpreters, three sermons (London, 1861); Charles Forster, *Spinoza Redivivus* (London, 1861); William Tait, *Inspiration and Justification* (London, 1861); Archibald Weir, *Revelation and Belief: A Word of Counsel to the Laity on the Present Theological Crisis* (Enfield, 1861).

22. Moses Margoliouth, *The End of the Law* (London, 1861).

23. Christopher Wordsworth, *The Inspiration of the Bible* (London, 1861), p. 4.

24. Wordsworth, *The Interpretation of the Bible* (London, 1861), p. 28.

25. Charles A. Heurtley, *The Inspiration of Holy Scripture. Constancy in Prayer* (Oxford, 1861).

26. Edward Hawkins, *The Province of Private Judgment and the Right Conduct of Religious Inquiry* (Oxford, 1861), p. 26.

27. Osborne Gordon, *A Sermon …* (Oxford, 1861); Edward H. Plumptre, *Dangers Past and Present* (Oxford, 1861). The latter acknowledged that there had been concealment and partisanship: 'We substitute the negation of a denial for the assertion of truth' (p. 20).

28. Samuel Wilberforce, *The Revelation of God the Probation of Man* (Oxford, 1861), pp. 32, 35, 40. See Standish Meacham, *Lord Bishop: The Life of Samuel Wilberforce* (Cambridge, MA, 1970), pp. 225–229.

29. 'A Layman' [Goldwin Smith], *The Suppression of Doubt is not Faith* (Oxford, 1861), pp. 9, 10, 12.

30. 'A Clergyman' [Richard St. John Tyrwhitt], *Concerning Doubt* (Oxford, 1861). Another, less temperate, reaction to Smith was *A Reply to the letter entitled 'The Suppression of Doubt is not Faith'* by One who doubts not, but fully believes that the Bible is the Word of God (Oxford, 1861).

31. 'A Layman', *Concerning Doubt. A Reply to 'a Clergyman'* (Oxford, 1861), p. 6.

32. John William Burgon, *Inspiration and Interpretation: seven sermons preached before the University of Oxford: with preliminary remarks: being an answer to a volume entitled 'Essays and Reviews'* (Oxford, 1861), pp. 76, 94.

33. *Ibid.*, pp. x, xxvi, xxvii of the preface.

34. *Ibid.*, pp. xix, xxviii, xliv, lxxx, ccx, lxx of the preliminary remarks. Burgon is treated as Jowett's counterpart by Nigel M. de S. Cameron, *Biblical Higher Criticism and the Defense of Infallibilism in 19th Century Britain* (Lewiston, NY, 1987), pp. 127–129. Thomas Carlyle also used the military metaphor: a sentry who deserts his post should be shot.

35. *Literary Churchman*, 7 (December 16, 1861): 468–469; *Ecclesiastic*, 23 (November 1861): 505, 508; *Guardian*, October 23, 1861, p. 974.

36. Charles Hume, *A Letter to a Friend on the Essays and Reviews* (London, 1861); 'Presbyter Septuagenarius', *Danger to the Bible from Licentious Criticism: Letters to Sons in the Universities* (London, 1861); William Sewell, *A Letter on the Inspiration of Holy Scripture, addressed to a student* (Oxford, 1861).

37. E. B. Pusey, *A Letter on the 'Essays and Reviews'* (London, 1861), reprinted from the *Guardian*; *Guardian*, March 6, 1861, pp. 214–215. Heurtley also declined to answer: 'the *errors* which the book contains have been refuted again and again. There are no new errors'. *Ibid.*, p. 215.

38. John Cairns, *Oxford Rationalism and English Christianity* (London, [1861]).

39. [W. J. Irons], *The Reviewers Reviewed and the Essayists Criticized: An Analysis and Confutation of each of the Seven 'Essays and Reviews'* (Oxford, 1861).

40. 'An American Layman', *A Critical Examination of the 'Essays and Reviews'*, edited by the Dean of Carlisle (London, 1861). A pirated edition of *Essays and Reviews* had been published by a Unitarian minister, Frederick H. Hodge, as *Recent Inquiries in Theology*. It was reviewed by several American journals; see Ieuan

Ellis, *Seven Against Christ: A Study of 'Essays and Reviews'* (Leiden, 1980), p. 140. Ellis also discusses German and French reviews.

41. *The 'Essays and Reviews' and the People of England. A popular refutation of the principal propositions of the essayists ...* (London, 1861); *'Another Gospel' Examined; or a Popular Criticism of each of the seven 'Essays and Reviews'* (London, 1861).

42. *Things That I Doubt:* dedicated to the authors of 'Essays and Reviews' by A Doubting Disciple (Oxford, 1861); 'Expectans', *The Grievance and the Remedy. An Essay in Verse ... concerning 'Essays and Reviews'* (London, 1861).

43. [Frances] Dowager Lady Shelley, *Thoughts on the Doubts of the Day* (London, 1861), mostly concerned with the 'development theory'; Henry Harris, *Scepticism and Revelation* (Oxford, 1861); Lord Lindsay, *Scepticism a Retrograde Movement in Theology and Philosophy* (London, 1861), part of a larger scheme of philosophy.

44. James Challis, *Creation in Plan and in Progress* (Cambridge, 1861); *The Witness of Prophecy* (Weston-super-Mare, 1861). The latter may have been by a dissenter.

45. Edward Hoare, *Inspiration: Its Nature and Extent* (London, 1861); John C. Miller, *Bible Inspiration Vindicated: An Essay on 'Essays and Reviews'* (Oxford, 1861); Henry Miller, *The Question of Inspiration Plainly Stated, in reference to certain views put forth by the authors of the book termed 'Essays and Reviews'* (Oxford, 1861), the dissentient.

46. Edward Girdlestone, *Remarks on 'Essays and Reviews'* (London, 1861); [F. O. Giffard], *Worn-out Neology; or, brief strictures upon the Oxford Essays and Reviews. By the author of the Hartley Wintney Tracts* (Basingstoke, [1861]); C. S. Absolom, *The Authors of Essays and Reviews judged out of their own mouth* (London, 1861), and *Jesus Christ and the Authors of Essays and Reviews Contrasted in their estimate of Scripture* (London, 1861).

47. *Must we Burn our Bibles? A few honest words about the 'Essays and Reviews'; addressed to honest people, by an Honest Man* (Bristol, 1861); [James Taylor, of Bakewell], *The 'Essays and Reviews' Examined, on the Principles of Common Sense ... by one who wishes to ascertain what is the 'True Faith of a Christian'* (London, 1861).

48. *Catholicity and Reason: A few considerations on 'Essays and Reviews'* (London, 1861); Henry Arthur Woodgate, *'Essays and Reviews' Considered in relation to the current principles and fallacies of the day* (London, 1861).

49. William Smith Burnside, *The Lex Evangelica: or, Essay, for the Times, proving that Holy Scripture is the only infallible interpreter to reason, in search after religious truth. Being a reply to a recent publication entitled 'Essays and Reviews'* (Dublin, 1861).

50. In probable chronological order, Robert Jermyn Cooper, *A Brief Defence of the Bible against the attacks of Rationalistic Infidelity: An Inquiry in reference to certain 'rationalist' opinions, especially those contained in the volume 'Essays and Reviews'* (London, 1861); *A Reply to the 'Essays and Reviews': or Christianity vindicated from the sceptical attacks of the Septem Contra Christum* by an M.A. of Cambridge (Cambridge, 1861); Charles F. R. Baylay, *Essays and Reviews compared with Reason and Revelation* (London, 1861); T. Collyns Simon, *An Answer to the Essays and Reviews* (London, 1861); John FitzGerald, *What is the Faith of the Essayists and Reviewers?* (London, 1861); *An Answer to the 'Essays and Reviews'. Showing the fallacy in believing the Scriptures are not written by divine inspiration. Also, proving the truth of their position in the final restitution of man* (London, 1862), actually 1861 (received by the British Museum 26 December 1861), unusual in agreeing

with Wilson on eternal punishment; [T. F. Cruise], *Letter to a Rural Dean on Neology* (Hastings, 1861).

51. C. H. Davis, *Anti-Essays: The 'Essays and Reviews' of 1860 Fallacious and Futile, 'at variance with each other and mutually destructive'* (Nailsworth, 1861), seven tracts bound together but published separately over five months, entitled *Preface and Introduction; Dr. Temple's Essay; Dr. Rowland Williams's Essay; The Late Rev. B. Powell's Essay; Mr. Wilson's Essay* (begun in the previous); *Mr. C. W. Goodwin's Essay; The Rev. Mr. Pattison's Essay and The Rev. B. Jowett's Essay. Theological Tracts for the Times* (London, 1861), five tracts: *The World at School; Miracles; The Historical Veracity of the Bible; The Supernatural in Christianity; Biblical Interpretations;* a further tract on *Prophecy* was separately published. John Howe Snell, *What is the End? or Observations on the Temple-Jowett Essays and Reviews,* no. 1 (London, 1861), seems to have been intended as the first of a series. Another series, begun in 1861, consisted of separately titled pamphlets by Charles Gooch: *Examination of Dr. Temple's Essay on the Education of the World* (London, 1861); *Examination of the Late Professor Powell's Essay on the Study of the Evidences of Christianity* (London, 1861); *Examination of Dr. R. Williams's Review of Biblical Researches* (London, 1861); *Record of Creation, considered in an Examination of Mr. Goodwin's Essay on Mosaic Cosmogony* (Cambridge, 1862); *Remarks on the Grounds of Faith suggested by Mr. Pattison's Essay on the Tendencies of Religious Thought* (Cambridge, 1862); *Interpretation of Scripture* (London, 1863).

52. I have discussed this common argument at length in 'The Mind of Victorian Orthodoxy: Anglican Responses to *Essays and Reviews*', *Church History,* 51 (June 1982): 186–197, reprinted in Gerald Parsons, ed., *Religion in Victorian Britain,* vol. 4: *Interpretations* (Manchester, 1988), pp. 28–40.

53. E. W. Hengstenberg was the leader of a reaction against advanced criticism temporarily prevailing in Germany.

54. W. H. Parker, *Brief Remarks on the Rev. Dr. Temple's Essay, on the 'Education of the World'* (London, [1861]), described as 'A New Edition'; *Challenge to Dr. Temple, in a Letter from a Godfather, on the subject of his Essay, 'The Education of the World'. By a Clergyman* (Huntingdon, [1861]), signed 'H. M.' 'A Working Man', *An Answer to Frederick Temple's Essay on 'The Education of the World'* (Oxford, 1861), dated 'Burford, May 4' and written by no working man; E. H. Hansell, *Notes on the first essay in the series called "Essays and Reviews"* (London, 1861); R. Blakelock, *Observations on the Rev. Dr. Temple's Essay on the Education of the World* (London, [1861]); C. S. Absolom, *Dr. Temple's Essay Examined* (London, [1861]); and belatedly Franke Parker, *A Light thrown upon Thucydides, to illustrate the prophecy of Daniel as to the coming of the Messiah ... to which is added, a review of Dr. Temple's essay on the Education of the World* (London, 1865).

55. Edward Henry Carr, *Of Miracles.* An argument in reply to the 3rd of the 'Essays and Reviews', being a lecture delivered in Trinity Chapel, Conduit St, Hanover Sq., March 14th, 1861 (London, 1861); C. P. Reichel, *The Christian Miracles: A Sermon Preached in St. George's Church, Belfast ... on April 21, 1861, in answer to the Rev. Baden Powell's contribution to 'Essays and Reviews'* (London, 1861); 'A. V.', *'Essays and Reviews'. Thoughts on Miracles, suggested by the late Rev. Baden Powell's 'Essay on the Study of the Evidences of Christianity'* (London, [1861]); W. Anderson O'Connor, *Miracles Not Antecedently Incredible. An Examination of Professor Powell's Argument in 'Essays and Reviews'* (Oxford, 1861); *Essays and Reviews. Examination of Mr. Baden Powell's Tractate on Miracles* (Dublin, 1861), reprinted from the *Christian Examiner;* [G. H. Forbes], *No antecedent Impossibility in Miracles. Some Remarks on the Essay of the late Rev. Baden Powell, and J. S. Mill* (Dublin, 1863).

56. Aside from Archdeacon Pratt's 4th edition, there was J. R. Young, *The Mosaic Cosmogony not 'Adverse to Modern Science': being an examination of the essay of C. W. Goodwin, M.A., with some remarks on the essay of Professor Powell* ... (London, 1861); followed belatedly by Benjamin Willis Newton, *Remarks on 'Mosaic Cosmogony', being the 5th of the 'Essays and Reviews'* (London, 1864), by a clergyman turned leader of the Plymouth Brethren.

57. Thomas H. Candy, *The Antidote; or, an examination of Mr. Pattison's Essay on the Tendencies of Religious Thought* (Cambridge, 1861).

58. John G. Cazenove, *On Certain Characteristics of Holy Scripture, with special reference to an essay on the interpretation of Scripture contained in 'Essays and Reviews'* (London, 1861), reprinted from the January 1861 *Christian Remembrancer* and remarkably fair; Robert C. Jenkins, *Scriptural Interpretation: The Essay of Professor Jowett briefly considered, in a Letter to the Rev. Professor Stanley, D.D.* (Oxford, 1861), and *A Word on Inspiration. Being a second letter on the essay of Professor Jowett, addressed to the Rev. Professor Stanley, D.D.* (Oxford, 1861).

59. Some of this ephemeral literature (especially provincial imprints) is not available in the deposit libraries, because it was not copyrighted. Titles which I know but have not seen are: 'Liverpool Clergyman', *The Faith of Eighteen Centuries*; C. Bridges, *Vain Philosophy the Spoiler of the Church*; J. Chapman, *The Foundation of the Temple* and *The Inspiration of Scripture*; Philip Gell, *Expiation*; J. W. Reeve, *The Scripture Cannot be Broken*; G. H. Robinson, *The Gospel of Christ*; C. T. Rust, *Patience and Comfort of the Scriptures*.

60. 'If to misquote is a fault, to charge misquotation is a crime. It is wonderful that, as no man has yet hit a blot in our book, so among all its assailants it has not found one with any sense of literary honour.' *Literary Churchman*, March 1, 1861, p. 96.

61. Leading article, 'The Truth and its Defenders', *ibid.*, April 16, 1861, pp. 145–146. By November 1, 1861, the *Literary Churchman* had noticed no less than 68 titles: Alvar Ellegård, *Darwin and the General Reader* (Göteborg, 1958), p. 106, n. 2.

62. 'S.T.', 'Modern Sceptical Writers – "Essays and Reviews"', *Journal of Sacred Literature*, 13 (April 1861): 85.

63. 'F. W. G.', 'Modern Sceptical Writers – On the Interpretation of Scripture, by Professor Jowett', *Ibid.*, 98–112, with a postscript in July, pp. 412–416; 'T.H.', 'Remarks on the Theory of Dr. Temple's Essay on "The Education of the World", in "Essays and Reviews"', *ibid.*, 14 (October 1861): 13–30.

64. 'D.E.F.G.' [Harvey Goodwin], 'A Letter on "Essays and Reviews"', *Macmillan's Magazine*, 4 (May 1861): 41–48.

65. 'Essays and Reviews', *Saturday Review*, 11 (March 2, 1861): 211–212.

66. 'The *Edinburgh* on "Essays and Reviews"', *ibid.* (May 4, 1861): 440. This was due to the intervention of the High Church proprietor, A. J. Beresford-Hope.

67. *The Times*, July 1, 1861, p. 8. This leader did not necessarily represent editorial policy, since leader writers were given considerable latitude in non-political matters which did not concern the editor, J. T. Delane. Thus a leader on August 31, 1861, regretted that 'the Episcopate of this country has too little hold over the intellect of the country' (p. 6). A lay general weekly, the *London Review*, followed the controversy assiduously and was critical of the Essayists.

68. Wilson to Pattison, July 25, 1860, and November 18 and 23, 1861, Bodleian Library Mss. Pattison 53, 54. The tenth edition was published in three printings of 1000 copies each in January, March and April of 1862.

69. *A Brief Examination of Prevalent Opinions on the Inspiration of the Scriptures of the Old and New Testaments. By a Lay Member of the Church of England.* With an

introduction, by Henry Bristow Wilson (London, 1861). Wilson's Liverpool friend John Macnaught had earlier written in defence of the Essayists, *Fallible or Infallible? A Lecture ... being a review of the arguments in a speech and sermon recently delivered on 'The Infallible Authority of Holy Scripture' by Rev. Hugh M'Neill* (London, 1861).

70. R. B. Kennard to Hamilton, February 20, 1861, Pusey House Hamilton Mss.

71. Robert Bruce Kennard, *Essays and Reviews. A Protest addressed to the rt. rev. the Lord Bishop of Salisbury on the appearance of the 'Episcopal Manifesto'. With a Letter to the Rev. Rowland Williams ... and an Appendix* (London, 1861).

72. Pusey House Hamilton Mss., March to May, 1861.

73. Kennard, *'Essays and Reviews'. Their Origin, History, General Character and Significance, Persecution, Prosecution, The Judgment of the Arches Court, – Review of Judgment* (London, 1863), with valuable inside information, and *The late Professor Powell and Dr. Thirlwall on the Supernatural* (London, 1864).

74. George J. Wild, *A Brief Defence of the 'Essays and Reviews': showing, by extracts from their works, that similar doctrines have been maintained by eminent divines and living dignitaries of our Church* (London, 1861). Ellis, *Seven Against Christ*, p. 129, errs in placing Wild in the diocese of Salisbury.

75. Francis Bodfield Hooper, *Reply to Dr. Wild and the 'Edinburgh': A defence of the bishops and the memorialists, in a letter to the Rev. G. J. Wild ...* (London, 1861).

76. Harry Jones, *Conscience versus the Quarterly. A Plea for Fair Play towards the writers of the Essays and Reviews* (London, 1861). For Jones, see Brian Heeney, 'Harry Jones and the Broad Church Pastoral Tradition in London', in P. T. Phillips, ed., *The View from the Pulpit: Victorian Ministers and Society* (Toronto, 1978), pp. 67–86.

77. Ellis J. Troughton, *Essays and Reviews* (London, [1861]), a letter to the proctors of Convocation, February 20; *An Hour with the Bishops about the 'Essays and Reviews'. Is Apostolical Succession a Safeguard against Error? By a Doctor of Divinity* (London, 1861); Robert Ainslie, *Discourses on the 'Essays and Reviews', delivered in Christ Church, New Road, Brighton* (London, 1861).

78. 'A Lay Graduate' [C. G. B. Daubeny], *A Few Words of Apology for the late Professor Baden Powell's Essay 'On the Study of the Evidences of Christianity', contained in the volume entitled 'Essays and Reviews'* (Oxford, 1861).

79. The full text of the address can be found in the *Guardian*, March 20, 1861, p. 271, and March 27, 1861, p. 294. See also Ellis, *Seven Against Christ*, p. 108. Among the signatories were T. H. Huxley, Charles Darwin, Sir Charles Lyell and Sir John Lubbock.

80. 'Toleration Within the Church of England', *Fraser's Magazine*, **63** (April 1861), 483–492.

81. John Cumming, *Popular Lectures on 'The Essays and Reviews'. Delivered in various places, and addressed to the common people* (London, 1861); John Campbell, *The Conquest of England: Letters to the Prince Consort on Popery, Puseyism, Neology, Infidelity, and the Aggressive Policy of the Church of Rome* (London, 1861), mainly on the danger of a Roman Catholic takeover, but Letters XV–XXII on *Essays and Reviews*; Edward Miall, *Bases of Belief*, 3rd edn (London, 1861), with a preface on *Essays and Reviews* (first published 1853).

82. M. H. M., *Exposition of the book entitled 'Essays and Reviews': being the substance of three lectures ...* (London, 1861); 'A Soldier of the Cross' [W. R. Aikman], *The Last Regret; or The Power of Divine Regeneration. A Poem: Illustrative of Truths of Inspiration assailed in a late work entitled 'Essays and Reviews'* (London, 1861), identifiable as nonconformist because profits were given to the Aged Pilgrims' Friend Society.

83. Jonathan Bayley, *Twelve Discourses on the Essays and Reviews by Seven Clergymen of Oxford* (London, 1862); [J. N. Darby], *Dialogues on the Essays and Reviews*. By one who values Christianity for its own sake, and believes it as a revelation from God, 2 vols (London, 1862), the longest tract of all.

84. James Buchanan, *The 'Essays and Reviews' Examined: a series of articles contributed to the 'Morning Post'. Revised and corrected by the author. With preface, introduction, and appendix, containing notes and documents* (Edinburgh, 1861).

85. The *Eclectic* and the *North British Review* had already spoken out in 1860. Robert Vaughan, the editor, wrote the articles in the *British Quarterly Review*. Those in the *North British* were by Isaac Taylor and Henry Rogers.

86. The author was H. W. Williams. See Willis B. Glover, *Evangelicals and Higher Criticism in the Nineteenth Century* (London, 1954), pp. 48–51.

87. [C. W. Russell], 'Anglican Neo-Christianity: The "Essays and Reviews"', *Dublin Review*, 49 (February 1861): 497. Russell was a professor at Maynooth.

88. [H. N. Oxenham], 'The Neo-Protestantism of Oxford', *Rambler*, n.s. 4 (January 1861): 287–314.

89. David Duncan, *'Essays and Reviews': A Lecture, delivered to the Manchester Friends Institute, on the 12th of 4th Month 1861*, 2nd edn (Manchester, 1861).

90. *Observations on a lecture delivered at the Manchester Friends' Institute by David Duncan, entitled 'Essays and Reviews'* (London, 1861); Joseph Binyon Forster, 'Dread of Controversy', *British Friend*, December 2, 1861, pp. 287–288. See John C. Kennedy, 'Heresy-Hunting among Victorian Quakers: The Manchester Difficulty, 1861–1873', *Victorian Studies*, 34 (Winter 1991): 227–253.

91. Robert B. Drummond, *Free Thought v. Dogmatic Theology: being two lectures on 'Essays and Reviews', delivered in St. Mark's Chapel, Edinburgh* (Edinburgh, 1861); John R. Beard, ed., *The Progress of Religious Thought as illustrated in the Protestant Church of France ... with an introductory essay on 'The Oxford Essays and Reviews'* (London, 1861).

92. *Jewish Chronicle*, March 8, 1861, p. 2, and March 22, 1861, p. 2.

93. John Bues Humperley, *Exoneravi Animam, or one radical reformer's way of thinking; containing a few suggestions touching the Essays and Reviews as appreciated by Convocation, and the discrepancy between genuine Jesusism and vulgar Christianity, still requiring reformation* (London, 1861).

94. 'A Layman' [Charles Bray], *Modern Protestantism: a few words on 'Essays and Reviews'* (London, [1862]), reprinted 1870; Joseph Barker, *An Essay on the celebrated 'Essays and Reviews', with remarks on the reception the work has met with from the Church and the State, and the lessons to be drawn therefrom* (London, [1863]). Barker oscillated between secularism and deism.

95. *Guardian*, July 17, 1861, p. 683.

Chapter 9

1. Hort to Westcott, February 15, 1861, in Arthur F. Hort, *Life and Letters of Fenton John Anthony Hort* (London, 1896), p. 439.

2. *Ibid.*, p. 439.

3. Hort to John Ellerton, February 15, 1861, in *ibid.*, p. 442.

4. See Ieuan Ellis, *Seven Against Christ: A Study of 'Essays and Reviews'* (Leiden, 1980), pp. 124–125.

5. Hort to Ellerton, April 9, 1861, in Hort, *Hort*, p. 444.

6. Maurice to Stanley, February 12, 1861, in Frederick Maurice, *The Life of Frederick Denison Maurice, Chiefly Told in His Own Letters*, 2 vols (London, 1884), 2: 383.

7. Maurice, *Maurice*, pp. 386–387.

8. *Tracts for Priests and People*, 1st series (Cambridge, 1861), p. 5.

9. Thomas Hughes, *Religio Laici* (Cambridge, 1861), p. 11.

10. F. D. Maurice, *The Mote and the Beam: A Clergyman's Lessons from the Present Panic* (Cambridge, 1861), pp. 6, 17, 30, 31, 38, 68.

11. Ellis, *Seven Against Christ*, p. 131.

12. Francis Garden, *The Atonement as a Fact and as a Mystery*, and John Llewelyn Davies, *The Signs of the Kingdom of Heaven: An Appeal to Scripture upon the question of Miracles* (Cambridge, 1861).

13. Maurice, *Maurice*, 2: 391. C. K. P[aul] and J. N. Langley, *On Terms of Communion* (Cambridge, 1861).

14. J. N. Ludlow and F. D. Maurice, *The Sermon of the Bishop of Oxford on Revelation, and the Layman's Answer* (Cambridge, 1861).

15. J. M. Ludlow, *Two Lay Dialogues* (Cambridge, 1861). The series was then bound together as *Tracts for Priests and People*, 1st series (Cambridge, 1861).

16. 'A curious compromise … They sin with both and hold with neither.' 'New Phases of Theology', *Literary Churchman*, 7 (November 1, 1861): 405.

17. *Spectator*, June 1, 1861, p. 588.

18. C. P. Chrétien, *Evidences for Those who Think and Feel More than They can Read* (Cambridge, 1861), p. 36.

19. J. M. Ludlow and Francis Garden, *Dissent and the Creeds*, and Sir Edward Strachey and F. D. Maurice, *Politics Ancient and Modern* (Cambridge, 1861).

20. J. Llewelyn Davies, *The Spirit Giveth Life* (Cambridge, 1862).

21. W. H. Lyttleton, *The Testimony of Scripture to the Authority of Conscience and of Reason* (Cambridge, 1862). Lyttleton, rector of Hagley, came from a noble family.

22. J. Llewelyn Davies and Francis Garden, *The Death of Christ: A review of the Bishop of Gloucester and Bristol's essay in 'Aids to Faith'* (Cambridge, 1862). This was William Thomson.

23. Richard H. Hutton, *The Incarnation and Principles of Evidence*. With a Letter to the Writer, by F. D. Maurice (Cambridge, 1862). See Olive J. Brose, *Frederick Denison Maurice: Rebellious Conformist* ([Athens, OH], 1971), p. 266.

24. The supplement was bound together with *Tracts for Priests and People*, 2nd series (Cambridge, 1862).

25. Pusey and Keble were approached but did not join in. See Ellis, *Seven Against Christ*, p. 123.

26. George Anthony Denison, 'Preface', *Faith and Peace. Being Answers to some of the 'Essays and Reviews'* (London, 1867), orig. 1862 as shown by a reference to the tracts being issued 'last year' (p. ix). Denison thought Pattison not worth a reply, and the respondent to Williams failed because of ill health. Denison found the root of the Essayists' errors to be 'the pride of human reason' (p.lv).

27. William Edward Jelf, *Supremacy of Scripture. An Examination into the Principles and Statements advanced in the Essay on the Education of the World. In a letter to the Rev. Dr. Temple* (London, 1861).

28. James Wayland Joyce, *The National Church. An answer to an essay on 'The National Church'. By Henry Bristow Wilson* … (London, 1861).

29. James Fendall, *Authority of Scripture. An examination into the principles and statements advanced in Professor Jowett's Essay on the Interpretation of Scripture* (London, 1861).

30. William Lee, D.D., *On Miracles. An examination of the remarks of Mr. Baden Powell on the Study of the Evidences of Christianity, contained in the volume entitled 'Essays and Reviews'* (London, 1861).

31. Edgar Huxtable, *The Sacred Record of Creation Vindicated and Explained: in answer to the essay 'On the Mosaic Cosmogony' in the volume of 'Essays and Reviews'* (London, 1861).

32. Denison, *Notes of My Life, 1805–1878* (Oxford, 1878), p. 319.

33. See 'Review of Position', 'Rugby School and Balliol College', and 'Judgment in Synod', pp. 2, 17–18, 20–22 in the first number of *Church and State Review*, 1 (June 1, 1862). Another of the Denison brothers weighed in against the Essayists: Col. Sir William Denison, Governor of Madras, *Remarks on 'Essays and Reviews'* (Madras, 1862).

34. John Nash Griffin, *Seven Answers to the Seven Essays and Reviews* (London, 1862), with an Introduction by Rt. Hon. Joseph Napier (late Lord Chancellor of Ireland).

35. Bourchier Wrey Savile, *Revelation and Science in respect to Bunsen's Biblical Researches, The Evidences of Christianity, and The Mosaic Cosmogony ...* (London, 1862), the longest Anglican pamphlet (384 pp.); Arthur T. Russell, *A Letter to the Right Rev. the Lord Bishop of Oxford, upon the Defence of the 'Essays and Reviews' in the April Number of the 'Edinburgh Review', 1861* (London, 1862), published with Wilberforce's permission; J. B. Heard, *New Wine in Old Bottles* (London, 1862); Sanderson Robins, *A Defence of the Faith*. Part 1: Forms of Unbelief (London, 1862), only part issued; [Robert Benton Seeley], *Is the Bible True? Seven Dialogues between James White and Edward Owen, concerning the 'Essays and Reviews'*, by the author of 'Essays on the Church' (London, 1862); and John G. Marshall, *Answers to 'Essays and Reviews'* (Halifax, N.S., 1862), by a former chief justice of Cape Breton Island.

36. For example, *Lux Mundi* (1889) and subsequent major Anglican theological volumes. See Josef L. Altholz, 'Periodical Origins and Implications of *Essays and Reviews*', *Victorian Periodicals Newsletter*, 9 (September 1977): 140–154.

37. 'Advertisement' to *Replies to 'Essays and Reviews'* (Oxford, 1862), p. ii. Wilberforce was thanked 'for advice and assistance also in making the necessary arrangements for producing such a volume'.

38. Robert Main, Radcliffe Observer, and John Phillips, reader in geology. Main's letter was later separately published: *A Letter from the Radcliffe Observer on the 'Essays and Reviews'* (Oxford, [1862]).

39. Preface to *Replies*, pp. vii–viii, ix–x.

40. E. M. Goulburn, 'The Education of the World', *Replies*, pp. 18, 21, 30.

41. H. J. Rose, 'Bunsen, the Critical School, and Dr. Williams', *Replies*, pp. 61, 70, 111, 121, 124. Rose charged (p. 122) that 'infidel societies have assisted in promoting the reading of these Essays in cities and large towns, by buying copies to cut them up and lend them out at a penny per Essay!'

42. Rose, 'Note on the "Edinburgh Review"', *Replies*, pp. 132–133.

43. C. A. Heurtley, 'Miracles', *Replies*, pp. 142, 152.

44. W. J. Irons, 'The Idea of the National Church', *Replies*, pp. 207–208, 209, 222, 235, 265, 273.

45. G. Rorison, 'The Creative Week,' *Replies*, pp. 297, 324, 336. Rorison made generous concessions as to biblical dating and authorship and accepted the nebular hypothesis, Lyell's geology and even a non-Darwinian 'evolution'. In the second edition of *Replies* (pp. 517–518), there was appended a letter of Darwin's opponent Richard Owen, upholding his view of the unbridgeability of the gulf between man and ape and the doctrine of Final Cause.

46. Arthur W. Haddan, 'Rationalism', *Replies*, pp. 350, 351, 405. Haddan had sent a proof of his article to Pattison with a mild rebuke for his insinuation of 'a kind of cloud of opinion': Haddan to Pattison, October 21, 1861, Bodleian Library Mss. Pattison 54.

47. Christopher Wordsworth, 'On the Interpretation of Scripture', *Replies*, pp. 422, 437, 454, 465, 498.

48. The *Record* remarked that 'there is a smack of High-Churchism throughout the whole volume'. *Record*, February 12, 1862, Supplement, p. 2.

49. H. Kirk Smith, *William Thomson, Archbishop of York: His Life and Times, 1819–90* (London, 1958), pp. 11, 157. Smith believes that Thomson 'himself had written a paper to be included in … *Essays and Reviews*, and that it failed to be included only because it was sent in too late' (p. 157). He acknowledges only one source, William Tuckwell, *Reminiscences of Oxford* (London, 1900), p. 226. Perhaps Tuckwell was thinking of *Oxford Essays*.

50. Thorold to Thomson, January 10, 1861, in Ethel H. Thomson, *The Life and Letters of William Thomson, Archbishop of York* (London, [1919]), p. 117. Thorold stressed that 'I am not writing entirely *ex proprio motu*' (p. 118).

51. Ellicott proposed Browne ('moderate High Church') and McCaul on April 4; *ibid.*, p. 122.

52. Thomson, Preface to *Aids to Faith; a Series of Theological Essays. By Several Writers. Being a Reply to 'Essays and Reviews'* (New York, 1862), p. 3.

53. Cited in G. W. Kitchin, *Edward Harold Browne, D.D., Lord Bishop of Winchester … A Memoir* (London, 1895), p. 209.

54. 'For the choice of contributors and the arrangement of subjects the Editor is responsible. Most of the writers gave their names without knowing those of their coadjutors … Each has written independently, without any editorial interference, beyond a few hints to prevent omissions and repetitions, such as must arise when several writers work without concert.' *Aids to Faith*, pp. 3–4.

55. H. L. Mansel, 'On Miracles as Evidences of Christianity', *Aids to Faith*, pp. 23, 25, 38, 39, 46. Mansel later published part of this essay as 'Critical Explanation of the Argument of Butler', an appendix to Joseph Napier, *The Miracles. Butler's Argument on Miracles, explained and defended: with observations on Hume, Baden Powell, and J. S. Mill* (Dublin, 1863).

56. William Fitzgerald, 'On the Study of the Evidences of Christianity', *Aids to Faith*, pp. 70, 75, 77–78.

57. Alexander McCaul, 'Prophecy', *Aids to Faith*, pp. 131, 135. McCaul originally intended to contribute another essay and undertook 'Prophecy' as 'a second paper, at short notice', when its intended author withdrew: 'Preface', p. 4.

58. 'It is impossible to separate the essential elements of Christ's teaching from the book of Daniel.' 'Prophecy', p. 142.

59. F. C. Cook, 'Ideology and Subscription', *Aids to Faith*, pp. 216, 210.

60. McCaul, 'The Mosaic Record of Creation', *Aids to Faith*, pp. 268, 269.

61. George Rawlinson, 'On the Genuineness and Authenticity of the Pentateuch', *Aids to Faith*, pp. 275, 327.

62. Cited in Kitchin, *Browne*, p. 210. Browne's object was 'to prove to doubting minds that, whatever difficulties might occur to them, as to degrees and modes of Inspiration … still there was abundant proof of a special miraculous and infallible Inspiration of Holy Scripture'.

63. Harold Browne, 'Inspiration', *Aids to Faith*, pp. 348–349, 359, 366, 370.

64. Narrower Churchmen found Browne dangerously tolerant. The *Record* (February 12, 1862, Supplement, p. 2) found his essay 'deficient in any clear apprehension

of what Inspiration is'. Thirlwall condoled with him: 'I am sorry to learn that the moderation and candour which you showed ... have exposed you to attack as ultra-liberal'. Kitchin, *Browne*, p. 213.

65. William Thomson, 'The Death of Christ', *Aids to Faith*, pp. 375, 418, 421. Thomson's remarks on one-sidedness evoked evangelical resentment: the *Record* regarded his article as 'defective' (February 12, 1862, Supplement, p. 2).

66. Charles James Ellicott, 'Scripture, and its Interpretation', *Aids to Faith*, pp. 432, 440, 471–472, 474, 479, 489, 503, 509.

Chapter 10

1. Owen Chadwick, *The Victorian Church*, 2 vols (London, 1966–70), 1: 468.

2. James Fraser, quoted in H. P. Liddon, *Walter Kerr Hamilton, Bishop of Salisbury* (London, 1869), p. 88.

3. Phillimore to Hamilton, March 11, 1861, Pusey House Hamilton Mss. See also the letters of March 8 and 26.

4. William Scott (editor of the *Christian Remembrancer*) to Hamilton, May 2, 1861, *ibid.*

5. *The Times*, May 23, 1861; *Record*, May 24, 1861, p. 3; *Guardian*, May 29, 1861, p. 497. The *Guardian* regretted Hamilton's action, a statement which began the alienation of Pusey and Keble from their erstwhile organ.

6. See the letters to Hamilton of Thirlwall, Dean E. B. Ramsay, James Fraser (Hamilton's former chaplain, a loving critic) and Lord Herbert of Lea (Sidney Herbert, a prominent layman of the diocese), Pusey House Hamilton Mss. But Hamilton received support from many local clergy and, in October, an address from 18 prominent laymen including a peer, two baronets and a MP.

7. Ieuan Ellis, *Seven Against Christ: A Study of 'Essays and Reviews'* (Leiden, 1980), pp. 179–180. Williams, though beneficed since 1859, did not resign at Lampeter (£500) and take up residence at Broad Chalke (nominally £311 but really about £80 less) until 1862. This was due to the need to rebuild the vicarage.

8. Walter Kerr [Hamilton], *A Charge* ... (Salisbury, 1861), p. 62–64.

9. Wilberforce to Fendall, October 23, 1861, in R. K. Pugh, *The Letter Books of Samuel Wilberforce* [Oxfordshire Record Society XLVII] ([Oxford], 1970), pp. 365–366. Wilberforce personally subscribed £200 with the promise of a further £200 if needed (it was); most of the subscriptions came from Ely diocesan clergy, including (secretly) Turton.

10. M. A. Crowther, *Church Embattled: Religious Controversy in Mid-Victorian England* (Newton Abbot, 1970), pp. 121–122.

11. Ellen Williams, *The Life and Letters of Rowland Williams, D.D.* (London, 1874), p. 46; Ellis, *Seven Against Christ*, p. 178. Williams' fund received contributions from non-Anglicans, including some Jews. The Essayists contributed £25 each to Williams' fund; Wilson to Pattison, August 25, 1861, Bodleian Library Mss. Pattison 54.

12. Leslie Stephen, *The Life of Sir James Fitzjames Stephen, Bart., KCSI, a judge of the High Court of Justice* (London, 1895), pp. 184–190; James A. Colaico, *James Fitzjames Stephen and the Crisis of Victorian Thought* (New York, 1983), pp. 173–174. Stephen was chosen because of his Broad Church sympathies, being recommended by Jowett: Wilson to Pattison, August 25, 1861, Bodleian Library Mss. Pattison 54.

13. Jowett, noting a 'friendship which has lasted about seventeen years', remarked

Lushington's 'singular purity of mind ... His life one of the happiest in the world ... His great simplicity'. Balliol College Jowett Mss., 'Brown Tin Box', Notebook K.

14. His recent biographer calls him a churchman 'of the old school', uninfluenced by any nineteenth-century school. S. M. Waddams, *Law, Politics and the Church of England: The Career of Stephen Lushington, 1782–1873* (Cambridge, 1992), pp. 55–56.

15. Jowett to Stanley, n.d., Balliol College Jowett Mss.

16. Even when approving the performance of his counsel, Williams wished that 'they could have dwelt more on the critical and Biblical justifications of my Prophetical views, to which I am not quite sure ... that they have done theological justice'. Williams to Kennard, January 17, 1862, in Williams, *Williams*, 2: 119.

17. Williams, *Hints to my Counsel in the Court of Arches*, extracted in Williams, *Williams*, 2: 53, 234n., 25, 27, 28.

18. Cited in Williams, *Williams*, 2: 58.

19. Quoted in *Court of Arches. Bishop of Salisbury v. Williams*, 1: 14. This is a curious document, a bound manuscript in the Department of Printed Books at the British Library (BM5155.k.11.), probably a fair copy of the shorthand reports prepared for the judge.

20. Quoted in *ibid.*, 1: 15. Phillimore had been the unsuccessful defence counsel for Heath, together with Stephen. There is a discussion of the 'exuberantly hetero-dox' Heath in Robert E. Rodes, Jr., *Law and Modernization in the Church of England: Charles II to the Welfare State* (Notre Dame, IN, 1991), p. 262.

21. *Ibid.*, 1: 27.

22. James Fitzjames Stephen, *Defence of the Rev. Rowland Williams, D.D. in the Arches Court of Canterbury* (London, 1862), pp. 2, 15, 37, 123, 126, 128.

23. *Ibid.*, p. xli, from the summary of the argument in the preface.

24. *Ibid.*, pp. 192, 193, 275, 295, 302.

25. *Ibid.*, pp. 321, 327, 330–331.

26. *Speech of Robert Phillimore, D.C.L., Q.C., in the case of 'The office of the Judge promoted by the Bishop of Salisbury against Williams'. Delivered on the 9th, 10th, and 11th of February, 1862* (London, 1862), pp. 1–2, 27, 45. '(From the Notes of the Shorthand Writer.)'

27. *Ibid.*, pp. 52, 54, 80, 116, 175.

28. *Court of Arches*, 3: 41, 47, 114; 4: 20, 70.

29. *Ibid.*, 3: 72, 106.

30. *Ibid.*, 4: 25, 65, 83–84.

31. *Guardian*, March 5, 1862, pp. 216–217.

32. Williams, *Williams*, p. 60.

33. Stephen, *Life of Stephen*, p. 187; Colaico, *Stephen and the Crisis*, p. 174. The latter has a summary of Stephen's argument on pp. 173–174.

34. The *Record*, in its year's-end leader, December 30, 1861, p. 2, had observed that if Stephen's defence prevailed, the Bible's 'authority as the Book of God would be at an end'.

35. Alexander M'Caul, *Testimonies to the Divine Authority and Inspiration of the Holy Scriptures*, as taught by the Church of England, in reply to the statements of Mr. James Fitzjames Stephen (London, 1862), pp. 3, 59.

36. Rowland Williams, *Persecution for the Word* (London, 1862), pp. 7, 14, 43, 44, 46. The pamphlet had not yet appeared when the interlocutory judgment was given, and it was published 'With a postscript on the interlocutory judgment and the present state of the case'.

Chapter 11

1. 'Judgment of the Lords of the Judicial Committee of the Privy Council on the appeal of Heath v. Burder, from the Court of Arches; delivered 6th June, 1862' (printed copy in Lambeth Palace Library), p. 2.
2. Ellen Williams, *The Life and Letters of Rowland Williams, D.D.* (London, 1874), p. 68, n. 1.
3. *Essays and Reviews. Judgment delivered on the 25th of June 1862 in the case of the Bishop of Salisbury versus Williams, and ... Fendall versus Wilson, by the Rt. Hon. Stephen Lushington, D.C.L., Dean of the Arches* (London, 1862), pp. 5, 6, 9, 11, 15, 16.
4. *Ibid.*, pp. 19, 22, 23, 26, 27, 31, 32.
5. *Ibid.*, pp. 33, 35, 36, 37, 40, 42, 44.
6. *Ibid.*, p. 44.
7. Lushington's biographer concludes simply that he 'failed' to achieve the object of construing the plain meaning of words. 'It seems that Lushington has swallowed the camel, but strained at the gnat.' S. M. Waddams, *Law, Politics and the Church of England: The Career of Stephen Lushington, 1782–1873* (Cambridge, 1992), pp. 343, 333.
8. Rowland Williams, letter, *Daily News*, June 28, 1862, p. 3. This was in response to a 'misleading' report of the case in *The Times*.
9. Williams, *Persecution for the Word*. With a postscript on the interlocutory judgment and the present state of the case (London, 1862), pp. 51–52, 61, 62.
10. [H. B. Wilson], 'Theology and Philosophy', *Westminster Review*, n.s. 22 (October 1862): 525, 527, 528.
11. *Ibid.*, n.s. 23 (January 1863): 256.
12. John Grote, *Essays and Reviews. An Examination of some portion of Dr. Lushington's Judgment on the admission of the Articles in the Cases of the Bishop of Salisbury v. Williams and Fendall v. Wilson. With remarks on the bearing of them on the clergy* (Cambridge, 1862), p. 35. Another pamphlet in support of Wilson on one point was 'A Clergyman', *Forgiveness After Death: Does the Bible or the Church of England affirm it to be impossible? A review of the alleged proofs of the hopelessness of the future state* (London, 1862).
13. Jowett to Lewis Campbell, July 16, [1862], Balliol College Jowett Mss.
14. Jowett to Florence Nightingale, about July 1862, *ibid.* This correspondence is partially reprinted by Vincent Quinn and John Prest, eds, *Dear Miss Nightingale: A selection of Benjamin Jowett's Letters to Florence Nightingale 1860–1893* (Oxford, 1987).
15. 'Essayism in a Court of Justice', *Guardian*, July 2, 1862, p. 629.
16. 'The Judgment in the Court of Arches', *Church and State Review*, 1 (August 1, 1862): 107.
17. Leading article, *Record*, June 27, 1862, p. 2. The article cited *Evangelical Christendom*, the organ of the Evangelical Alliance, for satirizing the judge as 'Archbishop Lushington'. The term had been coined by *Punch* in connection with Burder *v.* Heath.
18. 'Dr. Lushington's Judgment: Essays and Reviews', *Christian Observer*, 62 (August 1862): 609, 611.
19. [F. W. Newman], 'Essays and Reviews: Dr. Lushington's Judgment', *Westminster Review*, n.s. 22 (October 1862): 311.
20. 'Present Position of the Church of England', *Fraser's Magazine*, 66 (December 1862): 704. The article is unattributed in the *Wellesley Index* and not listed in

Leslie Stephen's life of his brother, but the fulsome praise of Fitzjames Stephen's speech (p. 701) suggests that he may have been the author; he reviewed himself anonymously on other occasions, and he wrote *Fraser's* review of the Privy Council decision.

21. 'Lushingtonianism in Little: Generals and Specials', *Punch*, July 12, 1863, p. 13.
22. Peter Hinchliff, *John William Colenso, Bishop of Natal* (London, 1964), p. 94. Hinchliff notes that Colenso had already been delated for the universalist views of his work on *Romans*, published in 1861.
23. J. W. Colenso, *The Pentateuch and Book of Joshua Critically Examined* (New York, 1863), pp. 10, 34.
24. Phillimore to Hamilton, June 28, 1862; Hamilton's diary, July 4, 1862; Pusey House Hamilton Mss. 'My object was not so much to determine the teaching of the Church as to protect one of my Parishes from false teaching.'
25. Phillimore to Hamilton, November 18, 1862, *ibid.*
26. A. C. [Tait], *A Charge ...* (London, 1862), pp. 7, 13, 16, 20, 22. Hampden also gave his Charge in 1862 but was too busy to publish it. He expressed distress at the rejection by the Essayists of the historical facts of the Bible. See Henrietta Hampden, *Some Memorials of Renn Dickson Hampden, Bishop of Hereford* (London, 1871), pp. 211–221, and Hamish F. G. Swanston, *Ideas of Order* (Assen, 1973), pp. 186–187.
27. *Guardian*, December 17, 1862, p. 1193.
28. Writing to the *Spectator*, which expressed surprise, Stephen pointed out that Williams would withdraw only those 'passages in which the court had held that he had identified himself with Baron Bunsen. As Dr. Williams did not adopt Baron Bunsen's opinions, and had not intended to advance them as his own, as it is the province of the court to say what was the legal effect of his words, and as the court had said that the legal effect of his words was to adopt those opinions', he offered to withdraw them, but 'refused explicitly' to withdraw his own opinion on a third passage. Quoted in Williams, *Williams*, p. 79.
29. Phillimore to Hamilton, December 16, 1862, Pusey House Hamilton Mss.
30. *Guardian*, December 17, 1862, p. 1194.
31. *Ibid.*
32. *Daily News*, December 16, 1862, p. 4. This remark was cited by the *Record*, December 17, 1862, p. 2, which did not criticize the decision.
33. [H. B. Wilson], 'Theology and Philosophy', *Westminster Review*, n.s. 23 (January 1863): 256. The comparison was with Heath.
34. Williams, January 19, 1863, quoted in Williams, *Williams*, p. 82.
35. 'The Judgment in the Court of Arches', *Church and State Review*, 2 (January 1, 1863): 22.
36. Josef L. Altholz, 'Publishing History of *Essays and Reviews*', *Notes & Queries*, n.s. 29 (August 1982): 312.

Chapter 12

1. See the lucid explanation in P. A. Howell, *The Judicial Committee of the Privy Council 1833–1876: Its Origins, Structure and Development* (Cambridge, 1979). Desmond Bowen, *The Idea of the Victorian Church* (Montreal, 1968), p. 94, calls the common lawyers 'a group of amateurs' in religious matters.
2. Phillimore to Hamilton, December 18, 1862, Pusey House Hamilton Mss. 'He might be dragged before the civil tribunal; he would not, as a Bishop of the

Church, appeal to it.' H. P. Liddon, *Walter Kerr Hamilton: Bishop of Salisbury* (London, 1869), p. 91.

3. Jeune had deftly turned aside a proposal to obtain a judgment of the university on the errors contained in *Essays and Reviews*: *Guardian*, April 10, 1861, p. 341.

4. Pusey to Keble, probably February 4, 1862, Pusey House.

5. *Case whether Professor Jowett in his Essay and Commentary has so distinctly contravened the doctrines of the Church of England, that a Court of Law would pronounce him guilty; with the Opinion of the Queen's Advocate thereon* (London, 1862).

6. *Case as to the Legal Position of Professor Jowett: with the Opinion of the Queen's Advocate thereon* (London, 1862).

7. The correspondence on this of Pusey and Keble is in Pusey House. Keble offered to contribute £100 towards the costs.

8. 'Small Debts and Heresies Court', *Punch*, February 28, 1863, p. 87, and March 7, 1863, p. 100.

9. *The Times*, February 15, 1863, p. 9.

10. *The Times*, February 19, 1863, p. 6.

11. Maurice, *The Times*, February 20, 1863, p. 9; Godfrey Lushington, February 21, p. 12; Pusey, February 23, p. 5, and letters of 'A Protestant' and 'M.A. (of Balliol)'; Maurice and 'Anglicanus' (Stanley's pseudonym), February 24, p. 9; 'A Looker-On', February 25, p. 5; Pusey and Newman, February 26, p. 9; Maurice, February 27, p. 9; 'The Oldest Lay Professor in the University of Oxford', March 3, p. 7; Pusey, March 4, p. 9, March 17, p. 5 and March 19, p. 11. Newman wrote to clear Pusey of involvement with Tract 90. There was a further side-controversy as to whether the liberals had saved Tract 90 from condemnation.

12. Geoffrey Faber, *Jowett: A Portrait with Background* (London, 1957), pp. 267, 270–271.

13. *Pusey and others v. Jowett. The Argument and Decision as to the Jurisdiction of the Chancellor's Court at Oxford* (Oxford, [1863]), pp. 41, 25.

14. Quoted in Evelyn Abbott and Lewis Campbell, *The Life and Letters of Benjamin Jowett, M.A., Master of Balliol College* (New York, 1897), p. 312.

15. Faber, *Jowett*, p. 270.

16. Pusey to Keble, 'S. Mark's Day' (April 25), 1863, Pusey House.

17. Balliol College Jowett Mss., 'Brown Tin Box', Notebook M (1879), f. 128, and Jowett to Stanley, [February 3, 1863].

18. Owen Chadwick, *The Victorian Church*, 2 vols (London, 1966–70), 2: 64.

19. W. R. Cosens to Hamilton, February 16, 1864, Pusey House Hamilton Mss., citing 'a friend of mine in the Council office'.

20. 'Coleridge thinks they have rather hostilely packed the court.' Phillimore to Hamilton, June 6, 1863, *ibid*. Phillimore cited the omission of the Lords Justices of Appeal, who had sat in similar cases. Samuel Wilberforce retailed the same story: Wilberforce to Bishop Gray, February 5, 1864, Bodleian Library Mss. Wilberforce d. 39.

21. Chadwick, *Victorian Church*, 1: 488–489. See also Timothy J. Toohey, *Piety and the Professions: Sir John Coleridge and His Sons* (New York, 1987), pp. 277–295.

22. Kingsdown (Pemberton-Leigh) was head of the chancery bar when he inherited a fortune in 1843. He retired from practice and became an unpaid member of the Privy Council, where he helped to organize the fledgling Judicial Committee. See Howell, *Judicial Committee*, pp. 62, 132–134. He had participated in the Gorham judgment.

23. Westbury later told Jowett 'that until theological questions came before the Courts he had believed what was ordinarily believed by members of the Church

of England. But when he began to examine for himself he was surprised to find how slender was the evidence … He was not always quite in good humour with the Church of England'. Jowett to Augusta Parker (Westbury's daughter), 1887, Balliol College Jowett Mss.

24.   Ellen Williams, *The Life and Letters of Rowland Williams, D.D.* (London, 1874), p. 138; Phillimore to Hamilton, June 23, 1862, Pusey House Hamilton Mss.: 'Stephen told me he had urged Dr. W. in vain to withdraw the passage'.

25.   H. B. Wilson, *A Speech delivered before the Judicial Committee of Her Majesty's Most Honourable Privy Council in the case of Wilson v. Fendall on appeal from the Arches Court of Canterbury* (London, 1863), pp. xx–xxi. The judges informally consulted Lushington on this point and followed his advice that 'it would be unfair to Wilson to put him in a worse position than if he had not opposed the articles at the interlocutory stage'. S. M. Waddams, *Law, Politics and the Church of England: The Career of Stephen Lushington, 1782–1873* (Cambridge, 1992), p. 343.

26.   *Ibid.*, pp. 38, 41, 42, 140, 151, 152.

27.   Williams, *Williams*, p. 141 and n. 2.

28.   *Ibid.*, p. 143.

29.   Westbury to Tait, September 5, [1863], Lambeth Palace Tait Mss., Vol. 80. Westbury hoped 'we shall agree on a very short judgment, simply stating the Law as now settled by decision, namely, that the passages libelled must be shown clearly to include or embody some doctrine or proposition contrary to the Articles or Book of Common Prayer, and that we do not find any passage which plainly and necessarily answers that description'. The procedure is explained by Howell, *Judicial Committee.*

30.   Longley to his son Henry, October 5, 1863, Lambeth Palace Longley Mss. 1838.

31.   Longley to Henry, November 26, 1863, *ibid.*

32.   Tait's diary, January 17 and 26, 1864, Lambeth Palace Tait Mss., vol. 44.

33.   Connop Thirlwall, Charge of 1863, in *Remains Literary and Theological of Connop Thirlwall,* J. J. Stewart Perowne, ed., 2 vols (London, 1877), 2: 9, 10, 12, 15.

34.   *Ibid.*, pp. 25, 17, 21, 24, 28, 29, 30, 33. Thirlwall had earlier (p. 8) condemned Williams' 'flippant and contemptuous tone'.

35.   *Ibid.*, pp. 47, 50.

36.   *Ibid.*, pp. 51, 52, 53.

37.   *Ibid.*, pp. 61, 67, 70, 72, 84.

38.   Stanley to Thirlwall, November 21, 1863, in John Connop Thirlwall, Jr, *Connop Thirlwall, Historian and Theologian* (London, 1936), pp. 233–234.

39.   A. P. Stanley, *A Letter to the Lord Bishop of London on the State of Subscription in the Church of England and in the University of Oxford* (Oxford, 1863). A bill had been introduced in Parliament for this purpose.

40.   W. Houghton, *Rationalism in the Church of England … with an appendix on 'Essays and Reviews'* (London, 1863).

41.   [Mark Pattison], 'Learning in the Church of England', *National Review,* 16 (January 1863): 187–220. He cited the Broad Church as 'the intelligence of Anglicanism' and referred specifically to *Essays and Reviews* as arousing indignation because of 'the transcendental treatment of religion from within': pp. 210, 216.

42.   D[uncan] Nimmo, 'Learning against religion, learning as religion: Mark Pattison and the Victorian crisis of faith', in Keith Robbins, ed., *Religion and Humanism* (Oxford, 1981), p. 320.

43.   Leslie Howsam, *Cheap Bibles: Nineteenth-Century Publishing and the British and Foreign Bible Society* (Cambridge, 1991), p. 181.

Chapter 13

1.   Pusey to Tait, December 6 and 25, 1863, and February 2, 1864, Lambeth Palace Tait Mss., vol. 80. The first stressed the danger of conversions to Rome if doctrine could not be enforced in the Church of England. The second emphasized the consequences of a denial of eternal punishment: 'nothing will keep men from the present pleasures of sin, but the love of God or the fear of Hell'. The third called it 'the greatest crisis the Church of England has gone through'.

2.   Pusey to Keble, January 29, 1864 (two letters), Pusey House. Already he was planning to agitate to get a declaration of doctrine from the bishops and to revise the court of final appeal. The letter, signed 'Senex', was printed in the *Record* on February 2.

3.   Longley to his son Henry, January 28, 1864, Lambeth Palace Longley Mss., 1838. Wilberforce to Bishop Phillpotts, January 29, 1864, Bodleian Library Mss. Wilberforce c. 5.

4.   Phillimore to Hamilton, January 27, 1864, Pusey House Hamilton Mss.

5.   Tait's printed opinion supplied some of the material for the final judgment. Randall Davidson and William Benham, *Life of Archibald Campbell Tait, Archbishop of Canterbury,* 2 vols (London, 1891), 1: 313.

6.   Report of Williams v. Bishop of Salisbury, Wilson v. Fendall, in *A Collection of the Judgments of the Judicial Committee of the Privy Council in Ecclesiastical Cases relating to Doctrine and Discipline,* George C. Brodrick and Rev. William H. Fremantle, eds (London, 1865), pp. 281–283.

7.   *Ibid.,* pp. 283, 285.

8.   *Ibid.,* pp. 286–289.

9.   *Ibid.,* pp. 289–290.

10.   The epitaph is attributed to Sir Philip Rose, but these lines are said to be by Charles Bowen, one of Jowett's pupils. J. B. Atlay, *The Victorian Chancellors,* 2 vols (London, 1906–8), 2: 264.

11.   Williams to A. Jessopp, February 13, 1864, in Ellen Williams, *The Life and Letters of Rowland Williams, D.D.* (London, 1874), p. 180.

12.   [H. B. Wilson], 'Theology', *Westminster Review,* n.s. 25 (April 1864): 547.

13.   An 1870 remark, cited in Ieuan Ellis, *Seven Against Christ: A Study of 'Essays and Reviews'* (Leiden, 1980), p. 192.

14.   Stanley to Tait, February 8, 1864, Lambeth Palace Tait Mss., vol. 81. See also *Spectator,* February 13, 1864, pp. 174–176.

15.   Hamilton to Pusey, February 13, 1864 (copy), Pusey House Hamilton Mss.

16.   Phillimore to Hamilton, February 12, 1864, *ibid.* Phillimore believed in the cause, not merely as an advocate.

17.   For the letter, see *Guardian,* May 4, 1864, p. 437. Preliminary to the visitation was a questionnaire for the clergy. In answer to a question about hindrances to ministry, Williams complained of the 'enforcement of the theology of Laud in the spirit of Titus Oates'. L. W. Cowie, 'The Church of England since 1837', in R. B. Pugh and Elizabeth Crittall, eds, *Victoria County History, Wiltshire,* III, (London, 1956), p. 70. Williams had to sit through Hamilton's Charge.

18.   W. K. [Hamilton], *A Charge* to the clergy and churchwardens of the Diocese of Salisbury, at his triennial visitation, in August, 1864 (Salisbury, 1864), p. 29. His

biographer sums it up: 'it was far better to have failed than to have done nothing'. H. P. Liddon, *Walter Kerr Hamilton Bishop of Salisbury* (London, 1869), p. 91.

19. The bill was £186, 14 s. F. Macdonald to Edward Hamilton, April 9, 1864, Pusey House Hamilton Mss.

20. The surplus was some £184. Archdeacon Hony to Hamilton, July 28, 1864, *ibid.* Of the total, some £813 had been collected by the archdeacons in 1862. There are many letters from contributors at Pusey House, including Archbishop Longley and Bishop T. Vowler Short (£100). Fendall's committee, as of June 8, had collected over £800 but was still £450 short. *Guardian*, June 8, 1864, p. 547.

21. *The Times*, February 10, 1864, p. 9.

22. 'The Judgment on the Essayists', *Guardian*, February 10, 1864, pp. 132–133. Also 'The Church *versus* the Judicial Committee of the Privy Council', *ibid.*, February 24, 1864, p. 180.

23. Pusey to Keble, February 12?, 1864, and Keble to Pusey, February 14?, 1864, Pusey House. The *Guardian*'s editor attempted to justify the paper: Martin R. Sharp to Pusey, February 13, 1864, *ibid.*

24. *Record*, February 10, 1864, p. 2. Also *Record*, February 17, 1864, p. 2.

25. [Maurice Swabey], 'The Privy Council Judgment', *Quarterly Review*, 115 (April 1864): 542, 546, 548. See Phillimore to Hamilton, April 9, 1864, Pusey House Hamilton Mss. Reform of the court was Phillimore's special theme.

26. 'A Lay Churchman' [J. F. Stephen], 'The Law and the Church', *Macmillan's Magazine*, 9 (March 1864): 440, 441.

27. [Stephen], 'The Privy Council and the Church of England', *Fraser's Magazine*, 69 (May 1864): 522, 532.

28. 'Public Affairs', *Christian Observer*, 64 (March 1864): 239–240.

29. 'The Recent Judgment in the Privy Council', *Christian Remembrancer*, 47 (April 1864): 493, 498.

30. 'The Law and the Church', *Church and State Review*, 4 (March 1, 1864): 94, 95.

31. 'The Privy Council Judgment', *British Quarterly Review*, 39 (April 1864): 423–424. The author was possibly Robert Vaughan, according to an entry for the *Wellesley Index to Victorian Periodicals*.

32. '*Essays and Reviews* – The Final Decision', *Liberator*, 10 (March 1, 1864): 42.

33. 'The Late Judgment of the Privy Council', *Dublin Review*, 55 (July 1864): 13, 22.

34. H. E. Manning, *The Crown in Council on the Essays and Reviews: A Letter to an Anglican Friend* (London, 1864), pp. 12, 27. Dated March 8, 1864.

35. H. E. Manning, *The Convocation and the Crown in Council: A Second Letter to an Anglican Friend* (London, 1864), p. 11.

36. In approximate chronological order, William Brock, *Infidelity in High Places* (London, [1864]), directed against Stanley; R[obert] Liddell, *The Inspiration of Holy Scripture, as not merely containing, but being, the Word of God. A Sermon ...* (London, 1864), by a noted ritualist; *The Present Crisis. A Letter to the Lord Bishop of London by one of his clergy, upon the recent judgment in 'Essays and Reviews'* (London, [1864]); A. C. Rowley, *A Pamphlet on the Judgment of the Privy Council in the case of 'Essays and Reviews'* (Bristol, 1864); and belatedly, Benjamin Willis Newton, *The Judgment of the Court of Arches and of the Judicial Committee of the Privy Council, in the case of Rowland Williams, D.D. ... considered* (London, 1866).

37. John Keble, *A Litany of our Lord's Warnings, (for the present Distress)* (Oxford, 1864), p. 19.

38. Pusey to Liddon, February 23, 1864, Pusey House.

39. Pusey to Hamilton, February 9, 1864, *ibid.* Pusey wrote in similar words to Wilberforce.

40. Geoffrey Rowell, *Hell and the Victorians* (Oxford, 1974), p. 94, cites for this constant 'note of *memento inferni*' a sermon of 1839: 'remember the parching flame, the never-dying worm ... Set heaven and hell before your eyes, so you may escape hell, and by God's mercy attain heaven'. The pastoral element in Pusey's ritualism is discussed in several studies by R. William Franklin, notably *Nineteenth-Century Churches: The History of a New Catholicism in Württemberg, England and France* (New York and London, 1987).

41. *Record*, February 19, 1864, p. 3. This was separately reprinted as *Dr. Pusey on the Privy Council Judgment* (London, 1864). A second letter, March 2, 1864, Supplement, p. 1, was a detailed critique of Westbury's judgment and assertion of 'the infallibility of Holy Scripture'.

42. *Ibid.*, February 19, 1864, p. 2.

43. Earl of Shaftesbury to Pusey, February 26, 1864, in H. P. Liddon, *Life of Edward Bouverie Pusey*, 4 vols (London, 1898), 4: 51. Pusey's link to the *Record* and to Shaftesbury was his brother-in-law Provost Cotton.

44. Pusey to Shaftesbury, February 28, 1864, *ibid.*

45. Pusey to Keble, January 29, 1864, *ibid.*, p. 46. There is an extensive correspondence on this in Pusey House.

46. Pusey attempted to draw W. E. Gladstone into this scheme. Pusey to Gladstone, February 18, 1864, Pusey House. But Gladstone, though he had followed the debate with great anxiety and deplored the judgment, did not think any action was desirable. Ellis, *Seven Against Christ*, pp. 208–209.

47. *Case as to the legal force of the judgment of the Privy Council, in re Fendall v. Wilson; with the opinion of the Attorney-General and Sir Hugh Cairns* (London, 1864), pp. 35–36, 5, 13, 16.

48. Pusey to Stanley, February 23, 1864, in Liddon, *Pusey*, 4: 63. There was much correspondence between Pusey and Keble about this.

49. Pusey to Stanley, February 28, 1864, *ibid.*, 4: 63. Stanley had criticized Pusey for publishing in the *Record*, 'the most unscrupulous of English newspapers'; Pusey argued the necessity of uniting with the party which read it.

50. Pusey to Stanley, March 5, 1864, *ibid.*, 4: 66.

51. Liddon to Stanley, March 10, 1864, in R. E. Prothero and G. G. Bradley, *The Life and Correspondence of Arthur Penrhyn Stanley, late Dean of Westminster*, 2 vols (New York, 1884), 2: 168–169.

52. Pusey to Keble, Ash Wednesday, 1864, Pusey House; Keble to Longley, February 13, 1864, Lambeth Palace Longley Mss. 7.

53. Longley to his son Henry, January 28, 1864, *ibid.*, 1838; Longley to Pusey, March 2, 1864, Pusey House.

54. *Guardian*, March 16, 1864, p. 248.

55. Charles Thomas [Longley], *A Pastoral Letter addressed to the Clergy and Laity of his Province* (London, 1864), pp. 4, 5, 10, 11, 12.

56. *Record*, March 18, 1864, p. 2. A Congregationalist minister criticized Longley's use of the word 'suffering': H. H. Dobney, *A Letter to his Grace, the Archbishop of Canterbury, on that portion of his recent pastoral letter which affirms 'The Everlasting Suffering of the Lost'* (London, [1864]).

57. This technicality, maintained by Cairns, has been described as 'carrying pedantry to extreme lengths'. In common law, the opinion of the court declares the law; and it was usual to speak of the opinion of the Judicial Committee as the

'judgment'. P. A. Howell, *The Judicial Committee of the Privy Council 1833–1876: Its Origins, Structure and Development* (Cambridge, 1979), p. 36. However, the report to the Queen, made effective by her Order in Council, stated only the result, not the reasons; and it was convenient for loyal and orthodox Churchmen that the Queen was not personally involved.

58. William Thomson, *A Pastoral Letter to the clergy and laity of the Province of York* (London, 1864), pp. 2, 22, 23.
59. Quoted in *Guardian*, April 20, 1864, p. 371.

Chapter 14

1. Wilberforce to Pusey, February 21, 1864, Pusey House.
2. Pusey to Liddon, n.d., *ibid.* Pusey drafted two items, the clergy declaration and a petition to the Queen for a royal commission on the constitution of the Judicial Committee in ecclesiastical cases. The latter was deferred.
3. The notice was in the form of placards, worded so as to invite all members of Convocation. The meeting was thus attended by several liberals, including Pattison, who wryly noted the confusion in his 1864 diary, Bodleian Library Mss. Pattison 130. The *Record* censured the liberals for attempting to disrupt the meeting: *Record*, February 29, 1864, p. 3.
4. *Ibid.*
5. Randall Davidson and William Benham, *Life of Archibald Campbell Tait, Archbishop of Canterbury*, 2 vols (London, 1891), 1: 313. The version in M. A. Crowther, *Church Embattled: Religious Controversy in Mid-Victorian England* (Newton Abbot, 1970), p. 123, represents a draft in which Pusey said 'plenary inspiration and authority' and did not say 'not only containing, but being'.
6. Copy in British Library.
7. *Punch* satirized this as 'Advertising a New Article', April 2, 1864, p. 139.
8. *Record*, March 23, 1864, p. 2.
9. Fremantle to Pusey, April 18, 1864, Pusey House, hoping for 12,000 signatures. *Record*, April 18, 1864, p. 4.
10. M'Neile's letter, *Record*, March 7, 1864, p. 3. Leading articles, *ibid.*, March 9 and 11, both p. 2.
11. Lathbury, *Guardian*, March 30, 1864, p. 309; Liddon, April 6, p. 322; Lathbury, April 13, p. 347; Liddon, April 20, p. 372; Lathbury, May 4, p. 428; Liddon, May 11, p. 451, with editorial note closing the controversy.
12. Goode's motivation can be made out from his letters to the *Record*, February 29, 1864, p. 3, and April 6, Supplement, p. 2, and Fremantle's letter, *ibid.*, April 8, p. 3.
13. *Record*, March 14, 1864, p. 2, and *Guardian*, March 16, p. 249.
14. H. P. Liddon, *Life of Edward Bouverie Pusey*, 4 vols (London, 1898), 4: 56.
15. *The Times*, March 5, 1864, p. 10.
16. *Ibid.*, March 8, 1864, p. 12.
17. *Ibid.*, March 9, 1864, p. 9. The rapidity of these responses was due to the Post Office, which maintained several deliveries a day in London and next-day delivery in the provinces. The dates given for these letters in Liddon, *Pusey*, are the dates of writing, not of publication.
18. *The Times*, March 11, 1864, p. 5.
19. *Ibid.*, March 12, 1864, p. 14. Maurice's comment on moral pressure echoed 'A Country Parson', *ibid.*, March 11, 1864, p. 5, who said that if he does not sign

'my own little world sets me down for a heretic'. He complained of 'a Fortieth Article, drawn up by private individuals, however eminent'.

20. *Ibid.*, March 15, 1864, p. 14.

21. For example, Denison, 'The Judgment and the Declaration', *Church and State Review*, 4 (May 1, 1864): 194: 'The question has been put to the Clergy of England, and the declaration is carried by a large majority.' See also 'S', 'Our Present Position: A Letter to a Friend', *Christian Observer*, 64 (June 1864): 427: 'such approach to unanimity'.

22. There were a few complaints about names being wrongly put on the list. See *Guardian*, July 6, 1864, p. 651 (Alexander D'Orsey); *ibid.*, July 13, 1864, p. 684 (William Lee).

23. The letters in the *Guardian* and *Record* are too numerous to cite. Allusion was made to this circumstance when the declaration was presented. See also (for Dean Hook of Chichester), Ieuan Ellis, *Seven Against Christ: A Study of 'Essays and Reviews'* (Leiden, 1980), p. 194.

24. Longley to Pusey, March 2, 1864, Pusey House.

25. *Guardian*, May 18, 1864, p. 479.

26. Ellis, *Seven Against Christ*, p. 194.

27. The story is told in W. H. Brock and R. M. Macleod, 'The Scientists' Declaration: Reflexions on Science and Belief in the Wake of *Essays and Reviews*, 1864–5', *British Journal for the History of Science*, 9 (March 1976): 39–66. They estimate some 5000 possible signatories, so the rate of assent was only one in eight.

28. Henry Parry Liddon, *The Whole counsel of God: or, the duty of the Clergy as Teachers of the people, with particular reference ... to the recent judgment in the case of 'Essays and Reviews'. A Sermon ...* (Oxford, 1864); Archer Gurney, *The Faith against Free-Thinkers; or, Modern Rationalism, as exhibited in the writings of Mr. Buckle, Bishop Colenso, M. Renan, and the Essayists* (London, 1864); William Charles Lake, *The Inspiration of Scripture, and Eternal Punishment. Two Sermons ... with a preface on the 'Oxford Declaration' ...* (Oxford, 1864); *An Answer to the Questions Raised by the 'Essays and Reviews', being a Sermon on Faith ...* (London, [1864]). Probably the last pamphlet dealing substantively with the book was *Church Reform and True Christianity* (London, 1867), by a layman.

29. James Randall, *A Charge ...* (Oxford, 1864), by one of the committee for the declaration. R. J. Eden, bishop of Bath and Wells, delivered an unpublished Charge: 'the recent judgment left the doctrines of the Church untouched ... the decision gives no latitude for holding or promulgating the heretical doctrines'. *Record*, April 8, 1864, p. 2. But Lord Arthur Hervey criticized the declaration in his archidiaconal Charge: *Guardian*, May 11, 1864, p. 456.

30. Evelyn Abbott and Lewis Campbell, *The Life and Letters of Benjamin Jowett, M.A., Master of Balliol College, Oxford* (New York, 1897), pp. 314–315. See also Liddon, *Pusey*, 4: 32–33.

31. Abbott and Campbell, *Jowett*, pp. 315–316.

32. *Guardian*, April 20, 1864, p. 370.

33. Hamilton's diary, April 24, 1864, Pusey House Hamilton Mss.

34. *Guardian*, April 20, 1864, p. 370.

35. *Ibid.*, April 27, 1864, p. 405.

36. A 'literate' is an ordinand without a university degree. Thirlwall had much experience of them in his Welsh diocese.

37. *Guardian*, April 27, 1864, pp. 406–407.

38. *Ibid.*, pp. 407–408.

39. *Ibid.*, pp. 408–411.

40. It is often said that Longley gave a 'casting' vote, but since he had not voted with the others, he merely gave his single vote afterwards.

41. *Guardian*, April 27, 1864, p. 411. The *Guardian*'s leader (p. 389) deplored 'the practice of censuring books'.

42. *Guardian*, June 22, 1864, pp. 597–598.

43. *Ibid.*, June 29, 1864, p. 629.

44. *Ibid.*, pp. 629–630.

45. *Ibid.*, pp. 630–631.

46. The Act for the Submission of the Clergy forbade synods to enact any canon, constitution or ordinance without previous royal licence. It had not been held to prevent resolutions such as condemnations of books. The last one passed was in 1711, and the attempted condemnation of Hoadly's sermon in 1717, which led to the suppression of Convocation for 150 years, was not claimed to be a violation of the statute. Rolt was substituted for Palmer in this opinion because the Attorney-General could not give a private opinion relating to the powers of the Crown.

47. This was a real possibility. Bishop Gray of Capetown, Colenso's antagonist, had told Longley that if the judgment were not repudiated by the Church he could not remain in communion with the Church of England. Gray to Keble, April 12, 1864, Keble College Keble Mss. 91. There was a frantic correspondence by Keble, Pusey and Wilberforce to hold Gray in line. A threat to secede to Rome was made by Wilberforce's son-in-law, H. J. Pye: Wilberforce to Pye, March 7, 1864, in R. K. Pugh, *The Letter-Book of Samuel Wilberforce* [Oxfordshire Record Society 47] (n.p., 1970), pp. 395–396. Pye was reassured by the action of Convocation: H. J. Pye, *Convocation. A Sermon, on the late synodical condemnation of the Essays and Reviews* (London, 1864), delivered on June 26. But in 1868 Pye and his wife converted to Rome.

48. *Guardian*, June 29, 1864, p. 631.

49. *Ibid.*

50. *Ibid.*, June 22, 1864, p. 597.

51. *Ibid.*, June 29, 1864, pp. 635–639.

52. *Ibid.*, July 6, 1864, pp. 662–668. To give a full report of the debate, the *Guardian* carried it through several weekly issues. I was aided in identifying the participants by an appendix to the dissertation of M. A. Crowther, then M. A. Worden, 'Conflicts over Religious Inquiry among the Anglican Clergy in the 1860s', Oxford, 1968.

53. Robert E. Rodes, Jr., *Law and Modernization in the Church of England: Charles II to the Welfare State* (Notre Dame, IN, 1991), p. 366.

54. 'Synodical Condemnation of *Essays and Reviews*', *Guardian*, June 29, 1864, p. 620. The writer was impressed by Stanley's performance.

55. 'The Month', *Church and State Review*, 4 (July 1, 1864): 13.

56. *The Times*, June 25, 1864, p. 11.

57. *Dramatis Personae* (1864), cited by L. E. Elliott-Binns, *English Thought 1860–1900: The Theological Element* (London, 1956), p. 6.

58. 'The Three Pastorals', *Edinburgh Review*, 120 (July 1854): 268–307. The third pastoral was that of Cardinal Wiseman, who commented on the lack of authority in the Anglican Church. I cite the article from the revised version as reprinted in A. O. J. Cockshut, ed., *Religious Controversies of the Nineteenth Century: Selected Documents* (Lincoln, NB, 1966), pp. 191–216. Cockshut remarks that the essay 'shows how Erastianism can, in the mind of a man like Stanley, be a truly religious principle' (p. 191).

59. *The Debate in the House of Lords on the Power of Convocation, July 15th, 1864 ...* (London, [1864]), pp. 38, 43; published by disestablishmentarians.

60. *Ibid.*, pp. 45, 46.

61. *Ibid.*, pp. 48, 49, 52–53, 54.

62. *Ibid.*, pp. 56, 59.

63. A. R. Ashwell and R. G. Wilberforce, *Life of the Right Reverend Samuel Wilberforce, D.D.* (New York, 1883), pp. 392–396; Francis Warre Cornish, *The English Church in the Nineteenth Century*, 2 vols (London, 1910), 2: 236; J. B. Atlay, *The Victorian Chancellors*, 2 vols (London, 1906–8), 2: 267.

64. *Guardian*, July 20, 1864, p. 701.

65. *Ibid.*, p. 708. Denison's *Church and State Review*, 5 (September 1, 1864): 74, put it more dramatically: 'Since the days of Jeffreys, no holder of the Great Seal has used such reckless violence of language.'

66. *The Gladstone Diaries*, ed. H. C. G. Matthew (Oxford, 1978), 6: 290. See Ellis, *Seven Against Christ*, p. 200.

67. *Record*, July 18, 1864, p. 2. The emphasis on the absence of lay representation in Convocation reflects the concerns of the *Record's* proprietor, Alexander Haldane, a Scot who never quite lost his presbyterian instincts. See Josef L. Altholz, 'Alexander Haldane, the *Record* and Religious Journalism', *Victorian Periodicals Review*, 20 (Spring 1987): 23–31.

Chapter 15

1. W. E. Gladstone to Pusey, February 19, 1864, Pusey House; Gladstone to Keble, March 31 and April 13, 1864, Keble Mss. K 90. For Gladstone's fuller position, see Ieuan Ellis, *Seven Against Christ: A Study of 'Essays and Reviews'* (Leiden, 1980), pp. 208–209.

2. Pusey to Gladstone, February 18 and 21, 1864, Pusey House.

3. The Judicature Act, 1873, reconstituted the Judicial Committee without the bishops. When implemented in 1876, a rota of bishops supplied theological assessors to advise the judges. P. A. Howell, *The Judicial Committee of the Privy Council 1833–1876: Its Origins, Structure and Development* (Cambridge, 1979), p. 71.

4. Ellis, *Seven Against Christ*, pp. 207–208. The debates were reported in the *Chronicle of Convocation* and the *Guardian*.

5. *Case, as to the legal force of the judgment of the Privy Council, in re Fendall v. Wilson; with the opinion of the Attorney-General and Sir Hugh Cairns* (London, 1864), pp. 20, 22.

6. Pusey, *The Times*, September 16, 1864, p. 10; Keble, *ibid.*, September 22, 1864, p. 7. Pusey had to explain a reference to the possibility of a 'Free Church' secession in his preface as 'a warning fact'.

7. The association was to uphold 'the right of the English Church to declare, maintain, and enforce her own vital doctrines among her own members'; it was proposed to suspend contributions to the Church endowment until orthodoxy was restored and to collect a fund to return favourable M.P.s. There is an extensive correspondence in Pusey House and Keble College.

8. Pusey to Gladstone, February 21, [1865], Pusey House. M. A. Crowther, *Church Embattled: Religious Controversy in Mid-Victorian England* (Newton Abbot, 1970), mentions a private meeting at Cuddesdon of eminent churchmen of both parties. The bishops as a body discussed the question but reached no agreement: H.

Kirk Smith, *William Thomson, Archbishop of York: His Life and Times* (London, 1958), p. 42.

9. See W. R. Ward, *Victorian Oxford* (London, 1965).

10. One of the original committee for the declaration complained of a 'clerical despotism' and stated that the union of High and Low 'was temporary and for a given end'. Rev. J. Miller to Tait, September 23, 1864, Lambeth Palace Tait Mss., vol. 81. Jowett noted that 'the English people don't like clerical tribunals and the Evangelicals are beginning to be afraid of being delivered into the hands of the High Church'. Jowett to Florence Nightingale, December 4, 1864, Balliol College Jowett Mss., vol. 1.

11. J. J. Stewart Perowne, ed., *Remains Literary and Theological of Connop Thirlwall*, 2 vols (London, 1877), 2: 132, 138, 142–143.

12. It is only slightly overpraised by a descendant as 'Thirlwall's greatest single theological contribution, because, speaking as a responsible authority, he delimited, for the first time in English history, the rights and powers of a church working within a sovereign state'. John Connop Thirlwall, Jr., *Connop Thirlwall, Historian and Theologian* (London, 1936), p. 241.

13. Pusey thought of a 'Society for the prosecution of heresy' to defray expenses: Pusey to Hamilton, February 22, 1865, Pusey House. Owen Chadwick, *The Victorian Church*, 2 vols (London, 1966–70), 2: 95. There is a delightful chapter on 'The Clergyman Who Subscribes for Colenso' in Anthony Trollope, *Clergymen of the Church of England* (London, 1866).

14. Chadwick, *Victorian Church*, 2: 90–97. The legal aspects are discussed in Robert E. Rodes, Jr, *Law and Modernization in the Church of England: Charles II to the Welfare State* (Notre Dame, IN, 1991), pp. 325–331. The best biography is Peter Hinchliff, *John William Colenso, Bishop of Natal* (London, 1964). Colenso is treated with respect in a chapter in John Rogerson, *Old Testament Criticism in the Nineteenth Century: England and Germany* (London, 1984).

15. There is a chapter on Voysey in Crowther, *Church Embattled*. Rodes, *Law and Modernization*, pp. 262–263, considers the Heath and Voysey cases together.

16. *Ibid.*, p. 275.

17. L. E. Elliott-Binns, *Religion in the Victorian Era*, 2nd edn (London, 1946), p. 289. The 'Speaker's Commentary', sponsored by Denison's brother, was a later attempt to mine the same vein.

18. H. D. McDonald, *Theories of Revelation: An Historical Study 1860–1960* (London, 1963), p. 58; see also pp. 46–48.

19. Owen Chadwick, *The Spirit of the Oxford Movement: Tractarian Essays* (Cambridge, 1990), p. 246. See also Chadwick, *Victorian Church*, 2: 75, and Desmond Bowen, *The Idea of the Victorian Church* (Montreal, 1968), p. 182.

20. John O. Johnston, *Life and Letters of Henry Parry Liddon* (London, 1904), p. 89, reports that the first edition of 2500 copies sold out; eight editions totalling 25,000 copies had been sold by 1880; further editions sold at the rate of 800 copies a year until Liddon's death in 1890. There evidently was a demand for the reassurance that Liddon provided.

21. Ellis, *Seven Against Christ*, p. 149–150.

22. Crowther, *Church Embattled*, pp. 147–148; Chadwick, *Victorian Church*, 2: 132–133.

23. Evelyn Abbott and Lewis Campbell, *The Life and Letters of Benjamin Jowett, M.A., Master of Balliol College, Oxford* (New York, 1897), pp. 317–320; Geoffrey Faber, *Jowett: A Portrait with Background* (London, 1957), pp. 340–342. This was £100 more than the motions of Stanley and Pusey had proposed, presumably to bring the salary up to the level of the other chairs.

24. 'I do not know how to get on without the character of a "martyr". To be a martyr is a delightful position ... As an unfeeling but sagacious friend once said to me, "Next to having a good place, there is nothing like a good grievance"'. Jowett to Robert Morier, March 7, 1865, in Abbott and Campbell, *Jowett*, p. 410.

25. 'Obloquy drove him back to the fastness. Five years later further obloquy made him drop the portcullis and draw up the bridge.' Chadwick, *Victorian Church*, 1: 552. See also Faber, *Jowett*, p. 325.

26. Jowett to Nightingale, September, 1864. Balliol College Jowett Mss., vol. 1. Nightingale was herself an amateur theologian.

27. Peter Hinchliff, *Benjamin Jowett and the Christian Religion* (Oxford, 1987), p. 92, the best analysis of Jowett's later theological positions.

28. Ellis, *Seven Against Christ*, pp. 256–257.

29. Rogerson, *Old Testament Criticism*, p. 238.

30. Cited in Ellis, *Seven Against Christ*, p. 242.

31. See the 'Preface to the Twelfth Edition' (London, 1865).

32. See the entries in *The Wellesley Index to Victorian Periodicals*, vol. 3 (Toronto, 1979). Pattison substituted for Wilson in October 1868.

33. Quoted in Ellen Williams, *The Life and Letters of Rowland Williams, D.D.* (London, 1874), p. 262.

34. 'It is plain that the antagonism between Science and Religion arises much more from a difference of spirit and temper in the students of the two than from any opposition between the two.' Quoted in David L. Edwards, *Leaders of the Church of England 1828–1944* (London, 1971), p. 295.

35. See Pattison's *Memoirs* (London, 1885); V. H. H. Green, *Oxford Common Room: A Study of Lincoln College and Mark Pattison* (London, 1957); and John Sparrow, *Mark Pattison and the Idea of a University* (Cambridge, 1967). I am indebted to Warden Sparrow for the text of Pattison's final statement of belief.

Chapter 16

1. P. T. Marsh, *The Victorian Church in Decline: Archbishop Tait and the Church of England 1868–1882* (London, 1969), p. 17.

2. The title page was not changed except for the date, with the confusing result that the 1869 edition is numbered the 'Twelfth', the same as the 1865 edition. See Josef L. Altholz, 'Publishing History of *Essays and Reviews*', *Notes & Queries*, n.s. 29 (August 1982): 312.

3. Wilson's words, quoted in Ieuan Ellis, *Seven Against Christ: A Study of 'Essays and Reviews'* (Leiden, 1980), p. 200.

4. Pusey to Liddon, November 13, 1872, in Henry Parry Liddon, *Life of Edward Bouverie Pusey*, 4 vols (London, 1898), 4: 208.

5. Pusey, October 7, 1869, *ibid.*, p. 207. Pusey frequently played with the idea of a 'Free Church' or non-juring secession.

6. Both quotations are from E. G. Sandford, ed., *Memoirs of Archbishop Temple, by Seven Friends*, 2 vols (London, 1906), 1: 281.

7. George Anthony Denison, *Analysis of 'Essays and Reviews'* (London, 1869), p. 3.

8. Denison, *The Synod of Canterbury and 'The Bishop of Exeter': A Letter, addressed to the Ven. the Prolocutor of the Lower House* (London, 1869), pp. 3–4, 8.

9. John W. Burgon, *Protests of the Bishops against the Consecration of Dr. Temple to the See of Exeter: preceded by a Letter to the Right Hon. and Right Rev. John Jackson, D.D., Bishop of London* (Oxford, 1870), giving a useful compilation of state-

ments by bishops who declined to consecrate; *Dr. Temple's 'Explanation' Examined* (Oxford, 1870).

10.   W. I. Trower, *A Letter to the Right Rev. the Bishop of Moray and Ross, Primus of the Scottish Episcopal Church, explanatory of opposition to the election of Rev. Dr. Temple, as Bishop of Exeter* (London, 1869), by a High Churchman; [William Keane], *Protest against Dr. Temple's Consecration to the Bishopric of Exeter* (privately printed, 1869); W. G. Cookesley, *A Letter to the Clergy of Bedfordshire on the Nomination of Dr. Temple to the See of Exeter* (London, 1869), protesting Gladstone's act as 'tyranny' but rejecting Pusey's call for separation; Edmund S. Grindle, *Episcopal Inconsistency; or, Convocation, the Bishops, and Dr. Temple* (London, 1869); James Mortimer Sangar, *Sacrilege! 'Who is on the Lord's Side?' A Word with Bishops, Clergy, and People about the proposed consecration to the See of Exeter of one of the 'Septem contra Christum'* (London, 1869); John Purcell Fitzgerald, *A Letter of Earnest Remonstrance to the Rt. Hon. W. E. Gladstone, M.P., First Lord of the Treasury, etc., upon his appointment of a co-writer with infidels to a Christian Bishopric* (London, 1870); John B. McClellan, *The Fourth Nicene Canon and the Election and Consecration of Bishops with special reference to the Case of Dr. Temple* (London, 1870).

11.   'An Ex-Incumbent of the Anglican Establishment', *A Defence of Mr. Gladstone's Church Policy, in the matter of 'The See of Exeter'* (London, 1869), ironic; J. N. D[arby], *Dialogue on Dr. Temple's Essay, with Preface in reference to the recent sermon and speech of the Lord Bishop of Exeter* (London, 1870?), the lengthiest.

12.   R. W. Church to Asa Gray, November 5, 1869, in Mary C. Church, ed., *Life and Letters of Dean Church* (London, 1894), p. 219.

13.   Owen Chadwick, *The Victorian Church*, 2 vols (London, 1966–70), 2: 87.

14.   Russell to Temple, November 26, 1869, in Sandford, *Temple*, 1: 279.

15.   Arthur C. Benson, *The Life of Edward White Benson, sometime Archbishop of Canterbury*, 2 vols (London, 1899), 1: 299.

16.   Quoted in Sandford, *Temple*, 1: 301. The letters of Browne, Wordsworth and Wilberforce are in *ibid.*, pp. 282, 283, 292.

17.   Temple to Coleridge, October 11, 1869, in *ibid.*, p. 285.

18.   Temple to Wordsworth, November 26, 1869, in *ibid.*, p. 293.

19.   Quoted in S. C. Carpenter, *Church and People, 1789–1889: A History of the Church of England from William Wilberforce to 'Lux Mundi'* (London, 1933), p. 289.

20.   Chadwick, *Victorian Church*, 2: 87–88; Sandford, *Temple*, 1: 291, crediting Canon Cook with managing the election. Archdeacon Philpotts, son of the late bishop, voted for election. Four prebendaries were absent.

21.   Sandford, *Temple*, 1: 291–292.

22.   Wilberforce to Burgon, Bodleian Library Mss. Wilberforce d. 47. Wilberforce wrote to Arthur Gordon, January 16, 1870: 'With a very high opinion of Temple personally, I deeply regret the appointment, because he has so obstinately refused to part himself from the "Essays and Reviews" in their censured parts.' A. R. Ashwell and R. G. Wilberforce, *Life of the Right Rev. Samuel Wilberforce, D.D.* (New York, 1883), p. 496.

23.   Browne's letter, December 16, 1869, in G. W. Kitchin, *Edward Harold Browne, D.D., Lord Bishop of Winchester …* (London, 1895), pp. 324–325.

24.   The others were Ellicott of Gloucester, James Atlay of Hereford and G. A. Selwyn of Lichfield. Four others agreed with the protests.

25.   Sandford, *Temple*, 1: 295.

26.   *Ibid.*, p. 301; Chadwick, *Victorian Church*, 2: 89. In fact, no further edition of *Essays and Reviews* appeared.

27. Denison to Speaker J. E. Denison, February 10, 1870, in Louisa Evelyn Denison, ed., *Fifty Years at East Brent: The Letters of George Anthony Denison 1845–1896 Archdeacon of Taunton* (London, 1902), p. 112.

28. Denison said that he only changed his mind once, and then to a more intransigent position. But this case must be added. See Robert E. Rodes, Jr, *Law and Modernization in the Church of England: Charles II to the Welfare State* (Notre Dame, IN, 1991), p. 299.

29. Quoted in Sandford, *Temple*, 1: 302–305.

30. *Ibid.*, 1: 3. 'In Temple we see a man publicly pilloried for theological opinions which he did not hold but which his honour forbade him to repudiate publicly.' A. O. J. Cockshut, *Anglican Attitudes: A Study of Victorian Religious Controversies* (London, 1959), p. 69.

31. John Owen, *The Ideal of the Christian Minister* (London, [1870]), p. 13.

32. Jowett to Nightingale, July 2, 1869, in Vincent Quinn and John Prest, eds, *Dear Miss Nightingale: A selection of Benjamin Jowett's Letters to Florence Nightingale 1860–1893* (Oxford, 1987), p. 170.

33. July 15, 1869, *ibid.*, p. 171. 'I should not wonder if the contributors are reduced to Mr. Wilson, Campbell & myself': July 25, 1869, *ibid.*, p. 174.

34. M. A. Crowther, *Church Embattled: Religious Controversy in Mid-Victorian England* (Newton Abbot, 1970), p. 124.

35. Jowett to Caird, January 28, 1870, in Evelyn Abbott and Lewis Campbell, *The Life and Letters of Benjamin Jowett, M.A., Master of Balliol College, Oxford*, 2 vols (New York, 1897), 1: 441. Another letter to Caird, February 24, 1870, is pp. 443–444.

36. Various mentions in *ibid.*, pp. 442, 443, and a list in Ellis, *Seven Against Christ*, p. 239.

37. *Ibid.*, pp. 239–241. These works were related to the revision of the English Bible, from which Jowett was excluded.

38. Abbott and Campbell, *Jowett*, 2: 13, 15.

39. *Ibid.*, 2: 41. Lushington, 90 years old, came up to vote for Stanley. He died four weeks later of bronchitis contracted on the journey. Stanley officiated at his funeral. S. M. Waddams, *Law, Politics and the Church of England: The Career of Stephen Lushington, 1782–1873* (Cambridge, 1992), pp. 346–347.

40. R. B. Kennard, *In Memory of the Rev. Henry Bristow Wilson, B.D.* (London, 1888).

Chapter 17

1. A recent scholar regards the conflict between biblical critics and their opponents as 'principally a conflict of method', rather like a Kuhnian paradigm shift, in which the methods of the two schools 'did not seriously interact with one another, because their premises were equally irreconcilable. The circles barely intersect'. Nigel M. de S. Cameron, *Biblical Higher Criticism and the Defense of Infallibilism in 19th Century Britain* (Lewiston, NY, 1987), pp. 275, 144.

2. Newman, *University Sermons* (1872), quoted by Robert Pattison, *The Great Dissent: John Henry Newman and the Liberal Heresy* (New York, 1991), pp. 115–116. Pattison points out that the term 'night battle', later used by Matthew Arnold in *Dover Beach*, originated with the fifth-century church historian Socrates Scholasticus, writing about the Arians.

3. Francis Warre Cornish, *The English Church in the Nineteenth Century*, 2 vols (London, 1910), 2: 238.

Selected Bibliography

Manuscript sources

London: Lambeth Palace (Longley, Tait Mss.)
Oxford: Balliol College (Jowett Mss.); Bodleian Library (Pattison, S. Wilberforce Mss.); Keble College (Keble, Liddon Mss.); Pusey House (Hamilton, Pusey Mss.)

Periodicals

Dailies: *Daily News; The Times*
Weeklies: *Christian Witness; Guardian; Jewish Chronicle; London Review; National Reformer; Punch; Record* (thrice weekly); *Saturday Review; Spectator; Unitarian Herald; Weekly Review*
Fortnightlies: *Church of England Magazine; Literary Churchman*
Monthlies: *Christian Advocate; Christian Observer; Church and State Review; Ecclesiastic; Evangelical Magazine; Fraser's Magazine; Liberator; Macmillan's Magazine; Rambler; Wesleyan Methodist Magazine*
Quarterlies: *British Quarterly Review; Christian Remembrancer; Dublin Review; Eclectic Review; Edinburgh Review; Journal of Sacred Literature; London [Quarterly] Review; National Review; North British Review; Quarterly Review; Theological Review; Westminster Review*
An effort has been made to list all separate publications involved in the controversy in the footnotes, which are bibliographic. A good list of the literature is in Ellis, *Seven Against Christ* (see below).

Selected modern works

Altholz, Josef L. 'The Mind of Victorian Orthodoxy: Anglican Responses to *Essays and Reviews*, 1860–1864', *Church History*, 51 (June 1982): 186–197. Reprinted in Gerald Parsons, ed., *Religion in Victorian Britain*, vol. 4: *Interpretations* (Manchester, 1988), pp. 28–40.
Cameron, Nigel M. de S. *Biblical Higher Criticism and the Defense of Infallibilism in 19th Century Britain* (Lewiston, NY, 1987).
Chadwick, Owen. *The Victorian Church*, 2 vols (London, 1966–70).
Cockshut, A. O. J. *Anglican Attitudes: A Study of Victorian Religious Controversies* (London, 1959).

Corsi, Pietro. *Science and Religion: Baden Powell and the Anglican Debate* (Cambridge, 1988).

Crowther, M. A. *Church Embattled: Religious Controversy in Mid-Victorian England* (Newton Abbot, 1970).

Ellis, Ieuan. *Seven Against Christ: A Study of 'Essays and Reviews'* (Leiden, 1980).

Faber, Geoffrey. *Jowett: A Portrait with Background* (London, 1957).

Hinchliff, Peter. *Benjamin Jowett and the Christian Religion* (Oxford, 1987).

Meacham, Standish. *Lord Bishop: The Life of Samuel Wilberforce* (Cambridge, MA, 1970).

Nimmo, Duncan. 'Learning against Religion, Learning as Religion: Mark Pattison and the "Victorian Crisis of Faith"', in Keith Robbins, ed., *Studies in Church History,* 17 (Oxford, 1981): 311-324.

Reardon, Bernard M. G. *From Coleridge to Gore: A Century of Religious Thought in Britain* (London, 1971).

Rodes, Robert E., Jr. *Law and Modernization in the Church of England: Charles II to the Welfare State* (Notre Dame, IN, 1991).

Rogerson, John. *Old Testament Criticism in the Nineteenth Century: England and Germany* (London, 1984).

Swanston, Hamish F. G. *Ideas of Order: Anglicans and the renewal of theological method in the middle years of the nineteenth century* (Assen, 1973).

Willey, Basil. *More Nineteenth Century Studies: A Group of Honest Doubters* (London, 1956).

Index

Abraham 161
Act of Uniformity 91
Admiralty Court 86
Aids to Faith 80, 84, 142, 168, 170, 171
Ainslie, Robert 71
alienation, spiritual 22, 24
American Quarterly Review 68
Anglicanism 1, 3, 4, 14, 36, 111, 134, 135
    liberal 4 *see also* Broad Church
    see also orthodoxy
Anselm 83
apologetics 28, 32
Arches, Court of 85, 87, 88, 98, 99, 101, 109, 149, 166, 172, 173, 174, 176
Arnold, Thomas 5, 6, 7, 15, 17, 46, 49, 124, 149
Articles, Thirty-Nine 22, 23, 24, 42, 44, 48, 52, 85, 87, 88, 89, 90, 91, 92, 93, 94, 95, 96, 97, 98, 99, 100, 102, 104, 105, 107, 108, 109, 115, 116, 131, 132, 133, 134, 138, 155, 176, 181
Atonement (doctrine) 3, 7, 16, 43, 64, 83, 102, 113, 161, 168
Augustine 92

Baden Powell *see* Powell, Baden
Bampton Lectures 4, 9, 80, 132, 134
Baring, Charles, Bishop of Gloucester 59, 161
Baur, Ferdinand Christian 31, 132, 153
Benson, Edward White 137, 158, 186
Bernard, Mountague 102, 103
Bernard, Thomas Dehany 132
Bible, books of *see also* Scripture
    Corinthians 7
    Daniel 18, 77, 81, 92, 96, 131, 132, 170
    Galatians 7, 16, 146
    Genesis 17, 18, 25, 26, 68, 69, 76, 78, 82, 96, 151, 160
    Isaiah 18, 77, 81, 132
    Job 18
    Jonah 18
    Joshua 18, 174
    2 Peter 97
    Romans 7, 146, 174
    Thessalonians 7, 146
Bible Society 35, 60, 107
Bickersteth, Edward 58, 59, 161
Bishop of Salisbury *v.* Williams 85, 86, 173, 177
Blakeney, Richard Paul 65, 161
Book of Common Prayer 89–90, 132, 176
Bowen, Charles 140, 177
Boyle, George David 13
Boyle, Robert 65
Brighton Observer 71
British Association for the Advancement of Science 12
British Quarterly Review 71, 112, 167, 178
British Standard 71
Broad Chalke (Wilts.) 11, 36, 85, 101, 157, 171
Broad Church movement 1, 4–8, 9, 10, 11, 14, 17, 48, 53, 97, 98, 128, 134, 135, 136, 140, 154, 155, 166, 171, 176
Browne, Harold 80, 82, 83, 121, 122, 137, 138, 170, 186
Browning, Robert 126
Buckle 41
Buckland, William 25, 151
Bungener, M. 22
Bunsen, Christian von 5, 16–19, 37, 40, 77, 89, 90, 92, 100, 105, 143, 147, 149, 150, 153, 154, 155, 160, 169, 174
Burder *v.* Heath 87, 88, 89, 93, 95, 173
Burgon, John William 66–7, 137, 146, 162, 185, 186
Butler, Joseph 3, 69, 76, 132, 145, 170

Caird, Edward 140, 187
Cairns, Hugh 113, 118, 123, 127, 129, 133, 179, 183
Cairns, John 67, 162
Calvinism 3, 22, 24
Cambridge Essays 9, 10, 12, 14, 15
'Cambridge three' 13
Cambridge University 6, 11, 145, 158
    King's 11, 158
    St. Catherine's 12
Cambridge University Press 9

Campbell, John 71, 166
Campbell, Lewis 140, 173, 175, 181, 184, 185, 187
Cape Colony 131
Carlyle, Thomas 162
Chapman, John 10, 39, 147
Chelmsford, Lord 104
Chretien, Charles Peter 75, 168
Christian Advocate 65, 154
Christian Observer 34, 36, 37, 38, 98, 111, 154, 173, 178, 181
Christian Remembrancer 36, 37, 112, 154, 155, 165, 171, 178
Christian Socialist movement 6, 9
Church, Richard William 137
Church and State 5, 6
Church and State Review 98, 125, 169, 173, 174, 178, 181, 182, 183
Church of England 1, 4, 12, 13, 22, 27, 35, 36, 38, 39, 40, 42, 43, 44, 47, 48, 51, 52, 59, 63, 88, 91, 93, 98, 104, 105, 107, 110, 111, 112, 113, 114, 115, 116, 118, 121, 122, 124, 126, 128, 129, 130, 131, 136, 137, 140, 141, 143, 151, 172, 176, 177, 182, 184
Church of England Magazine 36
Church Times 137
Clergy Discipline Act, 1840 85
Clerical and Lay Association for the Maintenance of Evangelical Principles 51
Clerical Journal 69
Clerical Subscription Act 132
Clerke, Charles Carr 119
Close, Francis 68
Cockin, W. 35, 154
Colenso, John William 99, 103, 106, 130, 131, 142, 143, 174, 181, 182, 184
Coleridge, John Duke 85, 86, 92, 100, 103, 105
Coleridge, Sir John Taylor 103–104, 175, 186
Coleridge, Samuel Taylor 5, 24, 32, 47, 81, 146, 150, 151, 152, 153
Comte, Auguste 40
Congregationalists 36, 71, 112, 179
conscience 16, 32, 33
Contemporary Review 140
Convocation of the Clergy 1
Convocation of the province of Canterbury 56, 57, 58, 59, 64, 65, 98, 103,
106, 107, 112, 117, 120, 123, 124, 125, 127, 128, 129, 131, 132, 137, 142, 143, 181, 183
Convocation of the province of York 59
Cook, Frederick Charles 81, 82, 170
Cowie, Benjamin Morgan 65
Cranworth, Lord 104
Cumming, John 65, 71, 161, 166

Daily News 100, 119, 133, 173, 174
Darby, John Nelson 71
Darwin, Charles 1, 14, 21, 34, 41, 64, 107, 131, 134, 143, 148, 150, 154, 155, 160, 165, 166
Davidson, Samuel 140
Davies, John Llewelyn 74, 75, 168
Deane, James Parker 86, 88, 89, 91, 92, 93, 100
deism and deists 3, 4, 26, 27, 28, 64, 69, 152, 160
de Morgan, Augustus 120
Denison, George Anthony 56, 57, 58, 59, 61, 62, 63, 65, 75, 76, 85, 98, 100, 112, 117, 120, 121, 124, 125, 129, 137, 138, 139, 159, 160, 161, 168, 169, 181, 183, 185, 187
Derby 51, 64
De Wette, W.M.L. 31
Disraeli, Benjamin 49, 63, 136, 160
divines, Anglican 1, 3, 6
Dorchester 51, 52
Dorset County Chronicle 70
Dublin 65
Dublin Review 72, 112, 167, 178
Duncan, David 72, 167

East Brent 137
Ebury, Lord 132
Ecclesiastic 34, 67, 154, 162
Eclectic Review 36, 71, 167
Eden, Robert John, Bishop of Bath and Wells 59, 161, 181
Edinburgh 140
Edinburgh Review 13, 34, 39, 42, 45, 60, 70, 77, 103, 126, 146, 156, 169, 182
Eichhorn, Johann Gottfried 18
Eliot, George 10, 60, 159
Elizabeth I 23, 85, 99
Ellicott, Charles John 80, 83, 84, 121, 136, 170, 171, 186
Elliott, Gilbert 140

Ellis, Ieuan 1–2, 32
Elton, Charles 133
English Church Union 57
Essayists 1, 2, 34, 35, 36, 37, 39, 40, 41,
43, 44, 45, 46, 47, 48, 49, 50, 53, 54,
55, 56, 57, 58, 60, 61, 63, 64, 65, 67,
68, 69, 70, 71, 72, 73, 74, 75, 76, 80,
82, 86, 97, 99, 100, 103, 105, 107,
109, 110, 124, 125, 131, 132, 133,
134, 135, 136, 142, 143, 145, 150,
154, 171, 178, 181
Essays and Reviews 1, 3, 4, 8, 9, 11, 13,
14, 15, 16, 20, 26, 28, 31, 32, 33, 34,
35, 36, 37, 39, 41, 42, 45, 46, 50, 51,
52, 53, 56, 57, 58, 59, 60, 61, 62, 63,
64, 65, 66, 67, 68, 69, 70, 71, 72, 73,
74, 75, 76, 77, 79–80, 83, 84, 86, 95,
100, 103, 105, 107, 111, 117, 120,
121, 123, 124–5, 128, 131, 134, 135,
136, 137, 139, 140, 141, 142, 143,
145, 146, 147, 148, 149, 150, 151,
152, 153, 154, 155, 156, 157, 158,
159, 160, 161, 162, 163, 164, 165,
166, 167, 169, 170, 171, 173, 174,
175, 176, 177, 181, 185, 186
Essays and Reviews (second edition) 140
'Essays and Reviews' Anticipated 60, 159
Evangelical Alliance 143, 155, 173
Evangelical Magazine 71
Evangelical Review 34
evangelicals 7, 27, 64, 68, 71, 72, 93, 98,
102, 111, 141, 167, 184
Evans, Marian *see* Eliot, George
evolution 26 *see also Origin of Species*
Ewald, H.G.A. von 18, 31, 150, 153
Exeter, bishopric and chapter of 137–8
Exeter Hall 35

Faith and Peace 63, 76
Fendall, James 75, 86, 99, 110, 124, 168,
171, 178
Fendall *v.* Wilson 75, 86, 93, 96, 173,
176, 177, 179, 183
Fitzgerald, William 81, 84, 170
Fortnightly Review 134
Fraser's Magazine 36, 37, 71, 98, 111,
134, 147, 155, 166, 173, 174, 178
Freeman, Edward Augustus 133
Freeman, Philip 139
Fremantle, W.E. 53, 158
Fremantle, William Henry 140

Fremantle, William Robert 117, 118, 180
Friends *see* Quakers
Fulham Palace 52, 53

Galileo, Galilei 25
Garbett, Edward 65, 154, 161
Garden, Francis 74, 75, 168
Geneva 22
Germany 5, 18
biblical criticism l, 5, 6, 8, 17, 19, 20,
22, 28, 31, 32, 33, 36, 44, 47, 50,
63, 64, 67, 69, 77, 81, 153
Gilbert, Ashhurst Turner, Bishop of
Chichester 59, 63
Gladstone, William Ewart 128, 129, 130,
136, 137, 179, 183, 186
Goode, William 118, 180
Goodwin, Charles Wycliffe 9, 11, 25–6,
31, 32, 37, 46, 56, 69, 82, 86, 106,
147, 148, 151, 160, 161, 164, 165
essay 14, 25–6
Goodwin, Harvey 56, 61, 62, 64, 69, 76,
78, 124, 134, 165
Gorham judgment, 1850 88, 89, 98, 101,
104, 108, 111, 112, 130, 146
Gospels 78, 82, 91, 122, 161
Goulburn, Edward Meyrick 77, 169
Graham, John, Bishop of Chester 60
Grant, Sir Alexander 13, 140
Gray, Robert 130, 131, 182
Great Staughton 36, 86
Gresley, William 64, 160
Griffin, John Nash 76, 169
Guardian 34, 35, 49, 56, 59, 67, 69, 72,
98, 102, 111, 113, 114, 118, 125, 127,
136, 137, 154, 156, 157, 158, 159,
160, 162, 166, 167, 171, 172, 173,
174, 177, 178, 179, 180, 181, 182, 183

Haddan, Arthur West 79, 170
Hamilton, Walter Kerr, Bishop of
Salisbury 50, 57, 58, 59, 61, 62, 63, 70,
85, 86, 99, 101, 110, 114, 121, 157,
166, 171, 174, 175, 176, 177, 178,
179, 181, 184
Hampden, Renn Dickson, Bishop of
Hereford 52, 53, 174
Hare, Julius Charles 6, 17
Harrison, Frederic 34, 37, 39, 40, 41, 42,
49, 50, 64, 142, 152, 155, 156
Havernick, H.A.C. 77

Hawkins, Edward 66, 148, 162
Heath, Dunbar 100, 131, 172, 184
Heaviside, James 62
Hengstenberg, Ernst Wilhelm 67, 69, 77, 164
Henry VIII, King 123, 133
Herschel, Sir John 120
heresy 21, 24, 58, 85, 88, 89, 91, 101, 102, 111, 131, 148, 151, 184
Heurtley, Charles 66, 78, 79, 102, 162, 169
High Church 3, 4, 10, 13, 27, 34, 37, 48, 49, 51, 57, 58, 59, 66, 67, 68, 75, 77, 79, 85, 92, 98, 103, 107, 112, 117, 118, 128, 129, 130, 131, 137, 141, 161
Hony, William 62, 178
Hooker, Richard 90
Hort, Fenton John Anthony 13, 73, 146, 167
Houghton, Lord (Monckton Milnes) 126, 128
Hughes, Thomas 73, 168
Hume, David 132, 170
Hutton, Richard Holt 75, 168
Huxley, Thomas Henry 12, 166
Huxtable, Edgar 76, 169

Inquirer 36
inspiration (of the Bible) 84, 90, 94, 104, 163
Irish Church 118
Irons, William Josiah 51, 58, 78, 162, 169

Jackson, John, Bishop of Lincoln 57, 121, 123, 124, 138, 161, 185
Jelf, Richard William 56, 59, 65, 68, 75, 158, 159, 161, 168
Jeune, Francis 101, 175
Jews 17, 19, 40, 72, 152, 171
Jones, Harry 71, 166
Journal of Sacred Literature 69, 165
Jowett, Benjamin 6, 7, 8, 12, 13, 14, 28–31, 32, 37, 39, 41, 42, 43, 46, 49, 52, 53, 54, 55, 57, 61, 67, 69, 73, 75, 79, 80, 81, 83, 86, 87, 98, 101, 102, 103, 106, 114, 120, 131, 133, 134, 135, 140, 145, 146, 148, 151, 152, 153, 155, 156, 158, 159, 160, 161, 162, 164, 165, 168, 171, 172, 173, 175, 176, 177, 181, 184, 185, 187
  essay 7, 8, 28–31

Joyce, James Wayland 75, 168

Keble, John 50, 85, 111, 112, 114, 120, 129, 130, 157, 168, 171, 175, 177, 178, 179, 182, 183
Kegan Paul, C. *see* Paul, John Kegan
Keil, Carl Friedrich 77
Kennard, Robert Bruce 70, 140, 166, 172
King's College, London 56
Kingsdown, Lord 104, 175

Lachmann, K.K.F.W. 7
Lambeth Conference 131
Lambeth Palace 52, 158
Lampeter, St. David's College 11, 36, 94, 171
Lancaster Independent College 140
Langley, J.N. 74
Lathbury, D.C. 118
Lee, William 76, 169
Lessing, Gotthold Ephraim 15, 31
Liberator 71, 112, 178
Liddell, Henry George 133, 178
Liddon, Henry Parry 50, 114, 118, 129, 132, 157, 171, 175, 179, 180, 181, 184, 185
Lightfoot, Joseph Barber 13, 73
Literary Churchman 67, 68, 69, 70, 154, 160, 162, 165, 168
Literary Gazette 34
Liverpool 60, 70
London Quarterly Review see *London Review*
London Review 36, 71, 154, 165
Longley, Charles, Archbishop of Canterbury 101, 105, 108, 114, 115, 119, 122, 123, 136, 161, 176, 177, 178, 179, 182
Longmans (publishers) 50, 70, 157
Lonsdale, John, Bishop of Lichfield 121
Lords, House of 126, 128, 183
Low Church 3, 4, 49, 51, 58, 59, 117, 118, 128, 130, 136, 141
Lowth, Robert 152
Ludlow, John Malcolm 74, 75, 168
Lushington, Stephen 87, 88, 89, 91, 92, 93, 95, 96, 97, 98, 99, 100, 101, 102, 104, 105, 107, 108, 109, 110, 111, 114, 117, 172, 173, 174, 175, 176, 187
Lutheranism 17
Lyell, Sir Charles 131, 166, 169

Lyttleton, William Henry 75, 168

Macaulay, Thomas Babington 21
Macmillan's Magazine 69, 111, 165, 178
Manchester 72
Manchester Friends' Institute 72, 167
Manning, Henry Edward 112, 178
Mansel, Henry Longueville 4, 33, 75,
  80–1, 84, 132, 146, 170
Margoliouth, Moses 65, 162
Martyr, Justin 47
Maurice, Frederick Denison 4, 6, 9, 20,
  65, 71, 73, 74, 75, 102, 118, 119, 158,
  168, 175
Mauricians 74, 75
McCaul, Alexander 51, 56, 58, 59, 62,
  64, 81, 82, 94, 117, 124, 155, 159,
  160, 170, 172
McNaught, John 60, 61
McNeile, Hugh *see* M'Neile, Hugh
Methodism 26, 36, 71
Miall, Edward 71, 166
Mill, John Stuart 9, 164, 170
Miller, Canon 35
Miller, Hugh 25, 40
Miller, John Cale 184
Milman, Henry Hart 13
Milton, John 31
miracles (biblical) 4, 20, 21, 33, 65, 69,
  76, 78, 80–1, 82–3, 106, 132, 161,
  164, 168, 170
M'Neile, Hugh 60, 118, 166, 180
Moberly, George 64, 160
Moses and Mosaic teaching 25, 64, 82,
  84, 99, 132, 151, 165, 169, 170
Mozley, James Bowling 132
Mudie's Circulating Library 50
Muller, (Friedrich) Max 13, 17, 50, 140,
  157

National Reformer 36, 44, 154, 156
National Review 75, 107, 176
neology 49, 65, 160, 163 *see* Germany,
  biblical criticism
New Jerusalem (Swedenborgian) Church
  71
New Testament 4, 29, 52, 81, 83, 88, 92,
  109, 140, 151, 165
Newman, Francis 10, 98, 173, 175
Newman, John Henry 9, 10, 24, 35, 44,
  46, 102, 141, 187

Newman, William Lambert 39
Niebuhr, Barthold Georg 5, 6
Nightingale, Florence 98, 133, 173, 184,
  185, 187
Noetics 13, 53, 66
Nonconformist 71
North British Review 36, 71, 155, 167

Ogilvie, Charles 102
Old Testament 4, 29, 52, 65, 72, 83, 88,
  91, 92, 107, 109, 131, 132, 140, 149,
  151, 153, 165, 184, 185
Ollivant, Alfred, Bishop of Llandaff 11,
  121, 123, 160
Origin of Species 1, 14, 34, 151
orthodoxy (Anglican) 3, 4, 7, 8, 13, 32,
  33, 37, 39, 41, 49, 50, 55, 68, 69, 71,
  73, 79, 80, 84, 107, 109, 115, 117,
  128, 129, 132, 142, 149, 161, 164
Owen, John 139, 140, 187
Oxenham, Henry Nutcombe 72
Oxford Convocation 61, 62, 63, 117–28
Oxford Essays 9, 10, 11, 14, 15, 148, 154,
  155, 167, 170
Oxford University 3, 4, 6, 15, 35, 36, 37,
  46, 50, 55, 56, 63, 66, 76, 86, 87, 101,
  103, 117, 119–20, 130, 132, 133, 145,
  149, 158, 184
  All Souls 62, 160
  Balliol 39, 54, 133, 140, 146, 148,
    153, 156, 158, 172, 175, 181, 184,
    185
  Christ Church 133
  Lincoln 9–10, 50, 57, 148
  Oriel 66, 148
  St. John's 9
  Wadham 39
  Vice Chancellor's Court 102
Oxford Movement 3, 68 *see also*
  Tractarians

Paley, William 3, 5, 20, 21, 27, 33, 69,
  76, 78, 145, 151
Palmer, Sir Roundell 113, 118, 129, 133,
  182
Palmerston, Lord 136
Parker, John Henry and James (publish-
  ers) 76, 157
Parker, John William (junior) 9, 50
Parker, John William (senior) 9, 10, 11,
  14, 50, 70, 146, 148

Parker, Theodore 36, 154
Parliament 1
Pattison, Mark 9, 10, 11, 12, 14, 26–8,
  31, 32, 35, 37, 38, 40, 46, 50, 53, 55,
  57, 64, 69, 79, 86, 103, 106, 107, 132,
  134, 140, 146, 147, 148, 152, 154,
  161, 164, 165, 168, 170, 171, 176,
  180, 185
  essay 26–8
Paul, St. 7, 28, 46, 83
Paul, Charles Kegan 74
Pears, Steuart Adolphus 64, 160
Pelham, John Thomas, Bishop of
  Norwich 59
Pentateuch 82, 99, 170, 174
Phillimore, Robert Joseph 85, 86, 88, 91,
  92, 93, 99, 100, 101, 102, 103, 104,
  105, 108, 110, 111, 171, 172, 174,
  175, 176, 177, 178
Phillpotts, Henry, Bishop of Exeter 52,
  114, 136, 158, 160, 177, 186
Philpott, Henry, Bishop of Worcester 52,
  138
Plato 133
Plymouth Brethren 71, 137, 165
Pooley's case, 1857 103
Pottinger, Henry A. 102
Powell, Baden 9, 13, 14, 20–1, 31, 32,
  37, 43, 46, 47, 53, 69, 71, 76, 78, 80,
  86, 105–6, 134, 148, 150, 153, 164,
  165, 166
  essay 14, 20–1
Pratt, John Henry 64, 151, 160, 165
Prayer, Book of Common *see* Book of
  Common Prayer
Presbyterians 65
Press 34
Privy Council, Judicial Committee of the
  88, 93, 95, 96, 97, 99, 100, 101, 103,
  108, 114, 117, 121, 122, 123, 125,
  126, 130, 131, 142, 149, 174, 175,
  176, 178, 179, 180, 183
prophecy 20, 33, 68, 69, 77, 90, 92, 96,
  134, 161, 170
Protestant Reformation Society 65
Protestant Truth Society 71
Punch 49, 102, 157, 160, 173, 175, 180
Pusey, Edward Bouverie 3, 12, 50, 61,
  67, 101, 102, 103, 108, 110, 111, 113,
  114, 116, 117, 118, 119, 120, 129,
  130, 131, 132, 136, 156, 157, 162, 168,
  171, 175, 177, 178, 179, 180, 182,
  183, 184, 185, 186
Puseyites 24, 118

Quakers 72
Quarterly Review 13, 34, 39, 42, 45, 46,
  48, 71, 74, 111, 142, 156, 178

Rambler 72
rationalism 26, 39, 41, 44, 66, 68, 72,
  155, 160, 170
Rawlinson, George 82, 84, 170
Record 35, 36, 37, 38, 56, 60, 65, 69,
  98, 108, 111, 113, 115, 118, 128, 143,
  146, 154, 155, 157, 158, 159, 160,
  161, 170, 172, 173, 178, 179, 180
Reeve, Henry 103
Reformation 140
Renan, Ernest 17, 103, 132, 181
Replies to 'Essays and Reviews' 79, 80, 142,
  169
Repton school 64
Revelation 4, 5, 17, 20, 24, 27, 32, 33,
  47, 61, 65, 66, 76, 81, 97, 122, 149,
  162, 169, 184
Rolt, John 123, 127, 182
Roman Catholicism 36, 48, 65, 72, 93,
  112, 114, 137, 166, 177
Rorison, Gilbert 78, 79, 169
Rose, Henry John 77, 78, 169
Rugby School 5, 6, 12, 15, 35, 36, 54,
  77, 86, 134, 136, 169
Russell, Lord (John) 137

St. Paul's School 13
salvation 22, 23, 24, 65
'Mr. Sanders' (Thomas Collett Sandars)
  10, 147
Saturday Review 49, 70, 157, 165
Schleiermacher, F.D.E. 6, 60
science 15, 20, 21, 25
Scott, Robert 54
Scottish Episcopalian Church 78
Scottish Free Kirk 36, 71
Scripture 3, 4, 6, 11, 16, 18, 19, 22, 23,
  24, 25, 26, 28, 29, 30, 34, 37, 40, 42,
  43, 45, 46, 47, 51, 52, 57, 58, 61, 62,
  63, 65, 66, 69, 70, 75, 77, 78, 79, 82,
  83, 84, 89, 90, 91, 92, 93, 94, 95, 96,
  97, 98, 99, 102, 105, 106, 107, 108,
  109, 111, 112, 115, 116, 117, 119,

120, 122, 123, 131, 134, 150, 153, 161, 163, 164, 165, 171, 172, 178, 179 *see also* Bible, Gospels
Selwyn, William 62
Shaftesbury, Earl of 60, 113, 132, 136, 137, 179
Sidgwick, Henry 49, 55, 158
Sion College 51, 65
Smith, Goldwin 66, 162
Smith, Payne 132
Society for Promoting Christian Knowledge 9
Society for the Propagation of the Gospel 139
South Africa 130, 182
Spectator 34, 60, 75, 159, 160, 168, 174
Stanley, A.P 4, 6, 7, 12, 13, 34, 41, 42, 45, 46, 47, 48, 49, 50, 54, 55, 61, 70, 71, 78, 86, 107, 110, 114, 120, 124, 125, 126, 131, 132, 134, 140, 142, 146, 148, 149, 151, 156, 157, 158, 165, 168, 172, 175, 176, 179, 182, 187
Stanleyites 13
Stephen, James Fitzjames 86, 89, 90, 91, 93, 94, 100, 111, 117, 171, 172, 174, 178
Stephen, Leslie 26, 152, 171, 174
Stephens, Archibald John 118
Strachey, Sir Edward 75, 168
Strauss, David Friedrich 31, 82, 132, 153
Sumner, Charles, Bishop of Winchester 50, 52
Sumner, John Bird, Archbishop of Canterbury 52, 57, 58, 59, 62, 63, 64, 90, 101, 136
Swabey, Maurice 86, 92, 93, 111, 178

Tait, Archibald Campbell 6, 49, 52, 53, 54, 55, 57, 58, 59, 60, 64, 65, 90, 99–100, 101, 105, 108, 110, 111, 115, 116, 122, 123, 124, 127, 131, 136, 138, 154, 156, 157, 158, 159, 162, 174, 176, 177, 180, 184, 185
Temple, Frederick 6, 9, 12, 14, 15, 16, 26, 31, 35, 37, 38, 40, 43, 46, 48, 49, 52, 53, 54, 55, 57, 69, 70, 71, 75, 77, 86, 106, 134, 136, 137, 138, 139, 142, 146, 147, 148, 149, 154, 155, 156, 158, 161, 164, 165, 168, 184, 185, 186, 187
   essay 14, 15–16, 40

Tennyson, Alfred 28, 152
Thirlwall, Connop 6, 11, 16, 21, 50, 52, 53, 57, 59, 60, 90, 105, 106, 107, 121, 122, 130, 131, 138, 147, 148, 150, 157, 158, 159, 166, 171, 176, 181, 184
Tholuck, Friedrich August 67
Thomson, William 13, 80, 83, 101, 115, 123, 168, 170, 171, 180
Thorold, Anthony Wilson 80, 170
Times, The 34, 49, 53, 55, 70, 102, 110, 118, 125, 129, 133, 137, 146, 157, 158, 173, 175, 180, 182
toleration 26
Tract 90 24, 35, 102, 175
Tractarians 3, 10, 36, 68, 85, 141, 184 *see also* Oxford Movement
Tracts for Priests and People 74
Traill, James Christie 118
Tregelles, Samuel 69
Trench, Richard Chenevix 47
Trinity College Dublin 76
Trower, Walter John 138
Turton, Thomas, Bishop of Ely 86
Twiss, Sir Travers 138

Unitarians 36, 72, 75, 107, 155

Victoria, Queen 109, 114, 115, 118, 136, 137, 138, 180
Voysey, Charles 131, 184

Watson, William Davy 36
Wellesley, Gerald 137
Wellington College 137, 158
Wesleyan Methodist Magazine 71
Westbury, Lord 104, 105, 108, 109, 110, 113, 115, 117, 120, 123, 126, 127, 128, 129, 175, 176
Westcott, Brooke Foss 13, 47, 73, 158, 167
Westminster Abbey 65, 114, 133, 134, 138
Westminster Review 10, 34, 37, 39, 40, 42, 44, 45, 48, 50, 60, 70, 98, 110, 134, 142, 147, 155, 173, 174, 177
Whately, Richard, Archbishop of Dublin 33, 148, 161
Wilberforce, Samuel, Bishop of Oxford 12, 34, 42, 43, 44, 45, 49, 50, 52, 53, 54, 57, 58, 59, 63, 66, 71, 74, 76, 77, 86, 113, 117, 120, 121, 122, 123, 124,

126, 127, 128, 130, 136, 137, 142,
143, 156, 157, 158, 159, 160, 162,
169, 171, 175, 177, 179, 180, 182,
183, 186
Wild, George John 71, 166
Willey, Basil 28, 49
Williams, Monier 50
Williams, Rowland 11, 13, 15, 16, 17,
18, 19, 20, 31, 32, 34, 35, 37, 40, 43,
46, 47, 49, 50, 53, 57, 58, 62, 67, 69,
70, 77, 79, 81, 85, 86, 87, 88, 89, 90,
91, 92, 93, 94, 95, 96, 97, 99, 100,
104, 105, 106, 108, 109, 110, 115,
117, 118, 120, 122, 123, 124, 125,
126, 131, 134, 139, 140, 142, 145,
147, 149, 150, 153, 154, 156, 157,
161, 164, 169, 171, 172, 173, 174,
176, 185
    essay 14, 16–20, 100
Williams and Wilson Appeal Fund 110

Wilson, Henry Bristow 9, 10, 11, 14, 15,
21–4, 28, 31, 32, 35, 37, 39, 40, 43,
44, 46, 47, 53, 60, 61, 64, 67, 70, 75,
78, 79, 81, 82, 86, 93, 95, 96, 97, 98,
100, 104, 105, 106, 108, 109, 110,
114, 115, 117, 118, 122, 123, 132,
134, 140, 142, 145, 146, 147, 148,
150, 151, 153, 155, 156, 159, 161,
164, 165, 166, 168, 171, 173, 174,
176, 177, 185, 187
    essay 14, 21–4
Wiseman, Nicholas, Cardinal 72, 182
'Word of God' 6, 22, 24, 30, 43, 45, 66,
79, 90, 93, 94, 95, 96, 104, 107, 108,
112, 115, 117, 119, 122, 132, 142, 162
Wordsworth, Christopher 56, 61, 62, 65,
66, 79, 125, 137, 138, 162, 170, 186

York, Chancery Court of 131
Young, George Malcolm 53